Venezuela

Ben Box

Credits

Footprint credits

Editor: Alan Murphy
Production and layout: Angus Dawson
Maps: Kevin Feeney

Managing Director: Andy Riddle
Commercial Director: Patrick Dawson
Publisher: Alan Murphy
Publishing Managers: Felicity Laughon, Nicola Gibbs
Digital Editors: Jo Williams, Tom Mellors
Marketing and PR: Liz Harper
Sales: Diane McEntee
Advertising: Renu Sibal
Finance and Administration: Elizabeth Taylor

Photography credits
Front cover: Lysithee/Shutterstock
Back cover: Zdorov Kirill Vladimirovich/Shutterstock

Printed in Great Britain by CPI Antony Rowe, Chippenham, Wiltshire

Every effort has been made to ensure that the facts in this guidebook are accurate. However, travellers should still obtain advice from consulates, airlines, etc about travel and visa requirements before travelling. The authors and publishers cannot accept responsibility for any loss, injury or inconvenience however caused.

Publishing information

Footprint *Focus Venezuela*
1st edition
© Footprint Handbooks Ltd
August 2011

ISBN: 978 1 908206 18 3
CIP DATA: A catalogue record for this book is available from the British Library

® Footprint Handbooks and the Footprint mark are a registered trademark of Footprint Handbooks Ltd

Published by Footprint
6 Riverside Court
Lower Bristol Road
Bath BA2 3DZ, UK
T +44 (0)1225 469141
F +44 (0)1225 469461
www.footprinttravelguides.com

Distributed in the USA by Globe Pequot Press, Guilford, Connecticut

The content of Footprint *Focus Venezuela* has been taken directly from Footprint's *South American Handbook 2012*.

MIX
Paper from responsible sources
FSC® C013604
www.fsc.org

Contents

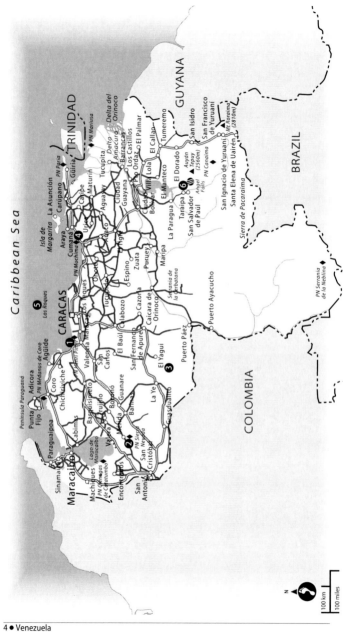

Caribbean Sea

TRINIDAD

GUYANA

BRAZIL

COLOMBIA

CARACAS

Maracaibo

Venezuela is where the Andes meet the Caribbean. The Orinoco river separates great plains from the table-top mountains of the Gran Sabana, where waterfalls tumble in sheer drops into the forest and lost worlds are easy to imagine. More recent innovations – cable cars up to the high peaks, hang gliders for jumping off them – are now part of the scene at Mérida, capital of Venezuela's Andes. Lying at the heart of the country – geographically and spiritually – are the llanos (plains), a vast area of flat savannah the size of Italy and home to an immense variety of birds, exotic mammals and reptiles, such as caiman (alligators), giant anacondas, anteaters, pumas, jaguars and giant otters, to name but a few.

These plains flood seasonally, but when the waters retreat, the birds and animals share their territory with cattle and the llanero cowboys, renowned for their hospitality towards visitors who can stay at one of the many luxurious hatos – cattle ranches – or rough it on a budget tour from Mérida. If the sea is more to your taste, head for the country's seductive coastline – the longest in the Caribbean at over 2500 km. Venezuela's waters play host to some of the best (and least known) diving in the region with three marine national parks. Pick of the bunch are Islas Los Roques, an archipelago of emerald and turquoise lagoons and dazzling white beaches. At the other end of the country, the Amazon is home to humid rainforests and rare plants and animals as well as over 20 different ethnic groups. This part of Venezuela is very much frontier territory and remains wild and untamed, as it was when the country received its first foreign visitor back in 1498. So overwhelmed was Columbus by what he saw that he described it as 'Paradise on Earth'.

Planning your trip

Where to go

Caribbean coast Venezuela has the longest coastline in the Caribbean with numerous palm-fringed beaches of white sand. **Caracas** is hidden from the Caribbean by Monte Avila, one of Venezuela's national parks, but you don't have to go too far beyond the mountain to find good beaches. Only a few hours west of the capital are some lovely little beaches. Further west is the Parque Nacional Morrocoy, with many islands close to the shore. North of Morrocoy is the historic town of Coro, surrounded by sand dunes, and the Paranaguá Peninsula. Parque Nacional Mochima, east of Caracas, has some excellent beaches and a multitude of islets to explore. Further east are unrivalled beaches on the Paria Peninsula, but they are harder to reach. Besides those islands already mentioned, there is Isla de Margarita, one of the country's principal destinations for local and foreign tourists. The Islas Los Roques, 166 km due north of the central coast, is a beautiful archipelago, still unspoilt despite the growth in tourist interest.

The Andes Venezuela's Andes have some gorgeous scenery, with snow-capped peaks and remote, historic villages. The main centre is Mérida, in the Sierra Nevada of the same name. It has accommodation, other services and tour companies, which can arrange treks, climbing and other excursions. Two of its claims to fame are the highest cable car in the world, ascending the 4776-m Pico Espejo, and the shop selling the largest number of ice cream flavours in the world.

The Llanos Life in the *llanos* revolves around the cycle of wet and dry seasons; the movement of cattle, the mainstay of the region's economy, depends on it. In the flat grasslands are slow running rivers which flood in the rainy season, creating a huge inland sea. When the rains cease, the whole area dries out completely. South of the cattle lands are forests and the tributaries of the Río Orinoco. Just after the May-November wet season, this is a paradise for nature lovers, with a spectacular variety of birds, monkeys, big cats, anaconda, river dolphins, caiman and capybara. Tours to the *llanos* are run from Mérida and there are ecotourism ranches which offer you the chance to get to know the lifestyle of the plains.

Guayana and the Orinoco Above the grasslands of the Gran Sabana rise *tepuis*, flat-topped mountains from which spring magnificent waterfalls and rivers. The Angel Falls, the highest in the world, are one such wonder, usually seen from a plane, but also reachable by a two- to three-day trip upriver. There are many other falls in the Gran Sabana and a few places to stay, the most popular being Canaima camp on a lagoon on the Río Carrao. Where Venezuela meets Brazil and Guyana is Mount Roraima; to reach its summit is one of the country's most adventurous excursions. The Orinoco delta is remote, but trips can be made from the small town of Tucupita. Amazonas is well off the beaten track, but accessible from Puerto Ayacucho. Much of the rainforest is protected and you need permission from the authorities to visit areas beyond the reach of a tour company.

When to go

The climate is tropical, with changes between the seasons being a matter of wet and dry, rather than hot and cold. Temperature is determined by altitude. The dry season in Caracas is December to April, with January and February the coolest months (there is a great difference between day and night temperatures at this time). The hottest months are July and August. The Caribbean coast is generally dry and rain is particularly infrequent in the states of Sucre, in the east, and Falcón, in the northwest. The lowlands of Maracaibo are very hot all year round; the least hot months are July to September. South of the Orinoco, in the Gran Sabana and Parque Nacional Canaima, the dry season is November to May. The same months are dry in the *llanos*, but the best time to visit is just after the rains, when the rivers and channels are still full of water and the humidity is not too high. In the Andes, the dry season is October to May, the best time for climbing or hiking. The days are clear, but the nights are freezing cold. The rains usually begin in June, but in the mountains the weather can change from day to day. **High season**, when it is advisable to book in advance is: Carnival, Easter, 15 July-15 September and Christmas to New Year.

Getting there

There are direct flights from France, Germany, Italy and Spain but not the UK. Where there are no direct flights connections can be made in the USA (Miami, or other gateways), Buenos Aires, Rio de Janeiro or São Paulo. **Main US gateways** are Miami, Houston, Dallas, Atlanta, New York and Los Angeles. If buying airline tickets routed through the USA, check that US taxes are included in the price. Flights from **Canada** are mostly via the USA, although there are direct flights from Toronto to Bogotá and Santiago. Likewise, flights from **Australia** and **New Zealand** are best through Los Angeles, except for the Qantas/LAN route from Sydney and Auckland to Santiago, and Qantas' route to Buenos Aires. Within **Latin America** there is plenty of choice on local carriers and some connections on US or European airlines.

Most airlines offer discounted fares on scheduled flights through agencies who specialize in this type of fare. If you buy discounted air tickets always check the reservation with the airline concerned to make sure the flight still exists. Also remember the IATA airlines' schedules change in March and October each year, so if you're going to be away a long time it's best to leave return flight coupons open. Peak times are 7 December-15 January and 10 July-10 September. If you intend travelling during those times, book as far ahead as possible. Between February and May and September and November special offers may be available.

Getting around

Air Most big places are served by Aeropostal *www.aeropostal.com*, Aserca *www.asercaairlines .com*, Avior *www.avior.com.ve*, Rutaca *www.rutaca.com.ve* and Venezolana *http://ravsa.com.ve*. Aereotuy/LTA *www.tuy.com*, connects the coast, the Orinoco Delta and their camp in Canaima National Park, Arekuna. Apart from Aserca, which is marginally better than the rest, none is great. Lost luggage is a frequent problem.

Delays and cancellations without compensation are common. Beware of overbooking during holidays, especially at Caracas airport; check in at least two hours before departure. If you book a ticket online with a credit card, you may be told at check-in that your tickets is 'reserved but not purchased'. Check with your card company that you have not been charged twice.

Bus and taxi Buses on most long-distance routes come in four standards, *normal*, *semi-ejecutivo*, *ejecutivo* and *bus-cama*. Fares are set by the authorities and you should see them posted on bus office windows. There are numerous services between the major cities and many services bypass Caracas, so you don't have to change buses in the capital. Buses stop frequently, but there may not always be a toilet at the stop. For journeys in a/c buses take a sleeping bag or similar because the temperature is set to freezing. This is most important on night journeys, which otherwise are fine. Also take earplugs and eyemask to protect against the loud stereo and violent Hollywood screenings. The colectivo taxis and minibuses, known as *por puesto*, seem to monopolize transport to and from smaller towns and villages. For longer journeys they are normally twice as expensive as buses, but faster. They are mostly 1980s US gas-guzzlers, in all states of repair (a shortage of original spare parts and brakeneck driving speeds make *por puestos* a dangerous mode of transport). They are, however, great places to meet the locals, learn about the area and discuss politics. If first on board, wait for other passengers to arrive, do not take a *por puesto* on your own unless you want to pay for the whole vehicle. They may be reluctant to take luggage, but for a bit of comfort you can pay for two front seats and place your luggage between you and the driver. Outside Caracas, town taxis are relatively expensive.

Hitchhiking Hitchhiking (*cola*) is not recommended as it is unsafe. It is illegal on toll roads and, theoretically, for non-family members in the back of pick up trucks. Avoid hitchhiking around Guardia Nacional posts, where foreign travellers, even if travelling on regular buses or *por puestos*, may be subject to harassment.

Maps *Guía Vial de Venezuela*, edited by **Miro Popic** (Caracas 1999), is a motoring guide with maps and tourist information. The best country map is the late Kevin Healey's, published by **International Travel Maps**, Vancouver, Canada, www.itmb.com; buy direct or at good travel agents.

Sleeping

Value for money is very low, with one or two exceptions, but many foreign-run, no-frills places catering for backpackers are opening up. The major cities, Isla Margarita, Los Roques, Guayana and Amazonas have higher room rates (eg US$15-20 in Caracas for a basic room). Add 10-15% for air-conditioning. In the Andean region prices are lower at around US$8-12 per person. If comfort and cleanliness is what you are after, the price of a basic 3-star (Venezuelan '4 star') hotel room with a/c, private bath and breakfast will be in our $$$ range (US$65-100), depending on location and whether it's a hotel or posada. There are no discounts or corporate rates for foreigners, unless arranged long in advance with tedious correspondence. A prior reservation will not guarantee you a

Sleeping and eating price codes

Sleeping

$$$$ over US$150   **$$$** US$66-150   **$$** US$30-65
$ under US$30

Prices include taxes and service charge, but not meals. They are based on a double room, except in the **$** range, where prices are almost always per person.

Eating

¶¶¶ over US$12   **¶¶** US$7-12   **¶** under US$7

Prices refer to the cost of a two-course meal, not including drinks.

room when you arrive. Always insist on seeing the room before paying; if you don't, you will almost certainly be given the worst possible room.

Elizabeth Kline's Guide to Camps, Posadas and Cabins in Venezuela 2009/2010, published every two years or so (purchasing information from notkalvin@yahoo.com) is incredibly detailed and doesn't pull its punches. *La Guía Valentina Quintero* also covers the whole country, suggesting routes, where to stay and eat, published biannually, www.valentinaquintero.com.ve. **Casa Tropical** (main office), CC Paseo Las Mercedes, Sector La Cuadra, Local 26, Caracas, T212-613 8343, www.casatropical.com.ve, offers interesting accommodation options in the Andes, Ciudad Bolívar and Tacarigua National Park, among other places.

Camping Camping in Venezuela is popular. Camping, with or without a vehicle, is not possible at the roadside. If camping on the beach, for the sake of security, pitch your tent close to others, even though they play their radios loud.

Eating and drinking

Eating out As with lodging, eating out is, by South American standards, very expensive and locals hardly ever do so. Some cities, like Puerto Ordaz, are notably costly. Midday used to be the cheapest time to eat and the best time to find fresh vegetables, but now many places offer only à la carte, quoting scarcity of supplies. In some places you can still find the three-course *menú ejecutivo* or *cubierto*, but it's increasingly rare. Minimum price for a meal is US$5-7, plus US$1 for drinks. Hotel breakfasts are likely to be poor. It is better and cheaper in a *fuente de soda* and cheaper still in a *pastelería* or *arepería*.

Food There is excellent local fish (such as *pargo* or red snapper, *carite* or king fish), crayfish, small oysters and prawns. Although it is a protected species, turtle may appear on menus in the Península de Paraguaná as *ropa especial*. Of true Venezuelan food there is *sancocho* (vegetable stew with meat, chicken or fish); *arepas*, bland white maize bread; toasted *arepas* served with various fillings or the local salty white cheese, are cheap, filling and nutritious; *cachapas*, a maize pancake wrapped around white cheese; *pabellón*, of shredded meat, beans, rice and fried plantains; and *empanadas*, maize-flour pies of cheese, meat or fish. At Christmas there are *hallacas*, maize pancakes stuffed with chicken, pork, olives, boiled in a plantain leaf. A *muchacho* (boy) on the menu is a cut of beef. *Ganso* is not goose but beef. *Solomo* and *lomito* are other cuts of beef. *Hervido* is chicken or beef with vegetables. *Contorno* with a meat or fish dish is a choice of fried chips, boiled potatoes, rice or yuca. *Caraotas* are beans; *cachitos* are filled *croissants*. *Pasticho* is what Venezuelans call Italian lasagne. The main fruits are bananas, oranges, grapefruit, mangoes, pineapple and pawpaws. *Lechosa* is papaya, *patilla* water melon, *parchita* passion fruit, and *cambur* a small banana. Excellent strawberries are grown at Colonia Tovar, 90 minutes from Caracas, and in the Andes. Delicious sweets are *huevos chimbos*, egg yolk boiled and bottled in sugar syrup, and *quesillo*, made with milk, egg and caramel. **Note** Venezuelans dine late!

Drink Venezuelan rum is very good; recommended brands are *Cacique*, *Pampero* and *Santa Teresa*. There are five good beers: *Polar* (the most popular, sold as Polar and Ice, and Solera and Solera Light), *Regional* (strong flavour of hops), *Cardenal* and *Nacional* (a *lisa* is a glass of keg beer; for a bottle of beer ask for a *tercio*); Brazilian *Brahma* beer (lighter than *Polar*) is now brewed in Venezuela. There are also mineral waters and gin. There is a good local wine in Venezuela. The *Polar* brewery joined with Martell (France) to build a winery in Carora. **Bodegas Pomar** (www.empresas-polar.com/marca-cerve_vinos.php) also sells a champagne-style sparkling wine. Look out for Pomar wine festivals in March and September. Liqueurs are cheap, try the local *ponche crema*. Coffee is very cheap (*café con leche* is milky, *café marrón* much less so, *café negro* is black); it often has sugar already added, ask for "sin azúcar". Try a *merengada*, a delicious drink made from fruit pulp, ice, milk and sugar; a *batido* is the same but with water and a little milk; *jugo* is the same but with water. A *plus-café* is an after-dinner liqueur. Water is free in restaurants even if no food is bought. Bottled water in *cervecerías* is often from the tap; no deception is intended, bottles are used as convenient jugs. Insist on seeing the bottle opened if you want mineral water. *Chicha de arroz* is a sweet drink made of milk, sugar and vanilla. Fruit juices are very good, ask for "jugo natural, preparado en el momento" for the freshest juice.

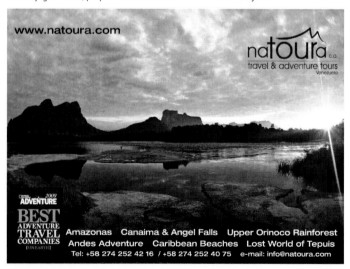

Essentials A-Z

Accident and emergency

Dial T171 for the integrated emergency system. **CICPC (Cuerpo de Investigaciones Científicas**, Penales y Criminalísticas), Av Urdaneta entre Pelota y Punceres; Edif Icauca, mezzanina 2, Caracas, T0212-564 7798, www.cicpc.gov.ve. For registering crimes, with agencies throughout the country.

Electricity

110 volts, 60 cycles. Plugs are 2-pin round and flat combined, 2-pin flat and 2-pin flat with optional D-shaped earth.

Embassies and consulates

The Ministry of Foreign Affairs website is www.mppre.gob.ve. For a list of Venezuelan embassies and consulates abroad visit www.anunsioscaracas.com.ve/embajadascon sulados.htm and sites such as www.embavenez-uk.org and www.embavenez-us.org.

Festivals and events

Public holidays

1 Jan; **Carnival** on the Mon-Tue before Ash Wed (everything shuts down Sat-Tue; book accommodation in advance), Thu-Sat of Holy Week, **19 Apr**, **1 May**, **24 Jun** (the feast day of San Juan Bautista, celebrated on the central coast where there were once large concentrations of plantation slaves who considered San Juan their special Saint; the best-known events are in villages such as Chuao, Cata and Ocumare de la Costa); **5 Jul**, **24 Jul**, **24 Sep**, **12 Oct**, **2 Nov**, **25 Dec**.

Other holidays

From 24 Dec-1 Jan, museums are closed, most restaurants close 24-25 Dec (except for fast-food outlets) and there is no long-distance public transport on 25 Dec, while other days are often booked solid. On New Year's Eve, everything closes and does not open for at least a day. Business travellers should not visit during Holy Week or Carnival. Extra holidays for banks: **19 Mar** (San José), nearest Mon to **6 Jan**, **Ascension Day**, **29 Jun**, **15 Aug** and **8 Dec**.

See *Atlas de tradiciones venezolanas*, Fundación Bigott/El Nacional (2005), a beautiful book with sections on festivals, gastronomy, music, *artesanías*, architecture and popular art. Also *Calendario de fiestas tradicionales venezolanas*, Cecilia Fuentes and Daría Hernández, Fundación Bigott (2003).

Money → *1 US$ = 4.30BsF (Jul 2011)*.

The unit of currency is the bolívar fuerte (BsF). There are coins for 1 bolívar fuerte, 50, 25, 12.5, 10, 5 and 1 céntimos, and notes for 2, 5, 10, 20, 50 and 100 bolívares fuertes. Have small coins and notes to hand, since in many shops and bars and on public transport large notes may be hard to change.

Venezuela has had an exchange control regime since 2003. The government determines the **exchange rate** for the bolívar fuerte, which remains overvalued in relation to the dollar and other currencies despite a devaluation in Jan 2010. All imports, since Jan 2011, are charged at 4.30 BsF (prices in this guide are calculated with this rate, so bear this fact in mind when estimating the cost of your trip). The 'parallel' (ie black) market exchange of currencies is illegal, but it is common practice among importers, exporters and travellers. It fluctuates, depending on many factors, including government foreign currency reserves and the price of oil. In Apr 2011 it fluctuated around US$1 = 8.60-9 BsF. Banks, *casas de cambio* and credit card transactions use the official rate; quoted rates in hotels tend to be worse than that.

If you do decide to change cash on the black market, a) find out what the unofficial rate is from as many sources as possible (you can check one of many web, facebook or twitter sites which change frequently owing to government crack-downs), and b) do the transaction with the most trusted person. The best method is with the senior staff in a European or US-run posada. If you don't take this option, the transaction will not be simple. You will probably not be offered the full parallel rate. If you run short of cash, your best and cheapest bet is to cross the border to Colombia (San Antonio to Cúcuta is easiest), spend the night in Cúcuta and withdraw as much as possible in Colombian pesos from an ATM. Then go to any *casa de cambio* and buy bolívares. Remember to count your money carefully and make sure that you do not receive damaged notes.

Plastic, TCs, banks and ATMs TCs can be changed in *casas de cambio* and some banks at the official rate, but not as easily as dollars cash. To convert unused bolívares back into dollars, you must present the original exchange receipt (up to 30% of original amount changed); only banks and authorized *casas de cambio* can legally sell bolívares. In *casas de cambio* rates for TCs will be poor and they insist on photocopying your passport, ask for proof of purchase of TCs, ask you to sign a form saying where cash dollars came from and may even photograph you. Beware of forged Amex TCs and US$ notes.

You can use Visa/Plus, Mastercard, Cirrus and Maestro for obtaining bolívares at the official rate only. There are cash machines for Visa, Plus, Mastercard, Maestro and Cirrus at Simón Bolívar airport, but they are not reliable. You should be wary of using cash machines; Visa and Mastercard transactions inside banks, although slower, are much safer. Queues at ATM machines attract thieves. Some ATMs require a Venezuelan ID number. **Citibank** will exchange Citicorp cheques and has Visa and Mastercard ATMs. For Visa ATMs, branches of **Banco de Venezuela**. For cash advances on Mastercard and ATM go to branches of **Banco Mercantil, Banco de Venezuela, Banco Exterior, Banco Occidental de Descuento** (BOD) and a few others. **Corp Banca** (part of BOD) is affiliated with American Express, no commission, some branches cash personal cheques from abroad on an Amex card; **American Express** travel services are handled by **Italcambio** agencies around the country. Mastercard assistance T0800-1-002902. Visa assistance T0800-1-002167.

Cost of travelling On the cheapest possible budget at the official exchange rate, you can get by on about US$50-60 pp per day, depending on which part of the country you visit. A less basic budget would be about US$120 per day, rising to US$350 and upwards for first class travel. Remember that these costs will be less if you use the parallel exchange rate. The average cost for using the internet varies from US$0.50-0.80 outside Caracas to US$1-2 per hour in the capital.

Opening hours

See also under Festivals and events, page 11.
Business hours Banks: Mon-Fri 0830-1530 only. **Government offices**: 0800-1200 are usual morning hrs, although they vary. Officials have fixed hrs, usually 0900-1000 or 1500-1600, for receiving visitors. **Businesses**: 0800-1800 with a midday break. **Shops**: Mon-Sat 0900-1300, 1500-1900.

Generally speaking, Venezuelans start work early, and by 0700 everything is in full swing. Most firms and offices close on Sat.

Safety

Venezuela is unfortunately quite a dangerous place to travel around. During the day is mostly trouble-free, as long as you are aware of where you are going. Ask your hotel where it is safe to go. Carry only as much money as you need, don't wear jewellery or expensive sunglasses. It is not advisable to walk after dark: always take a taxi, preferably a marked car, or get someone to recommend a driver who can give you his number and you can use him for the duration of your stay. This applies even to tourist centres like Mérida and Ciudad Bolívar. In many places services shut after 1800. You **must** speak at least basic Spanish to be able to get yourself around. Very few people in the street will be able to speak English, and even fewer in rural areas. As a tourist you will stand out, so it helps considerably to understand and be understood on a basic level.

Some statistics state that Venezuela's crime rate is the highest in South America and Caracas's murder rate is the world's highest. Muggings are common, particularly in the bigger cities and are often at gunpoint. Rape is sadly very common, but mainly in poor neighbourhoods where police do not dare or want to go after sunset.

Outside of the big cities you will feel less unsafe, but still need to be careful in quieter rural areas as there may not be many tourists around. The more popular destinations (such as beaches and national parks) are used to having travellers and are generally further away from the kind of problems that you might encounter in the large cities. You still need to watch out for scams, cons and petty thieving. Beaches can be packed at weekends and, while empty on weekdays, the detritus left by the weekend crowds may not be cleared up. If you are seeking an isolated beach, make enquiries about which are safe before setting out.

The marked divisions between pro- and anti-Chávez factions can cause tension on the street. Stay away from political rallies (unless you are there to join them).

Foreigners may find themselves subject to harassment or abuse, or to thorough police identity and body searches. Carry a copy of your passport and, if searched, watch the police like a hawk, in case they try to plant drugs to your bags. Do not photograph people without permission. Carry a mobile and be prepared to call your embassy or your contact in the country if a police search becomes threatening.

Tax

Airport tax   International passengers pay an airport tax of US$44.18 and exit tax of US$53 (at the official 4.30 exchange rate – check latest rates at www.aeropuerto-maiquetia.com.ve). The exit tax may be included in your flight ticket. Only locally-issued credit cards can be used for paying airport tax. Otherwise only dollars or bolívares are accepted, no TCs. (See page 12 above on ATM machines at the airport.) Children under 2 years do not pay tax. There is an 8% tax on the cost of all domestic flights, plus an airport tax of US$8.86. Exit stamps have to be paid by overland travellers at some borders, US$12.80 (BsF 55). Correct taxes are not advertised and you may be overcharged. **VAT/IVA**   12% (may be increased in 2011).

Telephone → *Country code +58.*

Ringing: long equal tones with equal long pauses. Engaged: short equal tones, with equal pauses. Mobile phone codes are generally 0412, 0414, or 0416.

Time

4 hrs behind GMT, 1 hr ahead of EST.

Tipping

Taxi drivers are not tipped if you agree the fare in advance. Usherettes are not tipped. Hotel porters, US$1; airport porters US$1 per piece of baggage. Restaurants 5-10% of bill;

some even charge on top of the service charge when it is included.

Tourist information

In charge of tourism is the **Ministerio del Poder Popular para el Turismo**, Av Francisco de Miranda con Av Principal de La Floresta, Edif Mintur (Frente al Colegio Universitario de Caracas), Chacao, Caracas, T0212-208 4511, www.mintur.gob.ve and www.inatur.gob.ve. **Venetur**, Centro Empresarial Centro Plaza, Torre B, p 16, Los Palos Grandes, Caracas, T0500-TURISMO (887 4766), www.venetur.gob.ve, Mon-Fri 0900-1730, is the state-owned and operated travel agency, aimed at facilitating travel for nationals and foreigners, making reservations and arranging tours. In Caracas, go to **Corpoturismo**, Parque Central, Torre Oeste, p 35, 36 y 37, T507 8800.

Outside Venezuela, contact Venezuelan embassies and consulates. Read and heed the travel advice at websites below.

Visas and immigration

See also Embassies and consulates, page 11. Entry is by passport and visa, or by passport and tourist card. Tourist cards (*tarjetas de ingreso*) are issued by airlines to visitors from all EU and other Western European countries, Australia, Canada, New Zealand, South Africa, USA and most South and Central American and Caribbean countries. To check if you need a visa, see www.mppre.gob.ve. Valid for 90 days, tourist cards cannot be extended. At some overland border crossings (including San Antonio) visitors are given only 30 days. Overstaying your tourist card may lead to arrest and a fine when you try to depart. For a **tourist visa**, you need 1 passport photo, passport valid for 6 months, references from bank and employer, onward or return ticket and a completed and signed application form. The fee is US$75. For a 90-day extension go to the Servicio Administrativo de Identificación, Migración y Extranjería, SAIME,

Av Baralt on Plaza Miranda in Caracas, T0800-SAIME00 or 0800-724 6300, www.saime.gob.ve (go to Extranjería, Solicitud de Visa de Turista or Prórroga de Visa); take passport, tourist visa, photographs and return ticket; passport with extension returned at end of day. SAIME offices in many cities do not offer extensions. Transit visas, valid for 72 hrs are also available, mostly the same requirements and cost (inward and onward tickets needed). SAIME in Caracas will not exchange a transit for a tourist visa. Consuls may give a 1-year visa if a valid reason can be given. To change a tourist visa to a business visa, to obtain or to extend the latter, costs US$75.

Note If you are not eligible for a tourist card, you must get a consular visa in advance. Carry your passport with you at all times as police do spot checks and anyone found without ID is immediately detained (carrying a certified copy of your passport and entry stamp is OK, though not always accepted). You will also be asked to provide details like name, address, passport number in restaurants and shops. Military checkpoints are in many areas, especially in border zones (eg on the roads from San Antonio to Maracaibo and Mérida), where all transport is stopped. Have documents ready and make sure you know what entry permits you need; soldiers may not know rules for foreigners. Searches at checkpoints are thorough and foreigners get closer attention than nationals. Do not lose the carbon copy of your visa as this has to be surrendered when leaving.

Weights and measures

Metric.

Contents

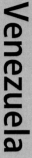

Venezuela

Caracas

Caracas is not the gentlest of introductions to South America. Some enjoy its pleasant, year-round climate, its parks and cosmopolitan nightlife. Others are drawn to see firsthand the Chávez revolution in action. For others, it's more like a slap in the face from a garishly dressed, loud mestizo with a taste for all things American. Founded in 1567, it lies in a rift in thickly forested mountains which rise abruptly from a lush green coast to heights of 2000 to 3000 m. The small basin in which the capital lies runs some 24 km east and west. By way of escape, there are several nearby excursions to mountain towns, the colonial district of El Hatillo, the Parque Nacional Monte Avila, beaches and Los Roques, a beautiful Caribbean atoll reached by a short flight.

Ins and outs → *Phone code: 0212. Population: about 4 million (city 2 million). Altitude: 960 m.*

Getting there The **airport** is 28 km from Caracas, near the port of La Guaira: Maiquetía and Aeropuerto Auxiliar for national flights and Simón Bolívar for international flights. The terminals are connected by an air-conditioned walkway. There are three main **bus terminals** in different parts of the city; where you arrive depends upon where you travelled from. ▶ *See also Transport, page 29.*

Getting around The metro is a/c, clean, safe, comfortable and quick, although poorly signed and often packed, especially at rush hours. MetroBuses are modern, comfortable, recommended but infrequent. Regular buses are overcrowded in rush hour and charge extra after 2100. Bus tickets cost US$0.05-0.15. *Por puesto* minibuses, known as *busetas, carmelitas* or *carritos* run on regular routes; fares depend on the distance travelled within the city. *Metrocable* systems opened 2010 from Parque Central (Line 4) to San Agustín barrio and from Palo Verde to Mariche. A bus system on dedicated lines is under construction.

Orientation In the centre, each street corner has a name: addresses are generally given as 'Santa Capilla and Mijares' (*Santa Capilla y* – sometimes *a – Mijares*), rather than the official 'Calle Norte 2, No 26'. In the east, 'y' or 'con' are used for street intersections. Modern multi-storeyed edifices dominate and few colonial buildings remain intact; many find the city lacking in character. A 10-km strip from west to east, fragmented by traffic-laden arteries, contains several centres: Plaza Bolívar, Plaza Venezuela, Sabana Grande, Chacaíto, Altamira, La California and Petare. The Avila mountain is always north.

Tourist offices Corpoturismo, Parque Central, Torre Oeste, p 35, 36 y 37, T507 8800.

Security Safety in Caracas has deteriorated in recent years and crime rates and kidnappings have risen significantly. You should be on the lookout from the moment you arrive; there are many pirate taxis and rip-off merchants operating at the international airport. It is best not to arrive in Caracas at night. Avoid certain areas such as all western suburbs from the El Silencio monument to Propatria, the areas around the Nuevo Circo and La Bandera bus stations, the area around the *teleférico*, Chapellín near the Country Club, and Petare. It is not advisable to walk at night in the city, except in the municipality of Chacao (Altamira, Chacao and Los Palos Grandes) and in Las Mercedes. Street crime is common, even armed robbery in daylight. Carry handbags, cameras etc on the side away from the road as motorcycle bag- snatchers are notorious. Do not to wear jewellery, carry valuables or openly display mobile phones or cameras. Car theft is common: always use car parks; never park on the street. Police checks are frequent, thorough and can include on-the-spot searches of valuables. Always carry your passport, or a photocopy (nothing else will be acceptable); bribes are sometimes asked for. If you have entered overland from Colombia, expect thorough investigation. See also Safety, page 12.

Sights

Centre
ⓘ *Many museums close on Mon and at lunchtime.*
The shady **Plaza Bolívar**, with its fine equestrian statue of the Liberator and pleasant colonial cathedral, is still the official centre of the city, though no longer geographically so. Much of its colonial surroundings is being restored. In the **Capitolio Nacional**, the National Assembly, which consists of two neoclassical-style buildings, the **Legislative Palace** and the **Federal Palace** ⓘ *Tue-Sun, 0900-1200, 1400-1700,* the Elliptical Salon has some impressive paintings and murals by the Venezuelan artist Martín Tovar y Tovar. The present **Cathedral** dating from 1674 has a beautiful façade, the Bolívar family chapel and paintings by Michelena, Murillo and an alleged Rubens 'Resurrection'. Bolívar was baptized in this Cathedral and the remains of his parents and wife are kept here.

The **Consejo Municipal** (City Hall) on Plaza Bolívar contains three **museums** ⓘ *all 3 open Tue-Fri 0930-1200, 1500-1800; Sat and Sun 0930-1800* and feature a collection of the paintings of Emilio Boggio, a Venezuelan painter; the Raúl Santana Museum of the Creole Way of Life, a collection of miniature figures in costumes, all handmade by Raúl Santana; and the Sala de Arqueología Gaspar Marcano, exhibiting ceramics, mostly discovered on the coast.

Casa Natal del Libertador ⓘ *Sur 1 y Este 2, Jacinto a Traposos, opposite Plaza El Venezolano, T541 2563, Tue-Fri 1000-1200, 1400-1700, Sun and holidays 1000-1300, 1400-1700,* is a fascinating reconstruction of the house where Bolívar was born (24 July 1783). Interesting pictures and furniture and murals tell Bolívar's life story. The first house, of adobe, was destroyed by an earthquake. The second became a stable, and was later pulled down. The **Museo Bolivariano** is alongside the Casa Natal and contains the Liberator's war relics.

San Francisco ⓘ *Av Universidad y San Francisco (1 block southwest of Plaza Bolívar),* the oldest church in Caracas, rebuilt 1641, should be seen for its colonial altars. **Santa Teresa** ⓘ *between La Palma and Santa Teresa, just southeast of the Centro Simón Bolívar,* has good interior chapels and a supposedly miraculous portrait of Nazareno de San Pablo (popular devotions on Good Friday).

Panteón Nacional ⓘ *Av Norte y Av Panteón, Tue-Sun 0900-1200, 1400-1630.* The remains of Simón Bolívar, the Liberator, lie here in the Plaza Panteón. The tomb of Francisco Miranda (the Precursor of Independence), who died in a Spanish prison, has been left open to await the return of his body, likewise the tomb of Antonio José de Sucre, who was assassinated in Colombia. Every 25 years the President opens Bolívar's casket to verify that the remains are still there.

Museo Histórico Fundación John Boulton ⓘ *Final Av Panteón, Foro Libertador, Casa N 3, next to the Panteón Nacional, T861 4685, www.fundacionboulton.com* contains good collections of 19th century art and objects, furniture, maps, metals and coins and a collection of objects and documents relating to the life of Simon Bolivar.

Museo de Arte Colonial ⓘ *Quinta Anauco, Av Panteón, San Bernardino, T551 8190, www.quintadeanauco.org.ve, Tue-Fri 0900-1130, 1400-1630, Sat-Sun and holidays 1000-1600, US$4.65.* This delightful house in the beautiful suburb of San Bernardino, was built in 1720 and was formerly the residence of the Marqués del Toro. Everything from the roof to the carpet has been preserved and the house contains a wealth of period furniture and sculpture and almost 100 paintings from the colonial era.

Sabana Grande and east of the centre
In the **Parque Central**, a concrete jungle complex between Avenida Lecuna (east end) and the elevated section of Avenida Bolívar, there are two, run-down octagonal towers

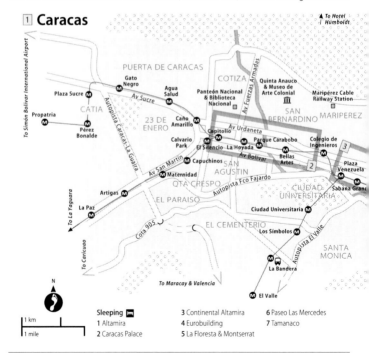

1 **Caracas**

Sleeping
1 Altamira
2 Caracas Palace
3 Continental Altamira
4 Eurobuilding
5 La Floresta & Montserrat
6 Paseo Las Mercedes
7 Tamanaco

(56 floors each) and four large, shabby apartment blocks with cafés and shops below. Four museums are located here: **Museo de Arte Contemporáneo** ⓘ *Parque Central, Cuadra Bolívar, T573 8289, www.fmn.gob.ve/fmn_mac.htm entrance beside Alba Hotel, 0900-1700, free.* It has some 3000 works on display, including modern sculptures and the works by, among others, Miró, Chagall, Matisse and Picasso, one of the finest collections of modern art in South America. The **Museo de los Niños** ⓘ *Parque Central, next to east Tower, Nivel Bolívar, T575 0695, www.maravillosa realidad.com, Mon-Fri 0900-1700, Sat-Sun and holidays 1000-1700, US$5.35, children US$4.65,* is an extremely popular and highly sophisticated interactive science museum. Also in the Parque Central complex, is the **Museo del Teclado** (Museum of Keyboard Instruments) ⓘ *T572 0713, www.museodelteclado.com.ve/pag/resena.html.*

Parque Los Caobos is a peaceful park with fountains and a cafeteria in the middle. It is a lovely place to wander if you are visiting the **Plaza de los Museos** (see below). It also contains **Bosque de las Esculturas**, an open-air sculpture exhibition near the Plaza de los Museos entrance. By the entrance in Avenida México is the cultural centre, **Ateneo de Caracas**, with a cinema, theatre, art gallery, concert room, bookshop and the imposing **Teresa Carreño theatre** complex. **Museo de Bellas Artes** ⓘ *Plaza de los Museos, T578 0275, www.fmn.gob.ve/fmn_mba.htm, free, Mon-Fri 0900-1600, Sat-Sun and holidays 1000-1700,* the oldest museum in Caracas, designed by Carlos Raúl Villanueva. It contains a good, permanent collection of contemporary and 19th century

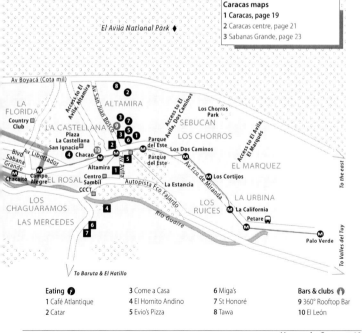

Caracas maps
1 Caracas, page 19
2 Caracas centre, page 21
3 Sabanas Grande, page 23

Eating ●		
1 Café Atlantique	3 Come a Casa	6 Miga's
2 Catar	4 El Hornito Andino	7 St Honoré
	5 Evio's Pizza	8 Tawa

Bars & clubs ●
9 360° Rooftop Bar
10 El León

works by mainly Venezuelan and South American artists and a good café surrounded by outdoor sculptures. Adjacent is the **Galería de Arte Nacional** ① *T576 8707, www.fmn. gob.ve/fmn_gan.htm, Mon-Fri 0900-1700, Sat-Sun and holidays 1000-1700*, displays the history of Venezuelan art, from colonial times to present day, and also houses the **Cinemateca Nacional** ① *www.cinemateca. gob.ve*, an arts and experimental cinemas. **Museo de Ciencias Naturales** ① *Plaza de los Museos, Los Caobos, T577 5103, www.fmn. gob.ve/fmn_mc.htm, Mon-Fri 0900-1700, Sat-Sun and holidays 1030-1800*, has archaeological, particularly pre- Columbian, zoological and botanical exhibits, interesting temporary shows.

Jardín Botánico ① *near Plaza Venezuela, entrance by Ciudad Universitaria, Mon-Sun 0830- 1630, www.fibv.org.ve/jardin*, is worth a visit, with extensive collections of over 2000 species; 10,000 trees belonging to 80 species grow in the arbetorium alone. Here you can see the world's largest palm tree (*Corypha Sp*) and the Elephant Apple with its huge edible fruit.

2 **Caracas centre**

Sleeping ▭
1 Alba Caracas
2 Avila
3 El Conde
4 Inter
5 Limón
6 Plaza Catedral

200 metres
200 yards

La Estancia ⓘ *just along from the Altamira metro exit, http://laestancia.pdvsa.com*, is a cultural centre with good exhibitions, regular activities and events including free yoga and music. It is set in a lovely park with beautiful trees and manicured lawns, the perfect place to escape from the hectic city.

Parque Nacional del Este (officially Parque Miranda) ⓘ *closed Mon, opens 0530 for joggers, 0830 for others, till 1700, reached from Miranda metro station*, is the largest park in Caracas and a popular place to relax, especially at weekends. A great place for a leisurely stroll and people watching, it has a boating lake, snake house, cactus garden, a number of different sunken lakes featuring caiman and turtles, monkeys and a caged jaguar as well as the **Humboldt Planetarium** ⓘ *T234 9188, www.planetariohumboldt.com*. **Museo de Transporte** ⓘ *Parque Nacional del Este (to which it is connected by a pedestrian overpass), T234 2234, www.automotriz.net/museo-del-transporte, Sun 0900-1700*, has a large collection of locomotives and old cars.

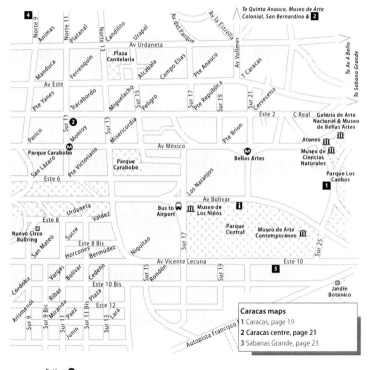

Caracas maps
1 Caracas, page 19
2 Caracas centre, page 21
3 Sabanas Grande, page 23

Eating ⓞ
1 El Parador
2 La Cocina Criolla de Francy
3 La Indicata

Other parks and urban excursions

The densely wooded **Parque Caricuao** ① *Tue-Sun 0900-1630: take metro to Caricuao Zoológico, then 5 min walk up Av Principal La Hacienda,* is at the southwest end of the Metro line, and forms part of the Parque Nacional Macuro. A pleasant day out. At the foot of the Avila mountain, the **Parque Los Chorros** ① *Tue-Fri 0830-1630, Sat-Sun 0830-1800, take bus from Los Dos Caminos station to Lomas de Los Chorros* has impressive waterfalls and forest walks. **El Calvario**, west of El Silencio, with the Arch of Confederation at the entrance, has a good view of Centro Simón Bolívar, but muggings have been reported. It has a small Museo Ornitológico, botanical gardens and a picturesque chapel.

El Hatillo ① *take a bus or taxi from central Caracas, about 20-30 mins' drive, depending on traffic*, once a separate village now subsumed by the city sprawl, is one of the few places in Caracas that has retained its colonial architecture. Built around a central plaza, its peaceful streets of multi-coloured houses offer a fine selection of cafés, restaurants, shops and small galleries. It is recommended as a wonderful spot to escape from the city and to shop for handicrafts, but it gets busy at weekends.

See also the cable car ride to the summit of **Monte El Avila** with fantastic views of Caracas, page 33.

3 Sabana Grande

Caracas maps
1 Caracas, page 19
2 Caracas centre, page 21
3 Sabanas Grande, page 23

N

200 metres
200 yards

Sleeping		Eating
1 Atlántida	6 Lincoln Suites	1 Arepanía 24 Horas
2 Crillón	7 Nuestro	2 Córdova Pollo's Ceviche
3 Cristal	8 Plaza Palace	3 El Arabito
4 Gran Meliá	9 Plaza Venezuela	4 El Arepazo
5 Las Américas	10 Savoy	5 Gran Café

Caracas listings

For Sleeping and Eating price codes and other relevant information, see Essentials, pages 9-11.

Sleeping

Caracas hotels are not cheap and the range of budget accommodation is poor. The cheapest hotels are in the downtown area, but this is not a safe part of town at night, or even in the day with a backpack. Sabana Grande, which has a wide range of hotels, is not safe at night if you are on your own. If you don't want to stay in the suburbs or centre, spend a little more and go to the upmarket Chacao, Altamira, La Castellana districts (all easily reached by metro), where it is relatively safe to stroll around during the day. There are hotels on the coast, close to the airport, if you do not want to go into the city. Some hotels listed below will charge an additional 17% tax; others include it in their price. If you book from abroad, make sure you receive written confirmation before beginning your journey. For apartment rental, consult *El Universal* daily paper, small ads columns. The business and commercial district is southeast of the centre, not on metro.

Central area *p17, map p21*
The cheapest hotels are around the Nuevo Circo bus terminal (not a safe area). Plaza Bolívar and its surrounding streets are busy by the day, but by night are deserted and unsafe.

$$$$ Alba Caracas, Av Sur 25 with Av Mexico, T503 5000. Ageing luxury hotel, formerly the Hilton, now run jointly by the state and a privately company. Business centre, city views, noisy (traffic and a/c), pool, but for this price there are better options elsewhere in the city.

$$$$ El Conde, Av Este esq El Conde, T860 1171. Well located for those wanting to stay in the historic centre, elegant lobby but rooms are a bit run down. Own restaurant and bar.

$$ Plaza Catedral, Blvd Plaza Bolívar, next to Cathedral, T564 2111. Central location just off Plaza Bolívar, Amex accepted, a/c, English spoken, good views over the Plaza but can be noisy. Good restaurant, includes breakfast. Recommended.

$ Inter, Animas a Calero, on corner of Av Urdaneta, near Nuevo Circo, T564 0251. Helpful, English spoken, very popular, poor restaurant, accepts credit cards.

$ Limón, Av Lecuna, Frente Parque Central, T571 6457, Bellas Artes metro. Safe, parking, well located for museums and galleries, often recommended.

6 Jaime Vivas
7 La Huerta
8 Sabas Nieves
9 Urrutia

Bars & clubs
10 El Encuentro de los Artistas
11 El Maní Es Así

San Bernardino

Residential area 2 km north of Bellas Artes metro.

$$$ Avila, Av Jorge Washington, T555 3000, www.hotelavila.com.ve. Modern, medium-sized hotel, set in tranquil tropical gardens around 20 mins' drive from the centre, very pleasant, good service, most staff speak English and German, fans, mosquito screens, pool, Metrobus nearby, very good restaurant and poolside bar, travel agency, phones accept Visa/Mastercard.

Sabana Grande/Chacaíto *p18, map p23*

This popular area with budget backpackers has restaurants and shops, but most close by early evening. Many hotels are in the Av Las Acacias/Av Casanova area, the majority are short stay.

$$$$ Gran Meliá, Av Casanova y El Recreo, T762 8111, www.gran-melia.com/en/. Top-ranking hotel with all facilities, business centre, generous gourmet buffets, restaurants (including Japanese and pizzería), fitness centre, spa, great pool area, piano bar.

$$$$ Las Américas, C Los Cerritos, at the end of Av Casanova, T951 7133, www.hotellasamericas. com.ve. Modern tower blocks, tiny roof pool and restaurant, taxi service to airport.

$$$ Crillón, Av Libertador, esq Av Las Acacias, T761 4411, www.hotelcrillon.com.ve. Near Plaza Venezuela metro. High-rise block, good service, comfortable, good bar.

$$$ Lincoln Suites, Av Franciso Solano, T762 8575, www.lincoln-suites.com.ve. Well-equipped with comfortable rooms, popular bar.

$$$ Plaza Palace, Av Los Mangos, Las Delicias, T762 4821, plaza_palace_hotel@hotmail.com. Old building with good facilities for business travellers, a/c, TV, helpful, English spoken.

$$$ Savoy, Av Francisco Solano López y Av Las Delicias, T762 1971. Well-established large hotel, good food, terrace, WiFi, secure car park, taxi service to airport.

$$ Atlántida, Av La Salle, Los Caobos, T793 3211. Modern, comfortable hotel with cable TV, restaurant, pool and fitness club.

$$ Plaza Venezuela, Av La Salle, Los Caobos, T781 7811. Modern, small but good rooms, helpful staff, good value.

$$-$ Cristal, C Real de Sabana Grande, Pasaje Asunción, just off Av Abraham Lincoln, near Sabana Grande metro, T761 9131. Comfortable, a/c, safe, good value, restaurant, English spoken, helpful staff.

$ Nuestro, also known as **The Backpackers Hostel**, Av Casanova, C El Colegio, T762 1788. Calls itself 'one of the only backpacker hostels in Caracas'. Basic rooms with bath, helpful staff, English spoken, can arrange airport transfers and tours, terrace and luggage lock, snacks and drinks sold. Good value. Works with recommended tour operator **Osprey**, T762 5975, www.ospreyvenezuela.com.

Chuao/Las Mercedes *map p19*

An upmarket commercial district southeast of the centre and Sabana Grande, no metro station.

$$$$ Tamanaco Inter-Continental, Av Principal Las Mercedes, T909 7111, www.ichotelsgroup.com. One of the better hotels in Caracas, good pool, sauna, luxury business hotel, courteous staff, good facilities, WiFi, excellent food. Midweek discounts available.

$$$$ Eurobuilding Hotel & Suites, Calle La Guarita, Chuao, T902 1111, www.eurobuilding.com.ve. 5-star, modern, has all-suite wing, well-furnished, a/c, includes breakfast, efficient service, large pool, gym, restaurants, many services, weekend rates.

$$$ Hotel Paseo Las Mercedes, CC Paseo Las Mercedes, Las Mercedes, T993 1244, www.hotelpaseolasmercedes.com. Located in the shopping mall with fine restaurants and bars on the doorstep. Comfortable, spacious rooms with good service. Close to the **Tamanaco** but a cheaper option.

Chacao, Altamira,
La Castellana *map p19*
These 3 districts, east of Gran Sabana and the centre, are adjacent to each other, and are a respectable commercial and residential zone.

$$$$ Caracas Palace, Av Luis Roche con Av Francisco Miranda, Altamira, T771 1000, www.caracaspalace.com. Popular high end hotel, good pool and spa.

$$$$ Continental Altamira, Av San Juan Bosco, Altamira, T261 0644, www.hotel-continental.org.ve. Smart, with breakfast, gardens and a good pool.

$$$$ Pestana Caracas, 1 Av Urb Santa Eduvigis, T208 1900, www.pestana.com. Brand new luxury hotel near Miranda Metro station and Parque del Este, business-oriented with all facilities, fitness centre, pool, restaurant and penthouse bar.

$$$ Residencia Montserrat, Av Avila Sur, T263 3533, F261 1394. Near Plaza Altamira and Altamira metro station, pleasant, well-run, helpful, a/c, hot water, TV, parking. Recommended for long stays.

$$$-$$ La Floresta, Av Avila Sur, T263 1955, www.hotellafloresta.com. Near Altamira metro, hot water, cable TV, restaurant, bar, parking, modern, some rooms renovated.

$$ Altamira, Av José Féliz Sosa, Altamira Sur, T267 4284 (do not confuse with **Altamira Suites Hotel**). Close to Altamira metro. Safe, modern, comfortable, credit cards accepted, helpful and efficient staff, changes dollars, secure parking. Most rooms with balcony. Recommended.

Near airport
See Litoral Central, page 35.

🍴 Eating

Central area *map p17, map p21*
There are plenty of eating places around Plaza Bolívar and, better still, around Plaza La Candelaria.

🍴 La Cocina Criolla de Francy, Av Este 2 y Sur 11, La Candelaria, T576 9849. Good

Spanish- Venezuelan food, best for weekend breakfasts and lunch. Recommended.

🍴 The restaurant in the **Museo de Arte Contemporáneo** serves great food, good value.

🍴 El Parador, Av Urdaneta, esquina Ibarras a Maturín No 18. Great Spanish food and service.

🍴-🍴 La Indicata, just off Plaza Bolívar. Good for breakfast, decent arepas, fresh juices and coffee.

Sabana Grande *p18, map p23*
This area has some cafés, bars (*tascas*) and restaurants. Good selection in CC El Recreo.

🍴🍴🍴 Urrutia, Fco Solano y Los Mangos. Good Basque food in this busy, relaxed restaurant

🍴🍴🍴-🍴 Jaime Vivas, C San Antonio, T763 4761. Best place to go for traditional Venezuelan food, especially *pabellón*.

🍴🍴🍴 La Huerta, Avda Fco Solano con 1ra Av de Las Delicias. A popular *tasca*, very good tapas. Popular with locals for watching Spanish football.

🍴 Córdova Pollo's Ceviche, Pasaje Asunción, Edif Rioja, Loc 11. Peruvian-owned ceviche restaurant, hole-in-the-wall, he puts chairs out on alleyway.

🍴-🍴 Gran Café, Sabana Grande. Great open air café-restaurant, good place to have a coffee or meal and watch the world go by.

🍴-🍴 Sabas Nieves, C Pascual Navarro 12. Homely, good value vegetarian restaurant.

🍴 El Arabito C Villaflor, just off Av Abraham Lincoln between metro stations Sabana Grande and Plaza Venezuela. Arabic food. Others in this area.

🍴 Areparía 24 Horas, Av Casanova y Av Las Acacias. Busy, inexpensive and very popular.

🍴 El Arepazo, 1 block south of Chacaíto metro station. Every kind of arepa filling you could want.

Chuao/Las Mercedes *map p23*
The area has a good selection of upmarket restaurants and US-style steakhouses and chains.

ᵀᵀᵀ Astrid y Gaston, Londres entre Av Caroní y Nueva York, T993 1119, Las Mercedes, www.astridygaston.com. Very nice Peruvian restaurant with open kitchen and friendly staff.

ᵀᵀᵀ Coco Thai and Lounge, CC Tolón, piso 3, Las Mercedes. Excellent Thai food in this sophisticated restaurant with roof terrace

ᵀᵀᵀ-ᵀᵀ La Castañuela, C Trinidad con C París. Live music at weekends, bar area, good Spanish food, generous portions, attentive service, popular.

ᵀᵀ La Carreta, Centro Uruguayo Venezolano, Av Arístides Calvani, Los Chorros, T234 0317. Atmospheric haunt of the Uruguayan community with fantastic meat and tango dancing on Wed and Sun nights.

ᵀᵀ La Taberna de Félix, Av Principal de las Mercedes, Multicentro las Mercedes. Lively Spanish restaurant and bar with live music and flamenco.

ᵀᵀ Nouveau Café, Av Principal De Valle Arribe, cruce con Av Orinoco. Well-priced, tasty Mediterranean food, including pastas, nice décor and terrace. Open Sun.

ᵀᵀ Persepolis, C California con C Mucuchíes, T993 3987. Good Iranian food.

Altamira, La Castellana *map p19*

ᵀᵀᵀ Avila Tei, Av San Felipe, Centro Coinasa, T263 1520. Excellent, elegant sushi restaurant, private booths available, closed Sun.

ᵀᵀᵀ Café Atlantique, Av Andrés Bello, Los Palos Grandes. Sophisticated bar and restaurant with good food

ᵀᵀᵀ-ᵀᵀ Catar, Cuadra Gastronómica, 6a Transversal. Relaxed, stylish café/restaurant with delicious thin crust pizzas and a melt-in-the-mouth chocolate pudding. Good selection for vegetarians. Closed Mon. Several other good restaurants in this gastronomic block.

ᵀᵀ Come a Casa, 1ra Avenida con 1ra Transversal, Los Palos Grandes. Popular Italian with terrace, cosy atmosphere and home made pasta dishes.

ᵀᵀ El Hornito Andino, 2da Transversal con 4ta Avenida, Campo Alegre. On the edge of Chacao, excellent, good value Andean breakfasts and lunches, vegetarian options. Good service.

ᵀᵀ Evio's Pizza, Av 4 between Transversales 2 y 3, Los Palos Grandes, Altamira. Best pizza in town. Live music from Thu to Sun.

ᵀᵀ Tawa, 1ra Avenida con 1ra Transversal, Los Palos Grandes. Peruvian fusion restaurant, good food with fine service.

ᵀᵀ-ᵀ Miga's, Av Luis Roche con 1ra Transversal, Los Palos Grandes, opposite **Altamira Suites Hotel**, www.migas.com.ve. Busy café/bakery/ deli chain with 6 outlets selling fresh breads, cakes, salads, sandwiches and meat dishes, some vegetarian options, open late.

ᵀᵀ-ᵀ St Honoré, 1ra Transversal con Av Andrés Bello, Los Palos Grandes. Popular café and bakery with covered terrace, good for lunch. Some of the best bread in town.

🔊 Bars and clubs

Caracas *p16, maps p19, p21 and p23*
Caracas has a vibrant nightlife. Clubs don't usually come to life until after 2300, and then go on to the early hours. Las Mercedes district is full of busy, trendy bars.

Bars
360° Rooftop Bar, 19th floor of **Altamira Suites Hotel**, 1ra Avendia, Los Palos Grandes. Hip, sophisticated wine bar with panoramic views of the city, snack on pizza or sushi and sip delicious cocktails. A must just for the views.

El Encuentro de los Artistas, Callejón Asunción (also known as the Callejón de las Puñaladas – Stab Alley!), Sabana Grande. Crowded, lively jazz bar with regular live music, popular with students.

El León, in Plaza La Castellana, T263 6014. Very popular outdoor bar, heaving at weekends, open daily 1200-2400.

El Naturista, 2da Transversal, La Castellana, next to McDonalds, T263 5350. Arepas by day, beer and bar at night, open daily, popular.

Puto Bar, also known as **NuvoBar**, Av Libertador con C El Muñeco, Chacao. Shoreditch and the Lower East Side meet Caracas, small, hip bar with live music.

Centro Comercial San Ignacio, see Shopping, has many fashionable, though pricey bars and the occasional nightclubs, popular with wealthy young Venzuelans. Try **Whisky Bar** (Nivel Blandín), usually packed, trendy and friendly crowd, long bar with terrace area, open daily. Or **Suka** (Nivel Blandín) with giant hammock and good cocktail menu.

La Suite bar, Centro Comercial Tolón Fashion Mall, PB, Las Mercedes, T300 8858. Another popular lounge bar, lavish décor, attracts wealthy 20-something crowd. Mix of music from house to 80s. Tango on Mon, boleros on Tue, jazz on Wed, varied music with invited DJ nights Thu-Sat.

U-Bar, CC Macaracuay Plaza, Macaracuay. Popular, university bar, giant screen, open 2200-0500.

Clubs

El Maní es Así, Av Francisco Solano y C El Cristo, Sabana Grande, T763 6671, www.elmaniesasi.com. Famous for its live salsa and dancing, casual, open Tue-Sun till 0400/0500.

Moulin Rouge, Av Francisco Solano, Las Mercedes. Club famous for its live rock music

⊕ Entertainment

Caracas *p16, maps p19, p21 and p23*
For details of cinemas and other events, see the newspapers, *El Universal* (the cinema page on www.el-universal.com has full listings), *El Nacional* and *Daily Journal*.

Concerts, ballet, theatre and film festivals at the **Ateneo de Caracas**, Paseo Colón, Plaza Morelos. **Centro de Estudios Latinoamericanos Rómulo Gallegos**

(CELARG), Av Luis Roche con 3ra Transversal, Altamira, T285 2721, www.celarg.org.ve. Cultural centre with cinema showing alternative films, theatre, exhibitions, talks.

Trasnocho Cultural, Urb Las Mercedes, Centro Comercial Paseo Las Mercedes, Nivel Trasnocho, T993 1910, www.trasnocho cultural.com. Theatre, cinemas, exhibitions, lounge bar with live DJs Thu-Sat, bookshop, café and yoga centre.

⊛ Festivals and events

Caracas

3 May, **Velorio de la Cruz de Mayo** still celebrated with dances and parties in some districts. **18-25 Dec**, Yuletide masses at different churches leading up to Christmas. Traditional creole dishes served at breakfasts.

○ Shopping

Caracas *p16, maps p19, p21 and p23*
Bookshops   American Bookshop, Nivel Jardín (bottom level) of CC Centro Plaza, Av Francisco de Miranda, Altamira metro, T286 2230/285 8779. Selection of second-hand English books.

Librorio, C París con Nueva York, Las Mercedes, T993 2841, www.libroria.com, Mon-Sat 0830- 1900, Sun 1400-1700. Good selection of English language books and English speaking staff.

Chocolate   La Praline Chocolatier, Av Andrés Bello con 3ra Transversal, Los Palos Grandes, T284 7986. Ultimate heaven for chocaholics, delicious chocolates crafted from Venezuelan cacao. The packets of hot chocolate make great gifts. **Blue Moon**, C La Paz, Plaza de El Hatillo, T963 3023. Divine chocolatier with small café selling hot chocolate mixes.

Handicrafts   Good quality Sun craft market between Museo de Bellas Artes and Museo de Historia Natural (metro Bellas Artes). **Hannsi**, C Bolívar, El Hatillo, T963 5577, www.hannsi.com. ve. A superstore of Venezuelan crafts and products made up of numerous small rooms displaying everything from candles to ceramics to hammocks and artesanías from the Amazon. Good adjoining café with wide coffee selection. Well worth a visit.

Jewellery Edificio La Francia, 'Esquina Caliente', Plaza Bolívar, Centro. Mon-Fri, 0900-1700, Sat 0900-1400, 10 floors of jewellery stores, central hub of Caracas' gold market.

Malls Most shopping takes place in Caracas' numerous malls.

Centro Sambil, Av Libertador, 1 block south of Chacao Metro. One of the largest in South America, with every type of shop, internet cafés, global brands, bookshops, *cambio*, CANTV centres and cinema. Open Mon-Sun 1000-2100.

CC El Recreo, Av Casanova y El Recreo, Sabana Grande. With shops, cinema, food court, open 1100-2100, Sun 1200-2000.

San Ignacio, several blocks north of Chacao Metro. Very exclusive. Cinema, banks and smart cafés, bars and restaurants too, open Mon-Sun 1000-2100.

Markets Mercado Quinta Crespo, off Av Baralt, El Silencio metro, daily, one of the largest central food markets, shabby but vibrant. **Mercado de Chacao**, Av Avila, 3 blocks north of Chacao metro, 0800-1200, daily except Sun. Good food, fruit and veg market.

Mercado Peruano, Colegio de Ingenieros metro, Boulevard Amador Bendayán, from 0900 on Sun, popular small Peruvian food market with ceviche stalls.

▲ Activities and tours

Caracas

Baseball The popular baseball season is from late Sep-Jan. The capital's local team, Los Leones del Caracas, plays at the Estadio Universitario, Los Chaguaramos. Tickets can be bought at the stadium's box office, www.leones.com.

Gym The gym and pool at **La Gran Meliá** are open to non-guests. A 'día del spa', use of the gym, pool for the day and a massage costs US$35.

Tours

There are numerous companies offering organized tours from standard packages to tailor-made trips. For details on climbing and mountaineering, contact **Asociación Venezolana de Instructores y Guías de Montaña (AVIGM)**, www.avigm.com.

Akanan, C Bolívar, Edf Grano de Oro, pb loc C, Chacao, T715 5433, www.akanan.com. Riding, cycling and other outdoor activities outside Caracas.

Alborada Venezuela, Plaza La Castellana, Torre IASA, oficina 101, T265 4052, www.alboradavenezuela.com. Tours focusing on nature conservation.

Alpiviajes, Av Sucre, Centro Parque Boyacá, Torre Centro, Los Dos Caminos, T283 1433, www.alpi-group.com. Tours throughout Venezuela, including fishing trips and adventure sports, English spoken, good for flights and advice. Flying safari tours in private plane. Recommended.

Backpacker Tours, www.backpacker-tours.com (see page 143). Numerous tours on offer including roundtrips, trekking, rafting and biking excursions. Good service.

Candes Turismo, Av Francisco de Miranda, Edif Roraima, p 3, of 3C, T953 1632, www.candes turismo.com. Well-established tour operator, range of destinations, helpful, efficient, English, Italian, German spoken.

Cóndor Verde, Av Caura, Torre Humboldt, M 3, Prados del Este, T975 4354, www.condor verdetravel.com. Operate throughout the country, well-established, German run.

Natoura Travel & Adventure Tours, C 31 entre Av Don Tulio y prol Av 6 No 5-27, Mérida 5101, T274-252 4216 (in US T303-800 4639), www.natoura.com. Tailor-made tours. Specialists in adventure tours and ecotourism. See also page 70.

Natura Raid, Av Principal de la Carlota, Centro Comercial Santa Cecilia, loc 3, T237 2648, www.naturaraid.com. Well-established and experienced agency, bilingual guides, works with local communities.

Orinoco Tours, Edif Galerías Bolívar, p 7, of 75A, Blvd Sabana Grande, T761 8431, www.orinocotours.com. German-owned, flights and tours, including trekking, birdwatching and 'flying safaris.' Very helpful.

Tucaya, Quinta Santa Marta, 1a Av Urbanización Campo Claro, Los Dos Caminos, T234 9401, www.tucaya.com. Small company with good reputation, popular with French speakers.

⊖ Transport

Caracas p16, maps p19, p21 and p23
Air

The airport, 28 km from Caracas at La Guaira port, has 2 terminals, Maiquetía (national) and Simón Bolívar (international), which are 5 mins apart, connected by an air-conditioned walkway. Airport information: www.aeropuerto-maiquetia.com.ve. Facilities include an **Inatur** tourist office (national terminal), casas de cambio, ATM machines, a bank, cafés, restaurants, car hire offices (national terminal) and duty free shops. In both terminals, many people will offer to change money on the black market. There is no way of knowing if they are trustworthy.

Always allow plenty of time when going to the airport, whatever means of transport you are using: the route can be very congested (minimum 45 mins, can take 2 hrs in daytime) and arrive, if possible, in daylight. Allow at least 2 hrs checking-in time before your flight.

It is vital that you do not arrive at the airport without having arranged a pick up. There has been an increase in foreigners getting taken in what seem to be marked taxis, only to be driven off, robbed and left in the middle of nowhere. If the hotel does not have its own taxis, ask them to contact a taxi company or someone they know for you. It is impossible to verify the trustworthiness of the freelance **taxi** drivers who crowd the

terminal. On no account go with an unlicensed driver. There are official taxis. The vehicles are all black, with an oval, yellow logo, which is also displayed at the counter in the arrivals hall where you buy a ticket for the journey into town. You will be accompanied to the taxi by a member of staff. Double check the driver's ID. Prices are listed by the sliding doors, outside which the taxis wait. The fare is about US\$\$40 (at the official rate) per vehicle to Caracas, price depends on time of day and district.

The airport **shuttle bus** (Bus Caracas) leaves from east end of terminal, left out of exit. To airport, catch it under the flyover at Bolívar and Av Sur 17, 250 m from Bellas Artes metro (poorly lit at night, not safe to wait here in the dark), or at metro stations such as Parque Central and Gato Negro. To the city 0700-1930, to the airport 0630-2130, every 30 mins, 1-2 hrs, depending on traffic, US\$5. If heading for a hotel in Chacao or Altamira on arrival, get off at Gato Negro metro station (same fare) and take metro from there (with luggage only at off-peak times). The shuttle bus or *por puesto* to airport can also be caught at Gato Negro metro station. Watch your belongings around Gato Negro. A much cheaper alternative is to take a bus to Catia La Mar and get out at the airport.

Airport information Passengers leaving Caracas on international flights must reconfirm their reservations not less than 72 hrs in advance by telephone or in person; not less than 24 hrs for national flights: if you fail to do this, you lose all rights to free accommodation, food, transport, etc if your flight is cancelled and may lose your seat if the plane is fully booked. Beware of forged tickets; buy only from agencies. If told by an agent that a flight is fully booked, try at the airport anyway. International passengers must check in at least 2 hrs before departure or they may lose their seat to someone on a waiting list.

Bus

Local See Getting around, page 16.
Long distance The *Terminal Oriente* at Guarenas for **eastern destinations** is clean, modern and relatively safe. It can be reached by numerous buses from the city centre and Petare. Take a taxi at night.

The La Bandera terminal for all **western** destinations is a 500 m, unsafe walk from La Bandera metro station on Line 3. City buses that pass are prominently marked 'La Bandera'. Give yourself plenty of time to find the bus you need although there are bus agents who will assist in finding a ticket for your destination. Tickets are sold in advance except for nearby destinations such as **Maracay** and **Valencia**. Those first on get the best seats so it is advisable to arrive an hour before departure. There is a left luggage office, telephone office, cash machines and a restaurant and many food and drink kiosks.

The more upscale **Aeroexpresos Ejecutivos**, Av Principal De Bello Campo, www.aero expresos.com.ve (timetables and prices available online), a private bus company, runs regular services to most major destinations. Prices are more expensive than others, but worth it for the more comfortable and modern buses and for the extra security.

Buses to places near Caracas leave from the old Nuevo Circo bus station (eg **Los Teques, Higuerote, Catia La Mar, La Guaira**).

Sat and Sun morning and public holidays are bad for travel into/out of Caracas. Always take identification when booking a long-distance journey. Times and fares of buses are given under destinations.
International buses Ormeño has 1 bus a week to **Cúcuta**, **Bogotá**, **Cali**, **Quito**, **Guayaquil**, **Lima**; safe, comfortable, a/c, video, toilet.

Car

Car hire Self-drive cars (**Hertz, Avis, Budget, Dollar, ACO**) are available at the airport (offices open 0700-2100, **Avis** till 2300, good service) and in town. See rates on page .

Metro

Operates 0530-2300, no smoking, luggage allowed only at off-peak times, www.metrodecaracas.com.ve. There are 4 lines: Line 1 (west-east) from Propatria to Palo Verde; Line 2 (north-south), from El Silencio to Las Adjuntas, with connection to Caricuao Zoológico and a new line from Las Adjuntas to Los Teques under construction; Line 3, south from Plaza Venezuela via El Valle to La Rinconada; Line 4 (west-east) from Capuchinos to Plaza Venezuela/Zona Rental, with a continuation through Las Mercedes and Chuao being built. A single ticket costs is BsF0.50, BsF0.90 return, whereas a 10-journey (*multi abono*) ticket is economical at BsF4.50. Student discounts are available with ISIC card; apply at Parque del Este station. Metrobuses connect with the Metro system: get transfer tickets (*boleto integrado*, BsF0.70-0.90) for services to southern districts, route maps displayed at stations; retain ticket after exit turnstile. Good selection of maps at shops in Altamira and La California stations.

Motorcycle

Motorcycles may not be ridden in Caracas between 2300 and 0500.

Taxi

Even though they are a legal requirement, meters are never used. Negotiate fares in advance; always offer 10% less than the driver's first quote and bargain hard. Most city trips are about US$8-10 during the day. Taxi drivers are authorized to charge an extra 20% on night trips after 1800, on Sun and all holidays, and US$1 for answering telephone calls. After 1800 drivers are selective about destinations. Beware of taxi drivers trying to renegotiate fixed rates because your destination is in 'a difficult area'. See warning above under Air about pirate taxis. See also under Air (or in Yellow Pages) for radio taxis. **Note** Never tell a driver it's your first visit to Caracas.

⊙ Directory

Caracas *p16, maps p19, p21 and p23*
Airline offices Domestic: Aeropostal, main office: Av Paseo Colón, Torre Polar Oeste, p 22, Los Caobos, T708 6211. **Aereotuy**, Boulevard de Sabana Grande, Edif Gran Sabana, N-174, T212 3110. **Aserca**, Edif Taeca, C Guaicaipuro, El Rosal, T0800-648 8356 (0700-2000, Sun 0800-1600). **Rutaca**, Centro Seguros La Paz, Av Fco de Miranda, Nivel Mezzanina, loc C-12, La California Sur, T624 5800. See Getting around, page 7 for websites. **International: Aerolíneas Argentinas**, Calle Guaicaipuro, Torre Hener p 1, of 1A, El Rosal, T951 6395, call centre 0800-100 5655, www.aerolineas.com, closed at weekends. **Air France**, Edif Parque Cristal, Torre Este, p 2, Los Palos Grandes, T208 7200, www.airfrance.com.ve. **American**, Av Principal, La Castellana, Centro Letonia, T209 8111, www.aa.com.ve. **Avianca**, Av Tamanaco, Torre Norte del edif JW Marriott, loc 21 y 22, El Rosal, T200 5725, 0800-100 5022. **Continental**, Centro Lido, Torre E, p 6, Av F de Miranda, T953 3107/0800-100 3198, www.continental.com. **Cubana** Av Casanova y Av Las Acacias, Torre Banhorient p 5, of 5F, T793 6319, ventascubanacaracas@yahoo.com.ve. **Delta**, Torre E, p 8, Centro Lido, Av Fco de Miranda, El Rosal, T958 1000 . **Iberia**, Av Fco de Miranda, edif Parque Cristal, Torre Este, p 9, Los Palos Grandes, T284 0020. **LAN**, Torre Kleper, of 3-1, Centro San Ignacio, Av Blandín, T263 9663, 0800-100 8600. **Lufthansa**, Centro Torre Conaisa, p 1, of 16, Av San Felipe, La Castellana, closed Sat-Sun.
Banks See also Money, page 11. Plenty of ATMs around the city and most of the banks have branches in the major shopping centres (Sambil, San Igancio, El Tolón). To change American Express TCs, try **Corp Banca**, Av

Principal de La Castellana, Plaza La Castellana, entre Blandín y Los Chaguaramas, Torre Corp Banca, Nivel E-3, La Castellana, T206 4521, mornings and afternoons. They ask for ID and proof of purchase. For money exchange and Amex travel services go to **Italcambio**, the official government exchange office and take ID. They also change Visa TCs, require proof of TC purchase, open Mon-Fri till 1630, Sat till 1200. Offices at Av Urdaneta, esq Animas a Platanal, Edif Camoruco, Nivel Pb, El Centro, T564 4111, Av Francisco de Miranda, CC Lido, Nivel Miranda, T953 9901, at CC Sambil shopping centre, Av Libertador, in Chacao, T265 7423, at Tamanaco Interncontinental Hotel, Las Mercedes, T993 5040, and others. **Italcambio** also at national and international terminals at airport (may limit transaction to US$100, open public holidays).
La Moneda, Centro Financiero Latino, Av Fco Solano, Edif San Germán, Sabana Grande, open Mon-Fri only. **Viajes Febres Parra**, Av Libertador, Edif CC Libertador, PB, Loc 4 y 5, La Florida, and at airport.
Cultural centres British Council, Torre Credicard, p 3, Av Principal del Bosque, Chacaíto, T952 9965, www.britishcouncil.org/ venezuela.htm. Opposite Chacaíto metro, great internet café, magazines, newspapers, film library, courses. **Asociación Cultural Humboldt (Goethe Institut)**, Av Jorge Washington con Juan Germán Roscio, San Bernardino, T552 7634, www.internet.ve/asohum. Library, films, concerts, Spanish and German courses. See also **Centro de Estudios Latinoamericanos Rómulo Gallegos** (CELARG), under Entertainment, and **La Estancia**, page 21, above.
Embassies and consulates Many are open to the public only in the morning, some are closed on Fri. For a full list of all foreign embassies see www.embassy.goabroad.com.
Ferries Conferry office for tickets to **Isla de Margarita**, Plaza Venezuela, Av Casanova con Av Las Acacias, Torre Banhorient, PB,

Sabana Grande, T0501-2663 3779, www.conferry.com. **Internet** Plenty of **CANTV** *centros de comunicaciones* and independent outlets around the city, eg Blvd Sabana Grande (Abraham Lincoln) with broadband, international faxes, and in shopping centres, eg CC Sambil, Chacao. See also **British Council**, above. **Language Schools** **Centro de Idiomas Berlitz**, CC Paseo Las Mercedes, Las Mercedes, www.berlitz.com. **Medical services** **Clínica Avila**, Av San Juan Bosco con 6ta Transversal, Altamira, T276 1111, www.clinicaelavila.com. **Post offices** Ipostel main branch at Urdaneta y Norte 4, near Plaza Bolívar, www.ipostel.gob.ve, for poste restante.

Overseas package service; packages should be ready to send, also at airport. **MRW**, throughout the city, T0800-304 0000, see www.mrw.com.ve for branches. 24-hr service, more reliable than Ipostel.

Telephones Public phones in Metro stations and along Blvd Sabana Grande (Abraham Lincoln). **Useful addresses** SAIME for visa renewal go to Departamento de Admisión, Av Baralt, Edif 1000, p 2, El Silencio, opposite Plaza Miranda, T483 2070/3581/2706. **Touring y Automóvil Club de Venezuela**, Torre Phelps, p 15, of A y C, Plaza Venezuela, T781 9743, desiree@ automovilclubvenezuela.com.

Around Caracas

Between the capital and the Caribbean coast is the national park of El Avila, not only a popular recreational area for caraqueños, but also a refuge for wildlife within earshot of the city and a good place for birdwatching and hiking. The coast itself is also a favourite weekend escape, although it can get busy. Nor, at weekends, can you expect to have Colonia Tovar to yourself, a German immigrant town to which city folk flock for the local produce and mild climate.

Waraira Repano/Monte Avila

The 85,192-ha **Parque Nacional El Avila** (renamed **Waraira Repano**) forms the northern boundary of Caracas. The green slopes rise steeply from both the city and from the central Caribbean coast. Despite being so close to the capital, fauna includes red howler monkeys, jaguar and puma. There are also several species of poisonous snake. Access is from Caracas, with several marked entrances along the Cota Mil (Avenida Boyacá), designed for hikers. The park is closed Monday and Tuesday morning. The website www.el-avila.com gives hiking routes (see below for suggestions and advice). See also www.warairarepano.gob.ve.

A **cable railway** (*teleférico*) runs up Monte El Avila ① *Tue 1300-1800, Wed-Sat 1000-2100, Sun 0900-1800, US$8, students with card US$4.65 and children 4-12 US$3.50, free for over 60s and under 4s, Final Av Principal de Maripérez (Simón Rodríguez), T901 5555 or 793 5960*. The 20-minute cable car ride offers fantastic views of Caracas on clear days and is highly recommended. Courting couples wander the restaurants, food stalls and skating rink at the summit, El Avila station. From here you can look down the other side of Monte Avila over the village of Galipán all the way to the Caribbean sea. The *Humboldt Hotel* on the summit has been refurbished and is open for guided tours but not for sleeping. From El Avila station you can take a 4WD *carrito* to the village of Galipán, a popular weekend excursion with *caraqueños*. The village has a number of good restaurants and numerous stalls selling food and local produce, strawberries and cream, jams and flowers. There are *posadas* for overnight stays. Also worth visiting is the old coffee hacienda Los Venados, where there is a zip wire (known as 'canopy') ① *Senderos Aéreos, T0416-177 4017, www.senderosaereos.com*. El Avila station can also be reached in 45 minutes by shared 4WD *carritos* that leave regularly from the entrance to the park at San Bernardino. A recommended trip is to ride up in a vehicle and hike back down (note that it is cold at the summit, around 13°C).

Listed below are three good places to start a hike. **Advice** Hikers should go in groups of at least three, for mountain and personal safety (Monte Avila is not a dangerous place, but muggings have been reported, especially on more remote paths; leave valuables at home). You should have a park permit from *Inparques* in Caracas to camp (Av F de Miranda, Parque Generalísimo Francisco de Miranda, opposite Parking 2, T273 2807). Always take water and something for the cold at altitude. The unfit should not attempt any of the hikes.

Pico Naiguatá (2765 m) This is a very strenuous hike. Take the metro to La California, then a bus going up Avenida Sanz, ask for the Centro Comercial El Marqués. From there walk up Avenida Sanz towards Cota Mil (Avenida Boyacá), about four blocks. At the end of Avenida Sanz, underneath the bridge, is the entrance to the Naiguatá trail. In about 40 minutes you reach La |Julia *guardaparques* station, where you have to pay US$0.50 entrance.

Pico Oriental (2600 m) From the Altamira metro station take a bus to 'La entrada de Sabas Nieves', where the *Tarzilandia* restaurant is. From here a dirt road leads up to the

Sabas Nieves *guardaparques* station, a steep 20-40 minute hike with good views of the city, popular with keep-fit *caraqueños*. The path to Pico Oriental starts at the back of Sabas Nieves and is extremely easy to follow. **Note** Paths beyond Sabas Nieves are shut in dry season (roughly February-June depending on the year) to prevent forest fires.

Hotel Humboldt (2150 m) This is a relatively easy route of three hours. Take the Metro bus from Bellas Artes station to El Avila stop, US$0.50; opposite is a grocery. Turn the corner and walk two blocks up towards the mountain. At the top of the street turn left; on your right is the park entrance. **Note** This area is not safe before 0800 or after dark. Many people take this route, starting 0830-0900, giving time to get up and down safely and in comfort.

Litoral Central

The Litoral Central is the name given to the stretch of Caribbean Coast directly north of Caracas. A paved road runs east from Catia La Mar, past the airport and then through the towns of Maiquetía, La Guaira and Macuto. This became the state of Vargas in January 1999 and in December that year was the focus of Venezuela's worst natural disaster of the 20th century. Prolonged heavy rains on deforested hillsides caused flash floods and landslides, killing and causing to disappear an estimated 30,000 people and leaving 400,000 homeless. From La Guaira a panoramic road runs to the beaches at Chichiriviche de la Costa, Puerto Cruz (nice beach, no shade, bars) and Puerto Maya (very nice beach with shade and services).

La Guaira, Venezuela's main port dates back to 1567. It achieved its greatest importance in the 18th century when the Basque Guipuzcoana Company held the royal trading monopoly. Much of the city was severely damaged in the 1999 floods.

Colonia Tovar and Guatopo → *Phone code: 0244. Population: 10,000. Altitude: 1890 m.*

This picturesque mountain town was founded in 1843 by German immigrants from Kaiserstuhl in the Black Forest; a small **museum** ⓘ *1000-1800, Sat-Sun and holidays*, tells the history of the founding pioneers. They retained their customs and isolation until a paved road reached the settlement in 1963. It is now very touristy, attracting hordes of weekend visitors, but the blond hair, blue eyes and Schwartzwald-accented German of the inhabitants remain. This *Tovarense* farming community make great bread, blackberry jam, bratwurst and beer. Colonia Tovar offers delightful landscapes, mild climate, old architecture and dignified hospitality.

From Colonia Tovar, Ruta 4 continues (paved but hair raising) south down the slopes for 34 km to La Victoria on the Caracas-Valencia Highway (see below); bus US$1; glorious scenery.

In **San Francisco de Yare** (*Phone code: 0239; 90 km from Caracas*), a celebration is held at Corpus Christi in early June (the eighth Thursday after Thursday of Semana Santa). Some 80 male 'Diablos' of all ages, dressed all in red and wearing horned masks, dance to the sound of their own drums and rattles. From Santa Teresa make a detour to the beautiful and little frequented **Parque Nacional Guatopo** on the road to Altagracia de Orituco (bus from Nuevo Circo marked 'El Popular', US$1.35). You must return to Santa Teresa to continue your journey to Yare. At the Parque Guatopo are various convenient places to picnic on the route through the forest and a number of good nature trails. Take insect repellent. Free camping at Hacienda La Elvira; take jeep from Altagracia de Orituco (US$1) and ask to be let off at the turn-off to the Hacienda. A permit must be obtained at the Inparques office in Caracas, which has some accommodation, or baggage can be stored temporarily while walking in the park.

Around Caracas listings

For Sleeping and Eating price codes and other relevant information, see Essentials, pages 9-11.

😴 Sleeping

Litoral Central *p34*

If you're arriving or leaving the airport at odd times, there are some good choices in Catia La Mar and Macuto as an alternative to Caracas. These places often provide transfers, or a taxi costs about US$5, 5-20 mins depending on traffic.

$$$$ Eurobuilding Express Maiquetía, Av La Armada, T7000 700, maiquetia@eurobuilding .com.ve. Useful business hotel with pool, tennis, cable TV, internet in rooms, airport transfer.

$$$$ Olé Caribe, Final Av Intercomunal, El Playón, 1160, Macuto, T620 2000, www.hotelolecaribe.com. A good, if expensive bet near the airport, a/c, TV, safe in room, breakfast, pool.

$$$-$$ Posada Il Prezzano, Av Principal de Playa Grande c/c 5, Catia La Mar, T351 2626, www.ilprezzano.com.ve. Italian-run, spotless, pleasant, good value, a/c, restaurant.

$$ Catimar, Urb Puerto Viejo Av Principal, Catia La Mar, T351 7906, www.hotelcatimar.com. Price includes transfers to and from airport (you may have to phone them from Asistencia al usuario desk), nice bar, restaurant, internet, basic rooms, expensive for what's offered. Near small Puerto Viejo beach, said to be safe, with a few restaurants (**Brisas del Mar, Puerto Mar**), snack bar.

$$ Santiago, Av La Playa, Urb Alamo, Macuto, T213 3500, www.hotelsantiago.com.ve. Comfortable, restaurant with live music, pool, secure parking, internet, 15 mins' drive to airport.

Colonia Tovar *p34*

There are many hotels, normally full at weekends. Rates, **$$** category and above,

include good, German-style food. Half-board prices are usually **$$$**. Credit cards widely accepted.

🍴 Eating

Colonia Tovar *p34*

Many places serve German delicacies.

† El Codazzi, in centre on C Codazzi. Traditional German and Hungarian dishes, strudel and biscuits, Wed-Sun 1100-1600. Recommended.

† El Molino, C Molino next to the old mill, 5 min walk from main plaza. Great *jugo de fresas*, wide selection of German dishes, open 0900-1000, 1200-1600, 1800-1900, Mon 0900-1400.

Café Munstall, opposite the church, interesting location in oldest house in Colonia Tovar. Excellent pastries and coffee at weekends.

Fruit, vegetables and flowers sold at **Frutería Bergman**, next to Lagoven station at east entrance to town; across the street is **Panadería Tovar** for delicious bread; many food stalls on weekends along Av Codazzi.

🥾 Activities and tours

Monte Avila *p33*

Centro Excursionista Caracas, Av Santa Sofia Sur, Zona Polideportivo, Urb Santa Sofia. El Cafetal, Caracas, cecaracas@cantv.net. This hiking club meets Sat 1430, day and weekend hikes, very welcoming; some English and German spoken.

🚌 Transport

Colonia Tovar *p34*

The 1½ hrs' windy drive up from Caracas on Ruta 4, through Antímano and El Junquito, is easy during the week, but murder (2½ hrs) on weekends: long traffic jams, few picnic spots or accommodation, definitely not recommended. It is generally easy to get a lift if there are no buses.

Bus From Av Sur 9 y El Rosario, next to Nuevo Circo, or, easier, from La Yaguara metro station, to El Junquito (1 hr, US$0.50), then change for Colonia Tovar (1 hr, US$1). *Por puesto* from Plaza Catia or O'Leary (more frequently), Caracas, 1 hr, US$2. Alternatively, take a *por puesto* from Plaza Capuchino to El Junquito, then one from there to Colonia Tovar, US$1.50. Last bus to Caracas 1800, later at weekends.

West from Caracas

The Central Highlands run through this varied region. North of the highlands is the Caribbean, with secluded coves and popular resorts such as Puerto Colombia. Straddling the mountains is the birders' paradise of Parque Nacional Henri Pittier. Two coastal national parks, Morrocoy, which lies offshore, and Los Médanos, around the old city of Coro, are further highlights of this area. West of Coro is the city and lake of Maracaibo, for most Venezuelans, a region summed up in three letters – oil. For others, it can be summed up in four letters – heat. Both are certainly true. To the south, though, are the eastern extremities of the Andean mountain chain, with quaint villages, lakes and high passes on the way to the Sierra Nevada de Mérida.

Maracay and around

Maracay is a hot, thriving industrial city and is the gateway to Henri Pittier national park. The city has some pleasant leafy residential neighbourhoods and is the centre of an important agricultural area. The great basin in which lies the Lago de Valencia and the industrial town of Valencia is 100 km west of Caracas. The basin, which is only 450 m above sea-level, receives plenty of rain and is one of the most important agricultural areas in the country.

Maracay → *Phone code: 0243. Population: 607,000. Altitude: 445 m.*
In its heyday Maracay was the favourite city of Gen Juan Vicente Gómez (dictator, 1909-1935) and some of his most fantastic whims are still there. **Jardín Las Delicias** (Avenida Las Delicias, en route to Choroní; take an Ocumare bus from terminal) with its beautiful zoological garden (closed Monday), park and fountain, built for his revels. The **Gómez mausoleum** (Calle Mariño) has a huge triumphal arch. The heart of the city is **Plaza Girardot**, on which stands the attractive, white **Cathedral**, dating back almost to the city's foundation in 1701. There is an interesting collection of prehispanic artefacts in the museum of the **Instituto de Antropología e Historia** ① *south side of the plaza, T247 2521, Tue-Sun 0800-1200, 1400-1800, free.* The opposite end of the same building has rooms dedicated to Gómez and Bolívar. At the rear of the building is the **Biblioteca de Historia** whose walls are lined with portraits of Bolívar. **Plaza Bolívar**, said to be the largest such-named plaza in Latin America, is 500 m east. On one side is the **Palacio del Gobierno**, originally the *Hotel Jardín*, built by Gómez in 1924. Also here are the **Palacio Legislativo** and the **opera house** (1973). The school and experimental stations of the Ministry of Agriculture are worth visiting. The **Museo Aeronáutico de las Fuerzas**

Aéreas Venezolanas ① *Av Las Delicias con Av 19 de Abril, 1 block from Plaza Bolívar, T233 3812, Sat-Sun 0900-1700*, has an interesting collection of aircraft and memorabilia. The San José festival is on 16-25 March. Tourist office for the state, **Iatur** ① *Av Las Delicias, Hotel Maracay pb, Municipio Girardot, T242 2284, iaturaragua1@ hotmail.com, open Mon-Fri 0900-1400; municipal website www.aragua.gob.ve.*

Parque Nacional Henri Pittier

A land of steep, lush, rugged hills and tumbling mountain streams, the 107,800 ha park, rises from sea-level in the north to 2430 m at Pico Cenizo, descending to 450 m towards the Lago de Valencia. Named after Swiss conservationist and engineer Henri Pittier, the park was established in 1937 and is the oldest in the country. It has 578 bird species, including seven different eagles and eight kites. It contains 43% of all species in Venezuela. The park is also home to pumas and jaguars. It extends from the north of Maracay to the Caribbean, excluding the coastal towns of Ocumare, Cata and Choroní, and south to the valleys of Aragua and the villages of Vigírima, Mariara and Turmero. The dry season is December-March and the rainy season (although still agreeable) is April-November. The variation in altitude gives a great range of vegetation, including impressive lower and upper cloud forests and bamboo. See *Parque Nacional de Henri Pittier – Lista de Aves*, by Miguel Lentino and Mary Lou Goodwin, 1993.

Two paved roads cut through the Park. The Ocumare (western) road climbs to the 1128 m high Portachuelo pass, guarded by twin peaks (38 km from Maracay). At the pass is Rancho Grande, the uncompleted palace/hotel Gómez was building when he died (in a state of disrepair). It is close to the bird migratory routes, September and October are the best months. There are many trails in the vicinity. Permits to visit the park and walk the trails near the **Rancho Grande biological research station** ① *T283 8264, museoebrg@cantv.net, open 0900-1600* are available here.

Aragua Coast

To Cata and Cuyagua The road to the coast from Rancho Grande goes through **Ocumare de la Costa** *(Population: 6140, 48 km from Maracay)*, to La Boca de Ocumare and **El Playón** (hotels and restaurants at both places). The road is very busy at weekends. Some 20 minutes west by boat is **La Ciénaga**, a pretty place, but little shade. A few kilometres east

Parque Nacional Henri Pittier

is **Bahía de Cata**, now overdeveloped, particularly at the west end, while the smaller beach at **Catita** is reached by fishing boat ferries (10 minutes, US$1), or a 20 minute walk, tricky over rocks at the start. In Cata town (5 km inland, population of town and beach 3120) is the small colonial church of San Francisco; devil dancers here fulfil an ancient vow by dancing non-stop through the morning of 27 July each year. Cuyagua beach, unspoilt, is 23 km further on at the end of the road. Good surfing, dangerous rips for swimmers. Devil dancers here too, on movable date in July/August.

To Choroní The second twisty and narrow (eastern) road through the Parque Nacional Henri Pittier is spectacular and goes over a more easterly pass (1830 m), to **Santa Clara de Choroní**, a small colonial town with attractive, pastel single-storey houses (no ATM). The Fiesta de San Juan on 31 May is worth seeing. Choroní is a good base for walking. There are many opportunities for exploring the unmarked trails, some originating in picturesque spots such as the river pools, 'pozos', of El Lajao (beware of the dangerous whirlpool), and Los Colores, 6 km above Choroní. Other recommended 'pozos' are La Virgen, 10 km from Choroní, and La Nevera, 11 km away.

Puerto Colombia and around → *Phone code: 0243. Population: 7000.*
Just beyond Choroní is the popular fishing village of **Puerto Colombia**, a laid back place with several narrow streets lined with colonial buildings. During high season, its small main bay attracts arts and crafts sellers. It is a good place to stay and spend a couple of days beach hopping with boat rides to different bays. Five minutes' walk across the river lies Puerto Colombia's main attraction; the dazzling long stretch of white beach, Playa Grande, lined with palm trees beneath mountains. There is a row of good fish restaurants at the beach entrance. At weekends drummers drum and dancers gyrate and the beach gets crowded with campers and families. At other times it's more peaceful, with brightly painted fishing boats in the river and frigate birds wheeling overhead. If swimming, beware the strong undertow. There are public showers at the entrance. Many fishing boats are for hire in the harbour, US$35 for a day trip. A very bumpy, 30-minute ride east goes to **Cepe**, another beautiful long beach with good swimming, popular with campers. About US$15, boats usually take 6-10 people, or *por puesto* fishing boat from the port US$1.50 per person. From the beach, there is a delightful 25-minute walk to **Pueblo de Cepe** through the Henri Pittier park. Several places on the beach serve fish, salad and *tostones* for US$5. Most locals bring their own supplies in the obligatory beer cooler. From the beautiful unspoiled beach there are fishing and scuba diving trips. The latter, with guide and equipment, explore the only bit of coral on this stretch of the coast. At Cepe's west end, you can climb the hill and descend to **Playa Escondida**, a deserted but more rocky beach. Other beaches include: to the east, before Cepe, Valle Seco (boat US$20, some shade, natural pool protected by reef) and **Chuao**. To the west are: Diario (small, no shade), Aroa (lovely, with river and palms, rough sea but one safe bathing area, no services, take everything with you, three hours' hike from Choroní, go early) and Uricao (also isolated); boat to Uricao US$15.

Maracay and around listings

For Sleeping and Eating price codes and other
relevant information, see Essentials, pages 9-11.

⊖ Sleeping

Maracay *p37*
Budget hotels are in streets around Plaza
Girardot.

$$$ Italo, Av Las Delicias, Urb La Soledad,
T232 1576, info@hotelitalo.com.ve. A/c, large,
modern 4-star, on bus route, pleasant, small
rooftop pool, good Italian restaurant, *El Fornaio*.
Recommended.

$$ Posada El Limón, C El Piñal 64, El Limón
suburb, near Parque Nacional Henri Pittier,
T283 4925, www.posadaellimon.com. Dutch
owned, some way from centre, Caracas
airport transfers US$125 cash in good car
with English-speaking driver, relaxed and
pleasant, family atmosphere, spacious rooms
with a/c and hot water, **$** in dorm, laundry,
pool, internet, good restaurant, parking, trips
to Parque with guide.

$$ Princesa Plaza, Av Miranda Este entre
Fuerzas Aéreas y Av Bermúdez, T232 2052.
Large commercial hotel, 1 block east of Plaza
Bolívar, convenient, a/c, inexpensive
restaurant.

$ Caroní, Ayacucho Norte 197, Bolívar,
T554 4465. A/c, hot showers, comfortable.
Recommended.

$ Mar del Plata, Av Santos Michelena 23,
T246 4313, mardelplatahotel@gmail.com.
Central, with a/c, cable TV, hot water, excellent.

$ Sao Vicente, Av Bolívar 03. Decent budget
option, a/c, central location, cable TV.

Parque Nacional Henri Pittier
p38, map 38
$ pp Campamento El Cocuy, Choroní
(**$$** full board), T243-991 1106, 0416-747
3833, www.cocuy.org.ve. Pleasant mountain
refuge, beautiful views, sleeping in
hammocks. Walking and birdwatching tours,
bilingual guides.

**$ pp Rancho Grande biological research
station**. Plenty of beds in basic dorms,
US$7.50 pp per night, use of kitchen facilities,
take warm sleeping bag, candles and food;
nearest supplies at El Limón, 20 km before
Rancho Grande.

Aragua Coast *p38*
Ocumare de la Costa
$$$ De La Costa Eco-Lodge, California 23,
T993 1986, 0414-460 0655,
www.ecovenezuela.com. Comfortable,
upmarket lodge near beach, with outdoor bar
serving food, restaurant, roof terraces with
good sea views, pool, landscaped gardens,
excursions, equipment hire, specialist
bilingual guides. Includes breakfast.

$ Posada Mis Tres Tesoros, Anzoátegui 46,
T993 1725, 0414-588 0149. 6 blocks from sea,
a/c, cable TV, simple rooms, hot water, very
good, helpful owners.

La Ciénaga
$$$ pp all-inclusive Coral Lagoon Lodge, La
Ciénaga, T0212-762 5975 at Angel-Eco Tours,
www.corallagoonlodge.com. A dive resort
accessible only by boat. Beautiful location on
waterfront with view of mountains. 6 rooms in
2 cabins sleeping 2-4 people, fans, solar power
with back-up generator, rainwater and
seawater used. Hammocks, deckchairs, kayaks
and snorkelling. Diving with PADI and SSI
instructors to underwater grottos, canyons,
reefs and wrecks.

Choroní
See www.choroni.info for listings and
locations of many hotels and posadas.
$$$ Hacienda El Portete, C El Cementerio,
T991 1255, www.elportete.com. Restored
cocoa plantation, colonial-style large grounds,
restaurant, a/c, pool, many children's facilities,
excursions.

$$$ Hacienda La Aljorra, 1 km south in La Loma, T0212-252 0002(Caracas), 218 8841 (Choroní), laaljorra@hotmail.com. On roadside, out of town, **$$** on weekdays, breakfast included, hot water, 300-year old cacao hacienda in 62 ha of wooded hillside. Large rooms, relaxing and peaceful.

$$ La Gran Posada, 5 km north of Choroní on a steep hillside above Maracay road, T217 0974. Small hotel right on the roadside with little open space. Neat, a/c pleasant bar and restaurant. Negotiate in low season.

$ Posada Colonial El Picure, C Miranda No 34-A, T991 1296, www.hosteltrail.com/posadaelpicure. Colonial house in village centre, backs onto river. Popular with travellers, welcoming, dorms and private rooms, restaurant with vegetarian options.

Puerto Colombia and around *p39*
There are dozens of posadas for all budgets in town, but most are fully booked during high season when prices rise by around 40%.

$$$ Hostal and Spa Casa Grande (also known as **Coco's**), Morillo 33, T991 1251. One of the best in town, attractive colonial décor, pool, gardens, parking. Excellent.

$$$ Posada Turpial, José Maitin 3, T991 1123, www.posadaturpial.com. Colonial house, a/c, with breakfast, well-organized, cosy, attractive, nice atmosphere, good restaurant, rooms around patio, TV, safety deposit box, German and English spoken. Book in advance. Owners run travel agency www.turpialtravel.com and organize local tours, dive trips. Recommended.

$$$-$$ Posada Pittier, on road to Choroní, 10-min walk from Puerto Colombia, T991 1928, www.posadapittier.com. Small, immaculate rooms, more expensive at weekends, a/c, good meals, helpful, WiFi, garden. Recommended.

$$ Costa Brava, Murillo 9, near Malecón, T991 1057, suarezjf@cantv.net. Cheaper in low season. Basic, cheaper without bath, fans,

laundry, good food, parking, English spoken, family run. Recommended.

$$ Hostal Vista Mar, C Colón at western end, T991 1250. On seafront, pleasant, terraces with hammocks, some rooms with sea view, some with a/c and TV, helpful, secure parking.

$$ La Posada de Choroní, Calle Principal, 2 blocks from Malecón, T991 1191, www.laposada dechoroni.3a2.com. Rooms with a/c and TV, cheaper without TV, cheaper with fan, hot water, colonial with rooms off central garden, parking.

$$ Posada Alonso, near checkpoint, T0416-546 1412 (mob). Quiet, hammocks, laundry. Recommended.

$$ Posada El Malecón, El Malecón 1, T991 1107. On seafront, a/c, hot water, less with fan, small, basic rooms. Discounts Mon-Thu (same owners as Vista Mar), secure parking.

$$ Posada La Parchita, Trino Rangel, T991 1233, 0416-832 2790. Including breakfast, rooms set around a lovely patio, very nice. Recommended, book in advance.

$$ Posada Xuchytlan, Av Principal, after Posada Cataquero, T991 1234. Charming, stylish colonial house, beautiful gardens, comfortable rooms, welcoming, a/c, parking, includes breakfast.

$$-$ La Montañita, Murillo 6, T991 1132, choroni_ indio@hotmail.com. Popular, nice courtyard, charming owners, packages available (**$$** full board).

$ Brisas del Mar, C Principal at the port. Above a bar, noisy but comfortable, a/c, TV, bit overpriced.

$ Casa Luna, next to Hostal Colonial, Morillo 35, no obvious sign, T951 5318, claudibeckmann@ web.de. Colonial house, basic rooms, German and English spoken. Tours to Pittier park, diving trips and airport transfers, jungletrip@choroni.net.

$ Hostal Colonial, on Morillo, opposite bus stop, T218 5012, colonial@choroni.net. Popular hostel, good value, with fan, laundry, German owner. Also good tours in the Pittier park.

$ La Abuela, near bridge to Playa Grande. Basic, fan, shared bath.

$ Posada Doña Enriqueta, Color 3, T991 1158, just off the seafront. Basic rooms, a/c, books tours, helpful, 40% discount Mon-Thu.

Camping is possible on Playa Grande, no permission needed and showers on beach; beware of theft. Crowded during high season.

Cepe and Chuao

Several *posadas* in Chuao, but some distance from the beach (those listed are closer). **La Luzonera ($$)**, on the plaza, T242 1284, is the best, but there are others (**$**), unsigned, basic. Camping is permitted on Chuao and Cepe beaches.

$$$ La Terraza del Morocho, Av Principal Las Tejerías 44, Chuao, T0414-450 3341. A/c, cable TV, helpful, ask about guides for excursions.

$$ El Gran Cacao, 200 m up the hill from the port at Chuao, T218 3604. Comfortable, with a/c or fan, some rooms with TV. Recommended.

$$ Posada Puerto Escondido, Cepe, T241 4645. Includes 3 meals, drinks and boat from Puerto Colombia, spacious rooms, with bath, hot water and fan, peaceful homely atmosphere, tropical gardens and pool area, diving. Recommended.

$ Rincón del Marino, near El Gran Cacao in Chuao. Basic, with fan.

🍴 Eating

Maracay *p37*

Many excellent restaurants in the Av Las Delicias area (eg **Mansión Imperial**, also has internet, bakery and supermarket). Lots of Chinese eateries and *loncherías*, *tascas* and cheap restaurants in streets around Plazas Girardot and Bolívar.

Puerto Colombia *p39*

¶¶¶-¶ Mango, Trino Rangel. Informal setting in patio, delicious catch of the day and pastas, generous portions. Recommended.

¶¶¶-¶ Willy, Vía Playa Grande 1, just after bridge along the river. Very popular, good seafood and meat dishes. In low season only opens Fri-Sun.

¶¶ Costa Café Terraza, just before bridge to Playa Grande. Upstairs terrace looks onto river, excellent fresh fish and tasty dishes. Good service, accepts credit cards.

¶¶-¶ El Abuelo, just before bridge to Playa Grande. Good food and value, accepts credit cards.

⚠ Activities and tours

Puerto Colombia *p39*
Claudia Beckmann and Emilio Espinoza, Unión 4, T951 5318, 0412-435 3056, jungletrip@ choroni.net. Good trips in the national park.

🚍 Transport

Maracay *p37*
Bus The bus station is 2 km southeast of the centre, taxi US$4. It has two sections, Terminal Oriente for long distance and Terminal Nacional for regional buses. *Por puesto* marked 'Terminal' for the bus station and 'Centro' for the centre (Plaza Girardot). To **Maracaibo**, Expresos los Llanos, US$17.50. To **Valencia**, US$3.50, 1 hr, and **Caracas**, US$4.75 by *autobus*, 5 daily, US$5.70 by *microbus*, 1½-2 hrs, and US$5.25 by *por puesto*. **Barinas**, US$12, 7 hrs. **Mérida** US$14-22, 12 hrs; **Ciudad Bolívar**, US$17.50, 10 hrs. To **Coro**, US$12, 7¾ hrs.

Parque Nacional Henri Pittier *p38, map*
Bus Depart from Maracay Terminal; pay full fare to **Ocumare** or hitch from the alcabala at El Limón. **Taxi** Hire in Maracay for day in the park, US$50.

Aragua Coast *p38*

El Playón

Bus From **Maracay**, 2-2½ hours, US$2.75. To **Cata** from El Playón US$0.50 from plaza, from Ocumare de la Costa US$1.

Choroní

Bus There is a single, new bus station between Choroní and Puerto Colombia, serving both. **Maracay-Choroní**, beautiful journey Henri Pittier park, every 2 hrs from 0630-1700, more at the weekend, US$2.75, 2½-3 hrs. Taxi US$7.25. Road congested at holidays and weekends.

Puerto Colombia *p39*

Bus From **Maracay** terminal leave from platform 5. Buses to Maracay depart every hour from 0500 till 1700, US$4.75, 2-3 hrs.
Taxi From **Maracay** US$8.50 pp, 1-1½ hrs.

🛈 Directory

Maracay *p37*

Banks See also Money, page 11. **Italcambio** (Amex), Av Aragua con C Bermúdez, C C Maracay Plaza, p 1, loc 110K, T235 6945, Mon-Fri 0830- 1700, Sat 0830-1200. *Cambio* in **Air Mar** travel agency, CADA Centro Comercial, Av 19 de Abril, Local 20, 2 blocks north of Plaza Girardot. 2.5% commission.
Internet Few places near Plaza Bolívar and CC La Capilla, Av Santos Michelena.

Puerto Colombia *p39*

Banks The nearest banks are in Maracay. Some *posadas* and restaurants change cash/TCs at poor rates, or give cash against credit cards (passport required). *Licorería San Sebastián*, by the bridge, changes cash and TCs and sells phone cards.

Valencia and around

Founded in 1555, Valencia is the capital of Carabobo State and Venezuela's third largest city. It's the centre of its most developed agricultural region and the most industrialized. Near the city are several groups of petroglyphs while the coast has some very popular beach areas. Best known of these is the Morrocoy national park, but you have to seek out the quiet spots.

Valencia → *Phone code: 0241. Population: 1,350,000. Altitude: 480 m.*

A road through low hills thickly planted with citrus, coffee and sugar runs 50 km west from Maracay to the valley in which Valencia lies. It is hot and humid with annual rainfall of 914 mm. Like its Spanish namesake, Valencia is famous for its oranges.

The **Cathedral** ① *daily 0630-1130, 1500-1830, Sun 0630-1200, 1500-1900,* built in 1580, is on the east side of **Plaza Bolívar**. The statue of the Virgen del Socorro (1550) in the left transept is the most valued treasure; on the second Sunday in November (during the Valencia Fair) it is paraded with a richly jewelled crown. See also **El Capitolio** ① *Páez, between Díaz Moreno y Montes de Oca,* the **Teatro Municipal** ① *Colombia y Av Carabobo,* the old **Carabobo University** building and the handsome **Plaza de Toros** ① *south end of Av Constitución beyond the ring road,* which is the second largest in Latin America after Mexico City. The magnificent former **residence of General Páez** (hero of the Carabobo battle) ① *Páez y Boyacá, Tue-Sun 0900-1500, free,* is now a museum. Equally attractive is the **Casa de los Celis** (1766) ① *Av Soublette y C Comercio, Tue-Sun 0800-1200, 1500-1700.* This well-restored colonial house and national monument served as a hospital for wounded soldiers during the Battle of Carabobo. It also houses the **Museo de Arte e Historia**, with pre-Columbian exhibits. Most of the interesting sights are closed on Monday.

Around Valencia

Most important of the region's petroglyphs can be found at the **Parque Nacional Piedras Pintadas**, where lines of prehispanic stone slabs, many bearing swirling glyphs, march up the ridges of Cerro Pintado. At the foot of Cerro Las Rosas is the **Museo Parque Arqueológico Piedra Pintada** ① *Sector Tronconero, vía Vigirmia, Guacara, T041-571 596, Tue-Sat 0900-1700, Sun 1000-1600, free,* has 165 examples of rock art and menhirs (tours, parking, café).

Other extensive ancient petroglyphs have been discovered at **La Taimata** near Güigüe, 34 km east of Valencia on the lake's southern shore. There are more sites on rocks by the Río Chirgua, reached by a 10 km paved road from Highway 11, 50 km west of Valencia. About 5 km past Chirgua, at the Hacienda Cariaprima, is a remarkable 35 m-tall geoglyph, a humanoid figure carved into a steep mountain slope at the head of the valley.

At 30 km southwest of Valencia on the highway to San Carlos is the site of the **Carabobo** battlefield, an impressive historical monument surrounded by splendid gardens. The view over the field from the *mirador* where the Liberator directed the battle in 1814 is impressive. Historical explanations are given on Wednesday, weekends and holidays.

Coast north of Valencia

Puerto Cabello (*Phone code: 0242, Population: 185,000*), 55 km from Valencia, was one of the most important ports in the colonial Americas, from which produce was transported to the Dutch possessions. Puerto Cabello has retained its maritime importance and is Venezuela's key port. Plaza Bolívar and the colonial part of town are by the waterfront promenade at Calle 24 de Julio. The **Museo de Antropología e Historia** ⓘ *C Los Lanceros 43, Tue-Fri 0900-1600, Sat 0900-1230*, is in one of the few remaining colonial houses (1790), in the tangle of small streets between Plaza Bolívar and the sea. It displays the region's history and has a room on Simón Bolívar.

To the east is **Bahía de Patanemo**, a beautiful, tranquil horseshoe-shaped beach shaded by palms. It has three main sectors, Santa Rita, Los Caneyes and Patanemo itself, with the village proper, further from the beach than the other two. All three have lodging, but it may be difficult to find meals midweek (try at posadas). Offshore is the lovely Isla Larga (no shade or facilities), best reached by boat from Quizandal, US$5, 15 minutes. There are several cafés along the beachfront. Nearby are two sunken wrecks that attract divers. From Puerto Cabello, take a *por puesto* from the terminal, 20 minutes, US$0.75, a taxi US$5.75.

Parque Nacional Morrocoy

Palm-studded islets and larger islands (*cayos*) with secluded beaches make up Parque Nacional Morrocoy. The largest and most popular of the islands within the park is **Cayo Sombrero**, with two over-priced fish restaurants. No alcohol is sold on this or other islands; be aware of hidden extra costs and take your own supplies. It is very busy at weekends and during holidays and is generally dirty and noisy. But there are some deserted beaches, with trees on which to sling a hammock. For peace and quiet, take boats to the farthest cayos. **Playuela** is beautiful and is considered to have one of the nicest beaches of all. It has a small restaurant at weekends and there's a nice walk to Playuelita. **Boca Seca** is also pleasant, with shade and calm water suitable for children, but it can be windy. **Cayo Borracho**, one of the nicest islands, has become a turtle-nesting reserve, closed to visitors. **Playa Azul**, a nice small cayo, has shallow water. The water at **Pescadores** is very shallow. **Los Muertos** has two beaches with shade, mangroves and palms. **Mero**'s beach is beautiful, with palms, but is windy. With appropriate footwear it is possible to walk between some of the islands. Calm waters here are ideal for water-skiing while scuba diving is best suited to beginners. Two things to note, though: a chemical spill in the 1990s destroyed about 50% of the coral in the park, so snorkellers will see very little. Only by diving to deeper waters will you see coral, although in all locations there are still fish to watch. Secondly, take insect repellent against *puri puri* (tiny, vicious mosquitoes) and flies. A number of muggings have been reported around Playa Sur.

Adjoining the park to the north is a vast nesting area for scarlet ibis, flamingos and herons, the **Cuare Wildlife Sanctuary**. Most of the flamingos are in and around the estuary next to Chichiriviche, which is too shallow for boats but you can walk there or take a taxi. Birds are best watched early morning or late afternoon.

Tucacas and Chichiriviche → *Phone code: 0259.*

Tucacas is a hot, busy, dirty town, where bananas and other fruit are loaded for Curaçao and Aruba. Popular and expensive as a beach resort, it has garish high-rise blocks and casinos. Its port area is gaining a reputation for rip-offs and robberies. A few kilometres beyond Tucacas, towards Coro, is Chichiriviche (*Population: 7000*), smaller, more relaxed, but lined with tacky shops, also dirty and not that attractive. Both provide access to Parque Nacional Morrocoy, each town serving separate *cayos*, but only as far as Cayo Sombrero. Apart from this and the diving options, no one has a good word to say about Tucacas or Chichiriviche.

Valencia and around listings

For Sleeping and Eating price codes and other relevant information, see Essentials, pages 9-11.

⊜ Sleeping

Valencia *p44*
There are hotels for all budgets on Av Bolívar, but it is a long avenue, so don't attempt to walk it.

$$$ Don Pelayo, Av Díaz Moreno y Rondón, T857 8793, www.hoteldonpelayo.com. Central, modern block, restaurant, a/c, includes buffet breakfast.

$$ Marconi, Av Bolívar 141-65, T823 4843. Small, modern hotel, simple rooms, a/c, helpful, safe, laundry, recommended (next to a petrol station), take bus or colectivo from bus station to stop after 'El Elevado' bridge.

$ Carabobo, C Libertad 100-37, esq Plaza Bolívar, T858 8860. Central, cold water, OK, with a/c lobby.

Coast north of Valencia *p44*
$$$ Posada Edén, Final Av Principal Los Caneyes, T0416-442 4955. The best posada in the region, small, comfortable, with a/c, TV, hot water, restaurant and pool.

$$$ Posada Santa Margarita, Bolívar 4-36, Puerto Cabello, T361 4112, www.posadasantamargarita.com.ve. Converted colonial house in historic part of town, 2 blocks from the waterfront promenade, local day trips, attractive rooms, roof terrace, restaurant, small pool, breakfast included. Reserve in advance.

At **Patanemo** there are hotels and *posadas* in the village (eg **Patanemo**, **Chachita** and **Iliana**).

$ Posada Natal Mar, at entrance to Caneyes sector, 100 m from turn-off to Bahía de Patanemo, T0412-536 7961. Small but clean rooms with a/c, TV, but no windows, restaurant upstairs.

Parque Nacional Morrocoy *p45*
Camping is allowed at **Cayo Paiclás** and **Cayo Sol** but you must first make a reservation with **Inparques** (National Parks), T800 8487 or 859 0530, daily 0800-2000; reserve at least 8 working days in advance; US$2.50 pp per night, 7 nights max, pay in full in advance (very complicated procedure). Very few facilities and no fresh water at **Paiclás**. **Playa Azul** and **Paiclás** have ecological toilets. At weekends and holidays it is very crowded and litter-strewn (beware rats).

$$$$ pp Villa Mangrovia on the Lizardo Spit between Tucacas and Chichiriviche, the only place to stay in the park. 3 rooms, excellent food and service, charming owner. Book via **Last Frontiers**, T01296-653000, or **Journey Latin America**, T0161-832 1441.

Tucacas *p45*
For a wider choice of budget accommodation stay at Chichiriviche rather than Tucacas. Most hotels and restaurants in Tucacas are on the long Av Libertador, the town's main street.

$$ Manaure, T812 0286. Modern, low-rise hotel, a/c, hot water, pool, good.

$$ Posada Villa Gregoria, C Mariño, 1 block north of bus stop behind the large water tank, T818 6359. Spanish-run, helpful, relaxing, good value, fan or a/c, laundry, small rooms, hammocks, garden, secure parking. Tours, English spoken.

$ Posada Amigos del Mar, C Nueva, near bus stop, beyond Hospital Viejo, T812 3962. Helpful staff, organizes trips to cayos and diving, use of kitchen, with fan. A good budget option.

Camping Gas in Tucacas or Puerto Cabello.

Chichiriviche *p45*
There are plenty of reasonably priced posadas.

\$\$ Capri, Av Zamora, T818 6026. Near docks, basic rooms, a bit shabby, shower, fan or a/c, pleasant, Italian owner, good restaurant and supermarket.

\$\$ Posada Sol, Mar y Arena, Mariño y Partida, T815 0306, posadasolmaryarena@cantv.net. Small rooms with a/c, TV, welcoming, upstairs terrace with a grill, 1 block from sea, changes US\$.

\$ Morena's Place, Sector Playa Norte, 10 mins walk from bus stop, T815 0936, posadamorenas@hotmail.com. Beautifully decorated house, fan, hammocks, helpful hosts, English spoken.

\$ Posada Alemania, Cementos Coro, T815 0912. German-run, runs tours, rents snorkel gear, 200 m from Playa Sur, nice garden.

\$ Posada Res Delia, C Mariño 30, 1 block from Gregoria, T818 6089. Including breakfast, **\$** with a/c, shared bath, organizes tours.

\$ Posada Tío José, on street parallel to main avenue, 1 block off, T898 0215. More pricey in high season, a/c, TV, cosy atmosphere, pleasant decor. Recommended.

🍴 Eating

Valencia *p44*
🍴🍴 **La Rinconada**, Plaza Bolívar. Recommended, open Sun.

Chichiriviche *p45*
Many fish restaurants along seafront, eg 🍴 **Txalupa**. Good seafood and Spanish dishes, efficient service. And **Veracruz**. Good fish.

⛰ Activities and tours

Tucacas *p45*
Bicycles can be hired in town.
Diving Equipment can be hired from near the harbour. There are several diving companies.
Submatur, C Ayacucho 6, near Plaza Bolívar, T812 0082, morrocoysubmatur1@cantv.net. Experienced owner, 4-day PADI course US\$350, day trip 2 dives from US\$65 (US\$45 with own

equipment); also rents rooms, **\$** , fan and cooking facilities.

🚍 Transport

Valencia *p44*
Air The airport is 6 km southeast of centre. Taxi airport-bus terminal US\$10.50.
Aeropostal flights daily to **Maracaibo** and **Porlamar**. Aserca flies to **Caracas, Maracaibo, Puerto Ordaz** and other cities (often via Caracas). **Dutch Antilles Express**, www.flydae.com, and **Insel Air**, www.fly-inselair.com, each fly to **Curaçao** 6 days a week.
Bus Terminal is 4 km east of centre, part of shopping mall *Big-Low* (24-hr restaurants). Entry to platforms by *ficha* (token), US\$2. Left luggage. Minibus to centre, frequent and cheap, but slow and confusing route at peak times; taxi from bus station to centre, US\$4.50 (official drivers wear ID badges). To **Caracas**, frequent buses with **Aeroexpresos Ejecutivos** from 0600-1900, 2½ hrs, US\$5.75. To **Maracay**, US\$3.50, 1 hr. **Mérida**, 10-12 hrs, US\$13-22; to **San Cristóbal**, 10 hrs, US\$19. **Barquisimeto**, US\$9, 3½ hrs. To **Maracaibo**, 2 evening buses with **Aeroexpresos Ejecutivos**, US\$15.50, 8 hrs. **Puerto Cabello**, US\$1, 1 hr. **Tucacas**, US\$2.50, or US\$5.25 by frequent *por puesto* service. To **Coro** US\$8.65, 4½ hrs. To **Ciudad Bolívar**, US\$18.25, 10 hrs.

Around Valencia *p44*
Parque Nacional Piedras Pintadas
Bus To **Vigírima** 20 km northeast of Valencia at regular intervals (US\$1), ask to get off at the 'Cerro Pintado' turnoff. Driving from Vigírima, turn left at a small blue 'Cadafe Tronconero' sign, then a further 3 km.

Carabobo
Bus To Carabobo leave from bottom of Av Bolívar Sur y C 75, or from Plaza 5 de Julio, Valencia, US\$0.50, ask for Parque Carabobo (1¼ hrs).

Parque Nacional Morrocoy *p45*

Ferry From Tucacas: prices per boat from US$20 return to **Paiclás** to US$40 return to **Cayo Sombrero** (max 7 per boat). Ticket office is left of the car entrance to the Park. Recommended boatmen are Orlando and Pepe. Boats to Boca Seca and Playuelita only leave from Tucacas. **From Chichiriviche**: tickets can be bought per person or per boat and vary according to distance; US$17.50 per boat to **Los Muertos**, 10 min trip, US$32-60 to **Cayo Sombrero**. Prices are set for each cayo and there are long and short trips. There are 2 ports: one in the centre, one at Playa Sur. Ask for the ticket system to fix price and to ensure you'll be picked up on time for return trip.

Tucacas *p45*

Bus Frequent *por puesto* from **Valencia**, US$5.25, bus US$2.50; to **Puerto Cabello**, take bus from the intersection of the coastal highway with the main avenue of Tucacas to **Morón** (35 mins, US$1.25), then from Morón to Puerto Cabello (15 mins, US$0.50); Tucacas- Morón bus goes on to Puerto Cabello, if there are enough passengers. To **Coro**, US$5.50, 3 hrs.

Chichiriviche *p45*

Bus To **Puerto Cabello**, frequent *por puestos* often via Valencia, 2 hrs, US$3.50; to **Barquisimeto** often via Morón, 3 hrs; to **Valera**, 9 hrs. To **Coro**, take a bus from the station on Av Zamora to **Sanare**, US$1, every 20 mins, then another to Coro, US$5.50, 3 hrs. Direct buses from **Valencia**, or take bus from Morón to Coro and get out at turnoff, 1½-2 hrs, US$4.65.

O Directory

Valencia *p44*

Banks See also Money, page 11. **Corp Banca**, Av Díaz Moreno, CC Colombia. Amex TCs changed. **Italcambio**, Av Bolívar Norte, Edif Talia, loc 2, T821 8173. Amex travel services, Visa TCs, a long way north of centre in Urbanización Los Sauces, get off bus at junction with C 132; also at airport, Mon-Fri 0830-1700, Sat morning only. **Consulates** British Honorary Consul, Dalca, Urb Industrial El Recreo, Calle B, Parcela 103, T878 3480, burguesdal@cantv.net.ve. **Telephones CANTV**, Plaza Bolívar, for international calls.

Tucacas *p45*

Banks **Banesco** gives cash advance on credit cards. Hotels and travel agents will change money but at very low rates, if they have enough cash. In **Chichiriviche**, many hotels will change dollars and euros but at very low rates.

Coro and around

The relaxed colonial city of Coro, with its sand-dune surroundings, sits at the foot of the arid, windswept Paranaguá Peninsula. Inland from Coro, the Sierra de San Luis is good walking country in fresher surroundings.

Coro → *Phone code: 0268. Population: 175,025. Mean temperature: 28°C.*

Coro, the capital of the Falcón state and former capital of the country, is a UNESCO World Heritage Site. Founded in 1527, it became an important religious centre for Christians and Jews alike. The city, 177 km from Tucacas, is relatively clean and well kept and its small colonial part has several shaded plazas and beautiful buildings, many of which date from the 18th century. Recently, efforts have been made to preserve and restore its colonial heritage. In the rainy season the centre may flood. The **tourist office** is on Paseo Alameda, T251 8033, English spoken, helpful. See also www.coroweb.com (in English, French and Spanish). State tourist office: **Fondo de Turismo**, Av Bolívar, CC Caribe, p3, loc 7, Punto Fijo, T246 7422, www.visitfalcon.com.

The **Cathedral**, a national monument, was begun in 1583. **San Clemente** church has a wooden cross in the plaza in front, which is said to mark the site of the first mass said in Venezuela; it is believed to be the country's oldest such monument ① *Mass Mon-Sat 1930*. It has been undergoing reconstruction. There are several interesting colonial houses, such as **Los Arcaya** ① *Zamora y Federación, also under reconstruction*, one of the best examples of 18th-century architecture, with the **Museo de Cerámica**, small but interesting, with a beautiful garden. **Los Senior** ① *Talavera y Hernández*, where Bolívar stayed in 1827, has the oldest synagogue in Venezuela (1853), if not South America. It houses a branch of the **Museo de Arte Alberto Henríquez** of the Universidad Francisco de Miranda (UNEFM) ① *open sporadically, usually only in the morning, less often in the rainy season*. Another branch of the museum is

Coro

N
200 metres
200 yards

Sleeping 🛏
1 El Gallo
2 Intercaribe
3 Miranda Cumberland
4 Posada Casa Tun Tun
5 Posada Don Antonio
6 Posada La Casa de los Pájaros
7 Taima Taima
8 Vila Antigua

Eating 🍴
1 Barra del Jacal
2 Dulzura y algo más
3 El Portón de Arturo
4 Mersi
5 Panadería Costa Nova
6 Posada Don Luis

on Paseo Talavera entre Bolívar y Comercio. Also on Paseo Talavera is the **Museo de Arte de Coro** ⓘ *T251 5265, www.fmn.gob.ve/fmn_coro.htm, free, Mon-Sat 0900-1900, Sun 0900-1700*, exhibiting some interesting modern artwork. Built 1764-1765, **Las Ventanas de Hierro** ⓘ *Zamora y Colón, Tue-Sat 0900-1200, 1500-1800, Sun 0900-1300, US$0.20*, is now the **Museo de Tradición Familiar.** Just beyond is the **Casa del Tesoro** ⓘ *C Zamora, T252 8701, free*, an art gallery showing local artists' work. There are other handicraft galleries in the centre, such as Centro Artesanal Generalísimo **Francisco de Miranda** near Plaza San Clemente. The **Jewish cemetery** ⓘ *C 23 de Enero esq C Zamora, visit by prior arrangement only, enquire at the Museo de Coro*, is the oldest on the continent. It was founded by Jews who arrived from Curaçao in the early 19th century.

The **Museo de Coro** 'Lucas Guillermo Castillo' ⓘ *C Zamora opposite Plaza San Clemente, T251 1298, Tue-Sat 0900-1200, 1500-1800, Sun 0900-1330, US$0.25*, is in an old monastery, and has a good collection of church relics, recommended.

Coro is surrounded by sand dunes, **Los Médanos de Coro**, which form an impressive **national park** ⓘ *www.losmedanos.com/; outside town on the main road to Punto Fijo: take bus marked 'Carabobo' from C35 Falcón y Av Miranda, or up Av Los Médanos and get off at the end, just after Plaza Concordia, from there walk 500 m to entrance, or take a taxi.* The place is guarded by police and is generally safe, but stay close to the entrance and on no account wander off across the dunes. Kiosk at entrance sells drinks and snacks; open till 2400.

The historic part of the town's port, **La Vela de Coro** (population: 25,275), is included in the UNESCO Heritage Site, with some impressive colonial buildings, lovely sea front, wooden traditional fishing boats and historic church. It has an unmistakable Caribbean feel, but it is in urgent need of facelift (taxi from Coro US$7). On the road to La Vela, near the turning, is the interesting **Jardín Botánico Xerofito Dr León Croizat** ⓘ *Sector Sabana Larga, T277 8451, Mon-Fri 0800-1200, 1300-1600, Sat and Sun 0900-1700, free, getting there: take Vela bus from corner of C Falcón, opposite Banco Coro, and ask to be let off at Pasarela del Jardín Botánico – the bridge over the road*. It is backed by UNESCO and has plants from Africa, Australia, etc. Tours in Spanish.

Paraguaná Peninsula → *Phone code: 0269. Population: 210,000.*

Punto Fijo and around This area is a must for windsurfers and is a great place for walking and flamingo spotting. The western side of the peninsula is industrialized, with oil refineries at Cardón and Amuay connected by pipeline to the Lago de Maracaibo oilfields. The main town is **Punto Fijo**, a busy, unappealing place, whose duty-free zone attracts shoppers with cheap electrical goods and alcohol. About 5 km away is the residential area of **Judibana**, a much nicer place to stay, with shopping centre, cinema and restaurants.

Adícora A quiet if run-down little resort on the east side of the peninsula. The beaches are very windswept and not great but they are popular with wind- and kite-surfers. There are three windsurfing schools in town. Adícora is also a good base for exploring the beautiful, barren and wild peninsula where goats and wild donkeys roam.

Cerro Santa Ana (830 m) is the only hill on the peninsula and commands spectacular views. The entrance is at El Moruy; take bus to Pueblo Nuevo (0730-0800), then take one to Punto Fijo and ask to be dropped off at the entrance to Santa Ana. From the plaza walk back to the signpost for Pueblo Nuevo and take the dirt road going past a white building; 20 m to the left is Restaurant La Hija. Walk 1 km through scrubby vegetation (watch out for dogs) to the *Inparques* office (closed Monday to Friday but busy at weekends). Register here before attempting the steep three-hour climb. It's safer to go on Saturday or Sunday. Some *posadas* in Coro arrange trips to the Peninsula.

Laguna Boca de Caño (also called Laguna Tiraya) is a nature reserve north of Adícora, inland from Supi, along a dirt track that is usually fit for all vehicles. There is abundant bird life, particularly flamingos. It is the only mangrove zone on the east of the peninsula.

Sierra de San Luis

South of Coro, on the road to Barquisimeto, the Sierra includes the **Parque Nacional Juan C Falcón**, with tropical forest, caves and waterfalls. Visit it from the picturesque village of **Curimagua**; jeeps leave from Coro terminal, US$4.65, one hour. The lovely colonial town of **Cabure** is the capital of the Sierra. Jeeps leave from Coro terminal, 58 km, 1¼ hours, US$4.65. As well as hotels, Cabure has restaurants, bars, a bakery, supermarket and pharmacy. A few kilometres up the road is a series of beautiful waterfalls, called the Cataratas de Hueque. **The Spanish Road** is a fantastic three-hour walk through orange groves and tropical forest from Curimagua to Cabure. You will see many butterflies along the way. The path is not well marked, so it is best to hire a guide. Take water. It's very muddy in rains; take insect repellent and good shoes and be prepared to get wet. Ask at any of the hotels listed below. To walk the Spanish Road from Coro in one day, take transport to Cabure, ask to be dropped at the turn-off for the **Posada El Duende** (see below) and walk uphill 1 km to the Posada, where you begin the trek. The path eventually comes out to the Curimagua-Coro paved road, where you can take transport back to Coro.

Coro and around listings

For Sleeping and Eating price codes and other relevant information, see Essentials, pages 9-11.

🛏 Sleeping

Coro *p49, map p49*
Coro has several excellent *posadas* catering for travellers; book well in advance, especially in Dec.
$$$ Miranda Cumberland, Av Josefa Camejo, opposite old airport, T252 2111, reservas@hotelescumberland.com. Large modern hotel, price includes breakfast, good value, restaurant, good pool area, travel agency.
$$ Intercaribe, Av Manaure entre Zamora y Urdaneta, T251 1844, intercaribe@cantv.net. Bland, modern, pool, a/c, small rooms.
$$ Posada Don Antonio, Paseo Talavera 11, T253 9578. Central, small rooms, a/c, internet, parking.

$ El Gallo, Federación 26, T252 9481, www.hosteltrail.com/posadaelgallo/. In colonial part, French/ Venezuelan owned, relaxed, spacious, internet, shared baths, courtyard with hammocks, dorms and private rooms, use of kitchen, some English spoken, see Eric for tours to Sierra San Luis, a 1-day tour includes lunch.
$ Posada Casa Tun Tun, Zamora 92, entre Toledo y Hernández, T404 4260, www.hosteltrail.com/casatuntun/. Run by knowledgeable and welcoming Belgian couple. Restored colonial house with 3 attractive patios, kitchen facilities, laundry, relaxing hammock areas and dipping pool, dorms and rooms with bath and lovely décor. Good value, nice atmosphere, free morning coffee, changes US$. Highly recommended.
$ Posada La Casa de los Pájaros, Monzón 74 entre Ampies y Comercio, T252 8215,

www.casadelospajaros.com.ve. Colonial house 6 blocks from centre, being restored by the owners with local art and antiques, rooms with and without bath, hammock space US$3.50, meals available, free internet, use of kitchen for small fee, laundry service, trips to local sights. Recommended.

$ Taima Taima, C 35 Falcón (away from centre), T252 1215. Small rooms, a/c, TV, some hot water, parking.

$ Villa Antigua, C 58 Comercio 46, T251 6479/ 0414-683 7433. Colonial style, a/c, TV, fountain in courtyard, restaurant, public phones.

Camping   About 30 km east of Coro at **La Cumara**, nice, good beach and dunes.

Punto Fijo *p50*

$$ Caraibi, Av Bolivia entre Peninsular y Ayacucho, T247 0227. With breakfast, good restaurant, parking, a/c, modern, accepts credit cards.

$$ Miami, C Falcón entre Av México y Bolivia, T245 8532. A/c, bit cheaper with fan, parking, restaurant. Recommended.

Judibana

$$ Jardín, on Av Mariscal y C Falcón, near airport, T246 1727. A/c, pool, restaurant, parking, accepts credit cards, changes US$ cash.
$ Luigi, C Oeste, P PB, T246 0970. A/c, pleasant, good restaurant, accepts credit cards.

Adícora *p50*

$$$ Hacienda La Pancha, Vía Pueblo Nuevo, 5 km from Adícora in the hills, T0414-969 2649. Beautiful, old, colonial-style house set in countryside, nice owners, restaurant, pool, no children.

$$-$ Archie's Surf Posada, Playa Sur, T988 8285, www.kitesurfing-venezuela.com. At entrance to Adícora, 5 mins' walk to centre. German-run, well established, organizes wind and kite surfing lessons. Also trips, horse riding and airport pick-ups. Furnished

bungalows for 4-12, apartments for 2-4, hammocks. Good reports.

$ Posada Kitzberger, C Comercio de Adícora, on Malecón, T988 8173. Fan and a/c, German owners, pleasant, cosy, no single rooms, good restaurant. Recommended.

Sierra de San Luís *p51*
Curimagua

$ Finca El Monte, Vía La Soledad, 5 km from the village, T404 0564, fincaelmonte@yahoo.com. Run by a Swiss couple on an eco-friendly basis. Peaceful, beautiful views, colonial style, hot water, meals, hammocks. Tours round the park include birdwatching and cave tours. English, German and French spoken. Highly recommended.

Cabure

In town are several budget options.
$$ Hotel El Duende, 20 mins uphill from village, T808 9066. A beautiful 19th-century posada and garden, price depends on size of room, fan, cold water, good restaurant, horse riding, walking, peaceful. Recommended.

🍴 Eating

Coro *p49, map p49*
🍴 **Barra del Jacal**, Av Manaure y C 29 Unión. Outdoors, pizza and pasta.
🍴 **El Portón de Arturo**, C 56 Toledo, towards Plaza Falcón. All kinds of regional meat.
🍴 **Mersi**, C 56 Toledo y Zamora. Good pizzas and *empanadas*.
🍴 **Posada Don Luis**, opposite airport. Serves local speciality, *chivo*, goat.

Cafés

Dulzura y algo más, on the corner of Paseo Alameda. Good ice cream and local sweets.
Heladería Brudrimar, Paseo Talavera 2, T253 1300. In historic centre, old fashioned, a real institution with good food and good for people watching. Recommended.

Panadería Costa Nova, Av Manaure, opposite *Hotel Intercaribe*. Good bread, sandwiches and pastries, open late.

Punto Fijo *p50*
♥ **Colonial**, C Libertad entre Colombia y Ecuador. Cheap, lunch only. Recommended. ♥ Good *panadería* opposite bus terminal.

Adícora *p50*
Hotel Falcon III, C La Marina, Vía Las Cabanas, T697 9267. On beachfront, white hotel, serves excellent, good value seafood and fish soup. Also rents a/c, basic rooms (**$$**).

✿ Festivals and events

Coro *p49, map p49*
26 Jul, Coro Week. **9-12 Oct**, state fair. **24-25 Dec**, Tambor Coriano and Parranda de San Benito (Coro, La Vela and Puerto Cumarebo).

⛰ Activities and tours

Coro *p49, map p49*
Contact *posadas* in town for tours, eg **La Casa de los Párajos**.

⊖ Transport

Coro *p49, map p49*
Air Airport open for domestic flights; see also Las Piedras, below, for flights.
Bus Terminal is on Av Los Médanos, entre Maparari y Libertad, buses go up C 35 Falcón, US$0.35, taxi US$2.75. To/from **Caracas** US$20, 6-8 hrs; **Maracaibo**, US$11.25 (US$15 with a/c), 4 hrs, *por puesto* US$15; **Tucacas**, every 20 mins, US$8, 3-4 hrs; **Punto Fijo**, *por puesto* US$2.

Punto Fijo *p50*
Air Airport at **Las Piedras**: *por puestos* from C Garcés y Av Bolívar (don't believe taxis who say there are no *por puestos* from airport to town); taxi from Punto Fijo US$5, from bus terminal US$3.50. Daily flights to **Curaçao** with **Insel Air**.
Bus Terminal on C Peninsular entre Colombia y Ecuador; *por puestos* to **Pueblo Nuevo, Adícora, Coro, Valencia** and **Maracaibo**. To **Maracay, Barquisimeto, Maracaibo** and **Caracas**: Expresos Occidente, on C Comercio entre Ecuador y Bolivia; to **Mérida, Barinas** and **Caracas**, Expresos San Cristóbal, C Carnevali behind Hotel América; **Expresos Alianza**, on Av Colombia between Carnevali and Democracia, to many destinations.

Adícora *p50*
Bus Several daily to and from **Coro**, from 0630- 1700, US$2, 1 hr; to and from **Pueblo Nuevo** and **Punto Fijo**, several daily from 0600-1730.

☉ Directory

Coro *p49, map p49*
Banks See also Money, page 11. **Banco Mercantil**, C 35 Falcón y C 50 Colina, Edif Don Luis, ATM and cash on Mastercard. **Banco Venezuela**, Paseo Talavera. ATM and cash on Visa and Mastercard. Try hotels and travel agents for cash and TCs. **Internet** Falcontech, next door to **Hotel Intercaribe**, Av de Manuare. **CANTV** Centro de Comunicaciones, Av Los Médanos, opposite bus terminal, also international calls.

Punto Fijo *p50*
Banks Many banks on Av Bolívar y Comercio accept Visa, Mastercard and others, eg **Banco de Venezuela, Banesco**. Banco Mercantil, Av Bolívar y C Girardot. Changes Citicorp TCs. **Casa Fukayama**, Av Bolívar entre C Altagracia y Girardot. Changes US$ cash. **Consulates** Dutch Consul in Punta Cardón, Judibana at Urb La Laguna, C Mucubaji 38, Roque Hernández, T240 7211. **Post offices** Ipostel at C Páez y Av Panamá, collection every 10 days. **Telephones CANTV** at C Falcón y Av México.

From Maracaibo to Colombia

To the heart of Venezuela's oil business on the shores of Lake Maracaibo: not many tourists find their way here. Those that do are usually on their way to Colombia via the border crossing on the Guajira Peninsula to the north. If you've got the time to stop and can handle the heat, Maracaibo is the only town in Venezuela where occasionally you'll see indigenous people in traditional dress going about their business and nearby are reminders of prehispanic and oil-free customs.

Maracaibo → *Phone code: 0261. Population: 1,800,000.*

Maracaibo, capital of the State of Zulia, is Venezuela's second largest city and oil capital. The region is the economic powerhouse of the country with over 50% of the nation's oil production coming from the Lago de Maracaibo area and Zulia state. The lake is reputedly the largest fresh water reserve in South America. A long cement and steel bridge, Puente General Rafael Urdaneta, crosses Lago de Maracaibo, connecting the city with the rest of the country. Maracaibo is a sprawling modern city with wide streets. Some parts are pleasant to walk around, apart from the intense heat (or when it is flooded in the rainy season), but as in the rest of the country, security is becoming an issue. By the time this edition goes to print, there should be some much-needed improvements in the centre. Plaza Bolívar is undergoing intensive reconstruction and is not considered safe at night. The hottest months are July to September, but there is usually a sea breeze from 1500 until morning. Just north of the regional capital is a lagoon where you can still see the stilt houses that inspired the Spanish invaders to christen it 'Little Venice'. The **tourist office** is Corzutur ⓘ *Av 18, esq C 78 (Dr Portillo), Edif Lieja, p 4, T783 4928, www.gobernacion delzulia.gov.ve.* Zulia state has returned a governor opposed to Chávez in the past two elections and the city is staunchly pro-market. Bear this in mind if expressing political opinions.

Sights The traditional city centre is **Plaza Bolívar**, on which stand the **Cathedral** (at east end), the **Casa de Gobierno**, the **Asamblea Legislativa** and the **Casa de la Capitulación** (or Casa Morales) ⓘ *Mon-Fri, 0800-1600, free,* a colonial building and national monument. The Casa houses the libraries of the Sociedad Bolivariana and of the Academia de Historia de Zulia, a gallery of work by the Venezuelan painter, Carmelo Fernández (1809-1887), several exhibition halls and a stunning interior patio dedicated to modern art. Next door is the 19th-century **Teatro Baralt**, hosting frequent subsidized concerts and performances.

Running west of Plaza Bolívar is the **Paseo de las Ciencias**, a 1970s development which levelled all the old buildings in the area. Only the **Iglesia de Santa Bárbara** stands in the Paseo; a new public park is to be opened here. **Calle Carabobo** (one block north of the Paseo de las Ciencias) is a very good example of a colourful, colonial Maracaibo street. One block south of the Paseo is **Plaza Baralt** ⓘ *Av 6, stretching to C 100 and the old waterfront market* (**Mercado de Pulgas**). The impressive **Centro de Arte de Maracaibo Lía Bermúdez** ⓘ *in the 19th-century Mercado de Pulgas building, Mon-Fri 0800-1200, 1400-1600, Sat-Sun 0930-1700*, displays the work of national and international artists. It is a/c, a good place to escape the midday heat and a good starting place for a walking tour of the city centre. Its walls are decorated with beautiful photographs of Maracaibo. The Centro has a café, internet, bookshops, cinema and holds frequent cultural events, including the Feria Internacional de Arte y Antigüedades de Maracaibo (FIAAM). The new part of the city round **Bella Vista** and towards the University is in vivid contrast with the small **old town** near the docks. The latter, with narrow streets and brightly painted, colonial style adobe houses, has hardly changed from the 19th century, although many buildings are in an advanced state of decay. The buildings facing **Parque Urdaneta** (three blocks north of Paseo de las Ciencias) have been well-restored and are home to several artists. Also well-preserved are the church of **Santa Lucía** and the streets around. This old residential area is a short ride (or long walk) north from the old centre. **Parque La Marina**, on the shores of the lake, contains sculptures by the Venezuelan artist, Jesús Soto (1923-2005). More of his work can be seen in the **Galería de Arte Brindhaven** (free), near Santa Lucía.

Paseo de Maracaibo, or Vereda del Lago, 25 minutes' walk from Plaza Bolívar, is a lakeside park near the *Hotel del Lago*. It offers walks along the shores of the lake, stunning views of the Rafael Urdaneta bridge and of oil tankers sailing to the Caribbean. The park attracts a wide variety of birds. To get there take a 'Milagro' *por puesto* or a 'Norte' bus northbound and ask the driver to let you off at the well-marked entrance. Opposite is the Mercado de los Indios Guajiros (see Shopping).

Maracaibo to Colombia

About one hour north is the Río Limón. Take a bus (US$1, from terminal or Avenida 15 entre C 76 y 77) to **El Moján**, riding with the Guajira Indians as they return to their homes on the peninsula. From El Moján, *por puestos* go to **Sinamaica** (US$2; taxi US$7).

Sinamaica is the entry point to the territory of Añu people (also known as Paraujanos) who live in stilt houses on Sinamaica lagoon. Some 15,000 Añu live in the area, although official numbers say there are only 4000. Their language is practically extinct (UNICEF is supporting a project to revive it: www.unicef.org/infobycountry/venezuela_37969.html; other reports say that one of the only two women still to speak it died recently aged 100). The Añu use fibers to make handicraft. To get to the lagoon, take a truck (US$1) from Sinamaica's main plaza on the new paved road to Puerto Cuervito (five minutes), where the road ends at the lagoon. Dozens of indigenous people will be waiting for water transport. You can hitch a ride on a shared boat to one of the settlements for a few bolívares, or you can hire a boat by the hour (US$20 per hour, ask for Víctor Márquez, recommended). Main settlements on the lagoon are El Barro, La Bocita and Nuevo Mundo. Nuevo Mundo has **Posada Nuevo Mundo**, basic bungalows on stilts on lagoon (**$**). There is small shop. There are several small eateries on the lagoon. **Parador Turístico de la Laguna de Sinamaica** has decent food, clean bathrooms and an excellent handicraft shop with local produce.

Beyond Sinamaica, the paved road past the Lagoon leads to the border with Colombia. Along the way you see Guajira Indians, the men with bare legs, on horseback; the women with long, black, tent-shaped dresses and painted faces, wearing the sandals with big wool pom-poms which they make and sell, more cheaply than in tourist shops. The men do nothing: women do all the work, tending animals, selling slippers and raising very little on the dry, hot, scrubby Guajira Peninsula.

Border with Colombia → *Colombia is 1 hr behind Venezuela.*

If you travel on the road between Maracaibo and the border, even if you are planning to visit just Sinamaica and its lagoon, carry your passport with you. This is tough area, with drug gangs and illegal immigrants (mainly from Colombia) attempting to cross the border. Police and army checkpoints are numerous. They are friendly but can get tough if you don't have your documents, or don't cooperate. The border operates 24 hours. You need an exit card and stamp, US$9.30 (BsF 40), to leave Venezuela, payable in bolívares only. Ask for 90 days on entering Colombia and make sure you get an entry stamp from the Colombian authorities (DAS). From the frontier to Macaio, it's a 15-minute drive. Check exchange rates; it may be better to change bolívares into Colombian pesos in Venezuela at the border rather than in Colombia.

From Maracaibo to Colombia listings

For Sleeping and Eating price codes and other relevant information, see Essentials, pages 9-11.

⊜ Sleeping

Maracaibo *p54*
It is best to reserve well in advance.
Reminder Prices are shown at official exchange rate.
$$$$ Best Western Hotel El Paseo, Av 1B y C 74, Sector Cotorrera, T792 4422, www.hotelelpaseo .com.ve. Closest competition to El Lago (see next entry), all rooms with breathtaking view of the lake. Very expensive but good. ♥ Garisol, revolving restaurant on top floor with great view, international dishes.
$$$$ Kristoff, Av 8 Santa Rita entre C 68 y 69, T796 1000, www.hotelkristoff.com. In the north of the city some distance from centre. Being refurbished throughout, a/c, nice pool open to non-residents, disco, laundry service, restaurant.
$$$$ Venetur Maracaibo, Av 2 (El Milagro), near Club Náutico, T794 4222, www.venetur.gob.ve. With 360 rooms, some overlooking the lake, this 5-star institution is easily the most luxurious hotel in Maracaibo. It was the Intercontinental, but is now part of Venetur.
$$$ Aparthotel Presidente, Av 11 N 68-50, entre C 68 y 69, T798 3133, ahpresi@intercable.com.ve. Self contained units, café and restaurant, pool and travel agency. Good for longer stays.
$$$ Gran Hotel Delicias, Av 15 esq C 70, T797 0983, www.granhoteldelicias.com.

North of the city. Old-fashioned modern hotel, bland, a/c, restaurant, pool, disco, accepts credit cards.
$$ Doral, C 75 y Av 14A, T717 5796, www.hotel doral.com. North of the city. A/c, safe, decent rooms, with breakfast, helpful. Recommended.
$ Acuario, C 78 (also known as Dr Portillo) No 9-43, Bella Vista, T797 1123. A/c, shower, safe, small rooms, safe parking, basic.
$ Paraíso, Av 9B, No 82-70, sector Veritas, T797 6149. With small sitting room, a/c, cable.
$ San Martín, Av 3Y (San Martín) con C 80, T791 5095. A/c, restaurant next door, accepts credit cards.
$ Victoria, Av 6-14, Plaza Baralt, T721 2654. Right in the centre, near Plaza Bolívar, unsafe area at night. Art nouveau structure, basic, private and shared bath, no hot water, a/c, no windows in some rooms, poor value but well located.

❶ Eating

Maracaibo *p54*
A range of US chain restaurants and Chinese restaurants (mostly on Av 8 Santa Rita, including restaurant **Hue Chie**) and pizzerías in the north of town. Many places to eat and bars on Calle 72 and 5 de Julio. Most restaurants are closed on Sun. Many restaurants on *palafitos* (stilts) in Santa Rosa de Agua district, good for fish (*por puesto* US$0.45 to get there); best to go at lunchtime.

¶¶¶ El Zaguán, on C Carabobo (see above).
Serves traditional regional cooking, friendly
service, good menu and food, pleasant bar.
¶¶¶ Paparazzi Ristorante, Av 20 entre C 69 y
70, T783 4979. Part of a nightclub, Italian and
international, one of the best in town.
¶¶ El Carite, C 78, No 8-35, T71878. Excellent
selection of fish and seafood, delicious and
moderately priced.
¶¶ Koto Sushi, Av 11 entre C 75 y 76, Tierra
Negra, T798 8954. Japanese food.
¶¶ Mi Vaquita, Av 3H con C 76. Texan steak
house, popular with wealthy locals, bar area for
dancing, pricey drinks. No sandals allowed.
¶¶ Peruano Marisquería, Av 15 (Delicias) y C
69, T798 1513. Authentic Peruvian seafood
dishes and international cuisine.
¶¶ Pizzería Napoletana, C 77 near Av 4.
Excellent food but poor service, closed Tue.
¶¶ Yal-la, Av 8 C 68, opposite Hotel Kristoff,
T797 8863. Excellent, authentic
Lebanese/Middle Eastern restaurant at very
reasonable prices. Great vegetarian food.
¶¶-¶ Café Baralt, Paseo de las Ciencias,
opposite Teatro Baralt. Recommended for
good value authentic local lunch, irregular
opening hours.
¶ Bambi, Av 4, 78-70. Italian run with good
cappuccino, pastries, recommended.
¶ Chips, Av 31 opposite Centro Comercial
Salto Angel. Regional fast food, *tequeños* and
patacones. Recommended. There are many
other good restaurants around the Plaza de la
República, C77/5 de Julio and Av 31, in Bella
Vista.
¶ Kabuki, C 77 entre Av 12 y 13. Nice café
with good food.
¶ La Friulana, C 95 con Av 3. Good cheap
meal, closes 1900. Repeatedly recommended.

☺ Festivals and events

Maracaibo *p54*
Virgen del Rosario, **5 Oct**; **24 Oct**; **18 Nov**,
NS de Chiquimquira (La Chinita),
processions, bullfights – the main regional
religious festival.

☺ Shopping

Maracaibo *p54*
There are several modern malls with all
services and amenities, including multiplex
cinemas. The most luxurious is **Centro Lago
Mall**.
Bookshops Librería Cultural, Av 5 de Julio.
Best Spanish language bookstore in town.
Librería Italiana, Av 5 de Julio, Ed Centro
América. Postcards and foreign publications.
Staff at the public library, Av 2, are helpful to
tourists.
**Handicrafts and markets El Mercado de
los Indios Guajiros**, open market at C 96 y Av
2 (El Milagro). A few crafts, some pottery,
hammocks, etc. **Las Pulgas**, south side of C 100
entre Av 10 y 14. The outdoor market,
enormous, mostly clothes, shoes, and
household goods. Most of the shops on **C
Carabobo** sell regional crafts, eg *La Salita*. **El
Turista**, C 72 y Av 3H, in front of Centro
Comercial Las Tinajitas, T792 3495.

☺ Transport

Maracaibo *p54*
Air La Chinita airport is 25 km southwest of
city centre (taxis US$20, no *por puestos*). Good
book- shop in arrivals sells city map; several
good but overpriced eateries; *Italcambio* for
exchange, daily 0600-1800, no commission;
car hire outside. Frequent flights with **Aserca,
Aeropostal** and **Avior** to **Caracas, Valencia,
Barquisimeto, San Antonio**, and **Porlamar**.
International flights to **Miami**.
Bus The bus station is 1 km south of the old
town. It is old and chaotic, unsafe at night.
Taxi to the city US$6.50-11. Ask for buses into
town, local services are confusing. Several fast
and comfortable buses daily to **Valencia**,
US$15.50, 8 hrs. **San Cristóbal**, US$18.75-20,
6-8 hrs, *por puesto*, US$21. **Barquisimeto**, 4
hrs in buseta, US$10.50. **Coro** US$11.25-15, 4
hrs. **Caracas**, US$19.50, 10-13 hrs
(**Aeroexpresos Ejecutivos** from Av 15 con C
90 – Distribuidor las Delicias, T783 0620), por

puesto US$40. **Mérida**, from US$11, 5-7 hrs, or *por puesto*, US$12.50, 6½ hrs.

Local *Por puestos* go up and down Av 4 from the old centre to Bella Vista. Ruta 6 goes up and down C 67 (Cecilia Acosta). The San Jacinto bus goes along Av 15 (Las Delicias). Buses from Las Delicias also go to the centre and terminal. From C 76 to the centre *por puestos* marked 'Las Veritas' and buses marked 'Ziruma'. Look for the name of the route on the roof, or the windscreen, passenger's side. Downtown to Av 5 de Julio in a 'Bella Vista' *por puesto* costs US$0.45-0.70, depending on distance. Taxis minimum US$4.65; from north to centre US$7 (beware overcharging, meters are not used). Public transport is being completely overhauled, but it will take years to complete. New large and small red public buses (government-owned) connect the north, centre and other parts of the city at US$0.45. Old private buses charge US$0.55.

An elegant light-rail system, **Metro**, is being developed. Six stations of the first line are in operation, from Altos de la Vanega, southwest of the centre, to Libertador, via Sabaneta and Urdaneta. Basic fare US$0.15. 5 more stations are under construction and more lines are planned.

Border with Colombia *p55*
Maracaibo-Maicao
Bus **Busven** direct at 0400. Other buses operate during the morning, US$15.50. Or take a *colectivo* from Maracaibo bus terminal (5 passengers), US$15.50 pp; shop around, plus US$1 road toll, 2-3 hrs. There are reports that border police are on the look out for bribes, so make sure your documents are in order. Some drivers are unwilling to stop for formalities; make sure the driver takes you all the way to Maicao and arrive before the last bus to Santa Marta or Cartagena (1630).

❸ Directory

Maracaibo *p54*
Banks See also Money, page 11. **Banco Mercantil**, on corner of Plaza de la República. Branches of **Banco de Venezuela**, including at airport, for Visa ATMs. Best for dollars and TCs is **Casa de Cambio de Maracaibo**, C 78 con Av 9B. **Italcambio**, C C Montielco, loc PA 1-1, entre Av 20 y C 72, T7832682, Amex rep. **Citibank**, Av 15 (Las Delicias) con C 77 (5 de Julio) for Citicorp TCs. All banks shut at 1530, exchange morning only. *Cambio* at bus terminal will change Colombian pesos into bolívares at a poor rate. **Consulates Germany**, Av 3F No 69-26, Sector Bellas Artes, T791 1416, herrmann@cantv.net. **Italy**, Av 17 entre C 71 y 55, Quinta La Querencia, Sector Baralt, T783 0834, consolato.maracaibo@ esteri.it. **Norway**, Auto Agro Maracaibo, CA; Av 4 (Bella Vista) No 85-150, T722 9096, autoagromcbo@telcel.net.ve. **UK**, Av 4 Bella Vista, Edif Centro Profesional Norte, of 3A, T797 7003, alexp@inspecciones.com. **Internet** Cyber Estudio, Av 10 No 66-110, 1100-2300. **Medical services** *Hospital Coromoto*, Av 3C, No 51, El Lago, T790 0017. **Post offices** Av Libertador y Av 3. **Telephones** CANTV, C 96, No 3-42, just off the main plaza. Centre for internet and international calls.

Barquisimeto and around

→ *Phone code: 0251. Population: 900,000. Altitude: 565 m. Mean temperature: 25°C*

The arid, fruit-growing area around the city of Barquisimeto leads to the lush Andean foothills of Trujillo state. Venezuela's fourth largest city was largely destroyed by an earthquake in 1812, but is a nice enough place to spend a few days when visiting the area. For information: **División de Turismo y Recreación** ⓘ *Cra 19 esq C 25, Palacio de Gobierno, T233 8239, www.cortulara.gob.ve.* See also www.barquisimeto.com.

Many fascinating corners have been preserved and a law prohibiting demolition of older buildings means more are being restored. The **Museo de Barquisimeto** ⓘ *Av 15 between C 25 and 26, Tue-Fri 0900-1700, Sat-Sun 1000-1700, free,* displays the town's history and contemporary art. More historic buildings line **Plaza Jacinto Lara**. The **San Francisco church** faces the plaza. On the opposite side is the small **Ateneo cultural centre** ⓘ *Cra 17 y C 23, Mon-Fri 0830-1200, 1500-1830, Sat 0900-1200, free,* with exhibitions in an 18th-century house. It also has a restaurant and occasional evening concerts. The **Cathedral** ⓘ *C 30 y Cra 26 (Venezuela),* is a modern structure of reinforced concrete and glass. At the heart of the old city is **Plaza Bolívar**, with a statue of the Liberator, the white-painted **Iglesia Concepción** and the **Palacio Municipal** ⓘ *Cra 17 y C 25,* an attractive modern building. **Parque Ayacucho** ⓘ *Cra 15 (Av Francisco de Miranda) between C 41-43,* has lush vegetation, fountains and a bronze statue of Mariscal Sucre. On Av Libertador Oeste, just out of the city **El Obelisco**, 75 m high (built 1952 to celebrate 400 years of the city), has a lift to the top, worth a visit.

About 24 km southwest of Barquisimeto is the busy agricultural centre of **Quíbor** (*Phone code: 0253, Population: 40,295*). Festivals on 18 January (NS de Altagracia) and 12 June (San Antonio de Padua). The **Centro Antropológico de Quíbor** exhibits work of the *indígenas* who used to live in the region. South of Quíbor and 40 minutes from Barquisimeto is **Sanaré** (1360 m), on the edge of the **Parque Nacional Yacambú**, where you can hike through tropical forest up the Fumerola, a sleeping volcano. About 60 km east of Barquisimeto is **Chivacoa** (*Population: 40,400*). South of the town is the sacred mountain of the María-Lionza cult, practised throughout Venezuela. Celebrations are held there at weekends with 12 October (Día de la Raza) being the most important day. There is a Catholic festival, La Inmaculada Concepción, from 8-14 December.

Barquisimeto and around listings

For Sleeping and Eating price codes and other relevant information, see Essentials, pages 9-11.

◯ Sleeping

Barquisimeto *p59*

Avenidas and Carreras run east to west, Calles run north to south.

$$ Hevelyn, Av Vargas (Cra 17) entre 20 y 21, T252 3986. Hot water, a/c.

$$ Príncipe, Av 18 entre C 22 y C 23, T231 2344. A/c, TV, pool, restaurant.

$$ Yacambú, Av Vargas/Cra 17 entre C 19 y C 20, T251 3022/3229. Accepts credit cards, a/c, bar and restaurant with Mediterranean food.

$ Avenue, Av Vargas/Cra 17 entre C 21 y C 22, T231 1367. A/c and fan, TV, parking, secure.

$ del Centro, Av 20 entre C 26 y C 27, T808 0378. Spacious rooms, a/c or fan, TV, cooled water dispenser on each floor.

$ Don Quijote, Cra 18 entre C 21 y C 22. Clean, cash only, parking, next to restaurant.
$ Lido, Cra 16 entre C 26 y 27, T231 5568. A/c, hot water, some rooms gloomy, cash only, poor value.

Sanaré
$ Posada Turística El Cerrito, T0414-550 4077. English spoken, small restaurant and bar, tours to local sights and Yacambú. Highly recommended.

🍴 Eating

Barquisimeto *p59*
🍴 **Barquipán**, C 26 entre Cras 17 y 18. Good breakfasts, snacks.
🍴 **La Maison de la Vargas**, Av Vargas entre C 21 y C 22. Panadería y pastelería, excellent choice of cakes, pastries, sandwiches. Lots of places to eat on and around Av Vargas.
🍴 **Majestic**, Av 19 con C 31. Breakfast and vegetarian meals.
🍴 **Sabor Vegetariano**, on C 24 entre Av 20 y 21, next to *El Rincón Griego* restaurant. Snacks.

⚙ Festivals and events

Barquisimeto *p59*
On **28 Dec** (morning) is the fiesta of **La Zaragoza**, when colourfully clad people are accompanied by music and dancing in the street. Huge crowds watch **La Divina Pastora** procession in early **Jan**, when an image of the Virgin Mary is carried from the shrine at Santa Rosa village into the city.

⊖ Transport

Barquisimeto *p59*
Air Jacinto Lara international airport is 8 km southwest of the centre, 10 mins, US$5.75 by taxi. Local buses outside, US$0.25. Flights to **Caracas** and **Maracaibo**.
Bus Terminal is on the edge of the city at Carrera 24 y C 42 (a new terminal, Estación Central Simón Bolívar, is under construction on the western edge of the city). To **Mérida**, 3-4 a day, at 1020 and several between 2000 and 0200, 8 hrs via Agua Viva and El Vigía, US$18.50 *bus cama*; to **Acarigua** (see page 84), 1 hr, US$4. To **Barinas**, 5 hrs, US$10. To **Valera** *por puesto*, 3½ hrs, US$8.75. To **Tucacas** every 2 hrs; to **Coro** at 1200 and by night, 7 hrs, US$13. To **Caracas**, US$13.25-15, 5½ hrs.

❶ Directory

Barquisimeto *p59*
Banks See also Money, page 11. **Banco de Venezuela**, Av 20 y C 31, No 31-08, ATM. **Capital Express**, Av Los Leones, Centro Comercial Paseo, next to C 90. **Italcambio**, Av Los Leones, C C París, loc 1-40, T254 9790, and at airport for Amex. **Post offices** Av 17 con C 25. **Telephones** C 30 entre Avs 24 y 25.

Valera to Mérida

From the lowland heat of Valera, roads climb towards the mountains, passing colonial towns and entering an increasingly rugged landscape.

Valera ➜ *Phone code: 0271. Population: 130,000.*

This is the most important town in Trujillo state. Here, you can choose between two roads over the Sierra, either via Timotes and Mucuchíes to Mérida, or via Boconó and down to the Llanos at Guanare. There are several upmarket business hotels, few decent budget ones, and lots of good Italian restaurants on the main street.

Trujillo ➜ *Phone code: 0272. Population: 44,460. Altitude: 805 m.*

From Valera a road runs via the restored colonial village of **La Plazuela** to the state capital, Trujillo. This beautiful historic town consists of two streets running uphill from the Plaza Bolívar. It's a friendly place with a warm, subtropical climate. The **Centro de Historia de Trujillo**, on Avenida Independencia, is a restored colonial house, now a museum. Bolívar lived there and signed the 'proclamation of war to the death' in the house. A 47m-high monument to the **Virgen de la Paz** ① *0900-1700, US$1*, with lift, was built in 1983; it stands at 1608 m, 2½ hours walk from town and gives good views to Lake Maracaibo but go early. Jeeps leave when full from opposite *Hotel Trujillo*, 20 minutes, US$1 per person. For **tourist information**, Avenida Principal La Plazuela, No 1-03, T236 1455, presidenciactt@hotmail.com, or fondomixto@formitru.org.ve.

Boconó and Niquitao

From Trujillo there is a high, winding, spectacular paved road to Boconó, built on steep mountain sides and famed for its crafts. The **Centro de Acopio Artesanal Tiscachic** is highly recommended for *artesanía* (turn left just before bridge at entrance to town and walk 350 m).

Niquitao, a small town one hour southwest of Boconó, is still relatively unspoilt. Excursions can be made to the Teta de Niquitao (4007 m), two hours by jeep, the waterfalls and pools known as Las Pailas, and a nearby lake. Southwest of Niquitao, by partly paved road is **Las Mesitas**; continue up towards **Tuñame**, turn left on a good gravel road (no signs), cross pass and descend to **Pueblo Llano** (one basic hotel and restaurant), from where you can climb to the Parque Nacional Sierra Nevada at 3600 m, passing Santo Domingo. Good hiking in the area.

Road to the high Andes

After **Timotes** the road climbs through increasingly wild, barren and rugged country and through the windy pass of **Pico El Aguila** (4118 m) in the Sierra de la Culata, best seen early morning, otherwise frequently in the clouds. This is the way Bolívar went when crossing the Andes to liberate Colombia, and on the peak is the statue of a condor. At the pass is the tourist restaurant **Páramo Aguila**, reasonably priced with open fire. People stop for a hot chocolate or a *calentado*, a herb liquor drunk hot. There are also food and souvenir stalls, and horses for hire (high season and weekends). Across from the monument is a small chapel with fine views. A paved road leads from here 2 km to a *CANTV* microwave tower (4318 m). Here are tall *frailejones* plants; nearby are large storage sheds for vegetables from Piñango cooperatives. Continuing north as a lonely track the road goes to the **Piñango lakes** (45 km) and the traditional village of **Piñango** (2480 m), 1½ hours. Great views for miles around. Eventually the road reaches the Panamerican and Lago de Maracaibo.

Santo Domingo (*Phone code: 0274; Population: 6000; Altitude: 2178 m*), with good handicraft shops and fishing, is on the spectacular road up from Barinas to Mérida, before the Parque Nacional Sierra Nevada. Festival: 30 September, San Gerónimo. The tourist office is on the right leaving town, 10 minutes from the centre.

Valera to Mérida listings

For Sleeping and Eating price codes and other relevant information, see Essentials, pages 9-11.

● Sleeping

Trujillo *p61*
$ Los Gallegos, Av Independencia 5-65, T/F236 3193. With hot water, a/c or fan, with or without TV. As well as several other places.

Boconó *p61*
$$ Estancia de Mosquey, Mosquey, 10 km from Boconó towards Biscucuy, T0272-414 8322, 0414-723 4246, www.estancia-mosquey.com. Family run, great views, rooms and cabañas, good beds, good restaurant, pool, recommended. There are other hotels and posadas in town, some on or near Plaza Bolívar, one opposite the bus station.

Niquitao *p61*
$$ Posada Turística de Niquitao, T0271-885 2042/0414-727 8217/0416-771 7860, http://posadaniquitao.com/. Rooms with bath, hot water, TV, some with bunks, restaurant, tours arranged with guide, also has small museum.
$ Na Delia, T0271-885 2113, on a hill 500 m out of town. With restaurant.

Road to the high Andes *p61*
Timotes
$$ Las Truchas, north entrance to town, T/F0271- 808 0500, www.andes.net/lastruchas. 44 cabins, with and without kitchen. Also has a Restaurant.
$ Carambay, Av Bolívar 41, T0271-828 9261.

Santo Domingo
$$$ La Trucha Azul, east end of town, T898 8111, www.latruchaazul.com. Rooms with open fireplace, also suites and cabins, expensive for what it offers.
$$$ Los Frailes, between Santo Domingo and Laguna Mucubají at 3700 m. T0274-417 3440, or 0212-976 0530, reservacioneshlf@gmail.com, www.hotellosfrailes.blogspot.com. Cheaper in low season, includes breakfast. Beautiful former monastery, specializes in honeymoon packages, rooms are simple, international menu and wines. Includes breakfast.
$$ Moruco, T898 8155/8070, out of town. Good value, beautiful, rooms and cabins, good food, bar.
$$ Paso Real, on the other side of the river from Los Frailes, no phone. A good place to stay.

● Eating

Niquitao *p61*
† † La Estancia, Plaza Bolívar. Owner Golfredo Pérez, helpful, kind, knows area well, pizzas.

● Transport

Valera *p61*
Bus The bus terminal on the edge of town. To **Boconó**, US$6, 3 hrs; to **Trujillo**, *por puestos*, 30 mins, US$1; to **Caracas**, 9 hrs, US$18.25 (direct at 2230 with **Expresos Mérida**); to **Mérida**, 4 daily with **Trans Barinas**, US$8.50, 4½ hrs; *por puestos* to **Mérida**, 3 hrs, US$11.50, leave when full

(travel by day for the views and, especially in the rainy season, safety); to **Maracaibo**, *micros* every 30 mins until 1730, 4 hrs, US$8.

Road to the high Andes *p62*
Santo Domingo

Bus Buses or *busetas* pass through in either direction at around 2 hr intervals all day.
Mérida 2 hrs, US$4.25 *por puesto*; **Barinas** 1½ hrs, US$4.75.

O Directory

Valera *p61*
Banks Corp Banca, Av Bolívar con C 5, changes Amex TCs, no commission. **Banco de Venezuela**, C 7 con Av 10, cash on Visa and Mastercard.

Trujillo *p61*
Banks See also Money, page 11. **Banco de Venezuela**, 1 block down from cathedral, has ATM.

Mérida and around

Venezuela's high Andes offer hiking and mountaineering, and fishing in lakes and rivers. The main tourist centre is Mérida (674 km from Caracas), but there are many interesting rural villages. The Transandean Highway runs through the Sierra to the border with Colombia, while the Pan-American Highway runs along the foot of the Andes through El Vigía and La Fría to join the Transandean at San Cristóbal.

The Sierra Nevada de Mérida, running from south of Maracaibo to the Colombian frontier, is the only range in Venezuela where snow lies permanently on the higher peaks. Several basins lying between the mountains are actively cultivated; the inhabitants are concentrated mainly in valleys and basins at between 800 m and 1300 m above sea level. The towns of Mérida and San Cristóbal are in this zone.

Mérida → *Phone code: 0274. Population: 300,000. Altitude: 1640 m.*

Mérida stands on an alluvial terrace – a kind of giant shelf – 15 km long, 2.5 km wide, within sight of Pico Bolívar, the highest in Venezuela. The mountain is part of the Five White Eagles group, visible from the city. The summits are at times covered in snow, but the glaciers and snow are retreating. Founded in 1558, the capital of Mérida State retains some colonial buildings but is mainly known for its 33 parks and many statues. For tourists, its claims to fame are the great opportunities for doing adventure sports and the buzz from a massive student population.

The heart of Venezuelan mountaineering and trekking is the Andes, with Mérida as the base, and there are several important peaks and some superb hikes. Bear in mind that high altitudes will be reached and acclimatization is essential. Suitable equipment is necessary and you may consider bringing your own. In the Sierra Nevada is mountain biking, whitewater rafting, para- penting and horse riding. See also the companies listed in Activities and tours, page 70.

Ins and outs

Getting around Mérida may seem a safe place, but theft and robbery does occur. Avoid the Pueblo Nuevo area by the river at the stairs leading down from Avenida 2, as well as Avenida 2 itself. The **airport** is on the main highway, 5 km from the centre. *Por puesto* into town US$0.35, taxi US$3.50. The **bus terminal** is 3 km from the centre of town on the west side of the valley, linked by a frequent minibus service to Calle 25 entre Avenidas 2 y 3, US$0.35. City bus fares rise at weekends. A trolley bus system from the southern suburb of Ejido to La Hechicera in the north has been opened for much of its length. ▸ *See also Transport, page 70.*

Information Tourist offices Next to the airport is the **Corporación Merideña de Turismo**, on Avenida Urdaneta y C 45, T262 2371/263 2782, cormetur@merida.gob.ve. It's open Monday- Saturday low season 0800-1200 and 1400-1800, high season 0800-1800. They supply a useful map of the state and town. Also at the airport in the waiting lounge, very informative, for the same low season hours, 0730-1330 in high season; in the bus terminal, same hours, have a map of the city (free). At Parque Las Heroínas, at the zoo in Chorros de Milla park and at the Mercado Principal, low season 0800-1200, 1400-1800, high season 0830-1830. **Inparques** (National Parks) Av Las Américas, C 2, sector Fondur, T262 1529, sierranevada .andigena.org. Map of Parque Nacional Sierra Nevada (mediocre) US$1; also, and easier, at Teleférico for permits.

Sights
In the city centre is the attractive **Plaza Bolívar**, on which stands the **cathedral**, dark and heavy inside, with **Museo Arquidiocesano** beside it, and **Plaza de Milla**, or **Sucre** ① *C 14 entre Avs 2 y 3*, always a hive of activity. The **Parque de las Cinco Repúblicas** ① *C 13, entre Avs 4 y 5, beside the barracks*, is renowned for having the first monument in the world to Bolívar (1842, replaced in 1988) and contains soil from each of the five countries he liberated (photography strictly prohibited). Three of the peaks known as the Five White Eagles (Bolívar, 5007 m, La Silla del Toro, 4755 m, and León 4740 m) can be clearly seen from here. **Plaza Las Heroínas**, by the lowest station of the *teleférico* (see below) is busy till 2300, an outdoor party zone, with artists exhibiting their work. Many tour operators have their offices here.

Less central parks include **Parque La Isla** ① *Prol Av Los Próceres*, which contains orchids, basketball and tennis courts, an amphitheatre and fountains. In the **Plaza Beethoven** ① *Santa María Norte*, a different melody from Beethoven's works chimes every hour; *por puestos/ busetas*, run along Avenida 5, marked 'Santa María' or 'Chorro de Milla', US$0.25. The **Jardín Botánico** ① *on the way to La Hechicera, www.botanica.ciens.ula.ve, open daily, 360 days a year*, has the largest collection of bromeliads in South America; also a canopy walkway. The **Jardín Acuario**, beside the aquarium ① *high season daily 0800-1800, low season closed Mon, US$0.25; (busetas leave from Av 4 y C 25, US$0.25, passing airport)*, is an exhibition centre, mainly devoted to the way of life and the crafts of the Andean *campesinos*.

Mérida has several museums: **Museo de Arte Colonial** ① *Av 4, Casa 20-8, T252 7860, fundacolonial@latinmail.com, Tue-Fri 0900- 1600, Sat-Sun 1400-1700 (1000-1700 high season), US$0.50*. More interesting is the small **Museo Arqueológico** ① *Av 3, Edif del Rectorado de la Universidad de los Andes, just off Plaza Bolívar, T240 2344, museogrg@ ula.ve, Tue-Sat 0800-1200, 1400-1800, Sun 1400-1800, US$0.50* with pre-Columbian exhibits from the Andes. **Museo de Arte Moderno** ① *Av 2 y C 21, Mon-Fri 0800-1600, Sat-Sun 0800-1300, free,* is in the Centro Cultural Don Tulio Febres Cordero, a run-down but impressive concrete building with political murals in front of its main entrance, several galleries and theatres. It is open sporadically.

Mérida listings

For Sleeping and Eating price codes and other relevant information, see Essentials, pages 9-11.

⊙ Sleeping

Mérida *p64, map p68*
Book ahead in school holidays and Feria del Sol.
$$$ Posada Casa Sol, Av 4 entre C15 y C16, T252 4164, www.posadacasasol.com. Renovated colonial-era house with lovely rooms in distinctive, tasteful style, modern art on walls, hot water, garden, free internet, large breakfast US$18, very helpful, English, German and Italian spoken, limited parking. Highly recommended.
$$ Apart Hotel Central, Av 3, No 16-11, T252 7629, aparthotelcentral@ hotmail.com. Good apartments for up to 12, TV, kitchen and parking.
$$ El Tisure, Av 4 entre C 17 y 18, T252 6061. Modern, colonial-style, very pleasant, disco.
$$ La Montaña, C 24 No 6-47 entre Av 6 y 7, T252 5977, www.posadalamontana.com. Hot water, TV, safe, fan, fridge, luggage store. Very helpful, English spoken, excellent restaurant.
$$ Mintoy, C 25 (Ayacucho), No 8-130, T252 0340. 10% discount for cash, comfortably furnished, breakfast, good value, parking, suites with separate sitting area (sleeps 5).
$$ Posada Doña Pumpa, Av 5 y C 14, T252 7286, www.donapumpa.com. Good showers, spacious rooms, cable TV, quiet, very comfortable, English-speaking owner, no breakfast, parking.
$$-$ Encanto Andino, C 24 No 6-53, entre Avs 6 y 7, T252 6929. **$** without bath, 5 rooms, easygoing, kitchen with fridge and microwave, no breakfast.
$$-$ Los Bucares de Mérida, Av 4 No 15-5, T/F252 2841, www.losbucares.com. Cheaper in noisier rooms at front, hot showers, TV, also has family rooms, nice patio with occasional live music, garage, safe, breakfast extra in *cafetín*.

$$-$ Montecarlo, Av 7 entre C 24 y C 25, T252 5981, F252 5910. Ask for back room with view of mountain, safe, parking, hot water, restaurant.
$$-$ Posada Alemania, Av 2 entre C 17 y 18, No 17-76, T/F252 4067, www.posadaalemania.com. **$** without bath, quiet, family atmosphere, leafy patio, popular with backpackers, discounts for long stay, breakfast and laundry extra, kitchen, book exchange, tourist information, English and German spoken, German owner. Adventure tours (trekking, rafting, riding, expeditions) with **Colibrí Tours**, T252 4961, www.colibri-tours.com, ask for Ricardo Torres.
$$-$ Posada Luz Caraballo, Av 2 No 13-80, on Plaza de Milla, T252 5441, www.andes.net/luzcaraballo/index.html. Colonial-style old building, hot water, TV, excellent cheap restaurant, good bar, parking.
$ El Escalador, C 23 entre Avs 7 y 8, T252 2411. Doubles or rooms with bed and bunks, hot water, TV, tourist information and tours, parapenting arranged, no breakfast.
$ Italia, C 19 entre Av 2 y 3, T252 5737. **$** in smaller rooms without bath, hot water, laundry, **Ayary Tours** travel agency, English, German and French spoken, changes dollars, Spanish lessons.
$ Luxemburgo, C 24, between Avs 6-7, T252 6865, www.andes.net/luxemburgo/index.html. In same group as
$$ Nevada Palace, C 24, No 5-45, www.andes.net/nevadapalace/ index.html. Cold water, safe, with restaurant, modern, with **Palace Cyber**.
$ Posada Casa Alemana-Suiza, El Encanto, Av 2 No 38-120, T263 6503, info@casa-alemana.com. Very nice, airport pick-up, parking, discount for long stays, laundry, English and German spoken. Also runs good tours and activities as **Carnaval Tours**, T263 6503.

$ Posada Familiar Mara, C 24 No 8-215, T252 5507. Pleasant, hot water, luggage store, no TV, no breakfast.

$ Posada Guamanchi, C 24, No 8-86, T252 2080, www.guamanchi.com. Owned by tour operator of same name, if on a tour you are guaranteed a room. Rooms of varying size, some with bath, some with good view, 2 kitchens, cable TV room, terrace with hammocks, good, no parking.

Eating

Mérida *p64, map p68*
Many places offer student lunches for US$1-1.50. Good restaurants in Centro Comercial La Hechicera, Av Alberto Carnevalli, northeast of the centre: **La Chistorra**, T244 0021, a seafood bar and restaurant, open 1200-2400, Spanish food. Next door is **Sushi'tei**, with Japanese chef, very friendly, wide range of dishes, sushi, sashimi and traditional Japanese recipes.

Buona Pizza, Av 7 entre C 24 y 25, T252 7639, with Express branch opposite and 2 other branches, open 1200-2300 daily, very good pizza.

Café Atico, C 25 near Plaza Las Heroínas. Excellent lunch for US$2.50. Recommended.

Chipen, Av 5, No 23-67, T2525015. The oldest restaurant in Mérida, serving Spanish and Venezuelan food, excellent trout and cordon bleu.

El Museo, Av 2, C12-13. Nice patio, lots of graffiti, good food, pleasant place for a drink.

El Reencuentro, Av 4 y C 29, at Hotel Chama, T9352602. Offers international and Venezuelan cuisine, chicken, meat and seafood, open 1200-2200 (till 2300 Fri-Sat, Sun till 1800).

La Abadía, Av 3 entre C 17 y 18, T251 0933, www.grupoabadia.com. Excellent, varied menu, including vegetarian, 30 mins free internet time with each meal. Has other outlets including **La Abadía del Angel**, C 21 entre Avs 5 y 6, café and restaurant, with internet.

La Astilla, C 14, No 2-20, Plaza de Milla. Plants, nostalgic music, bar, varied menu including pizza, frequented by locals and groups.

La Mamma, Av 3 and C 19. Good pizza, pasta, set lunches and salad bar, popular in the evening, live music at weekends, local wine.

Cheo's Pizzería, 3 separate restaurants on Plaza Las Heroínas, one serves pizzas, the 2nd chicken and meat, the 3rd trout. Also hotel on the plaza.

El Sabor de los Quesos, on Plaza de Milla. Very good and cheap pizzería, very busy, painted green and white.

El Tinajero, C 29/Av 4. Clean, simple place.

Federico's, Pasaje Ayacucho No 25-24. Vegetarian and pizza.

La Esquina de Pajarito, C 25 esquina Av 6. Simple but good local food, cheap set lunch.

La Montaña, C 24 between Av 6 and 7 (next to *posada*). Good, cheap food, pleasant setting.

El Sano Glotón, Av 4 y C 18. Vegetarian. Recommended. Next door but one is a great snack bar with excellent *empanadas*.

Cafés

Café Express, Av 4, No 23-54, upstairs No 2A. Cosy café on the 1st floor of this old building, with good cakes.

Café Mogambo, Av 4 y C 29, T2521011. A classic style café, open Tue-Sun 1730-2230. Good salads, paninis and gourmet dishes, a wide variety of coffees. Also serves breakfast, but you must go through **Hotel Chama**. Credit cards accepted.

Heladería La Coromoto, Av 3 y C 29, T523525, Tue-Sun 1415-2100, offers 750 flavours of ice cream, at least 60 choices daily, eg trout, avocado.

T-Café, Av 3 Independencia y C 2, diagonally opposite **Heladería La Coromoto**. Homemade food, breakfast, good lunches, dinners, juices, coffee and cakes, and nice music.

Mérida p64, map p68
There is no cover charge for nightclubs but
always take your passport or a copy.

Alfredo's, C 19 y Av 4, 0900-2300. Bar,
popular, also vegetarian café and internet.
Birosca Carioca, Av 2 y C 24. Popular, with
live music, take care outside.

Mérida

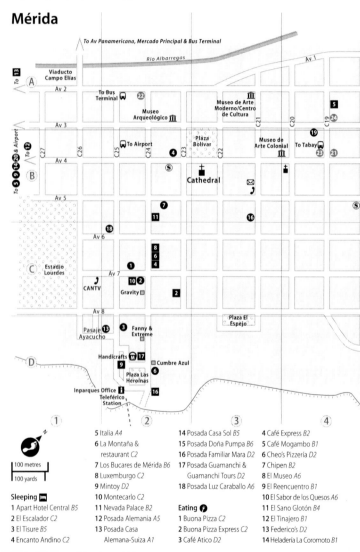

5 Italia A4	14 Posada Casa Sol B5	4 Café Express B2
6 La Montaña &	15 Posada Doña Pumpa B6	5 Café Mogambo B1
restaurant C2	16 Posada Familiar Mara D2	6 Cheo's Pizzería D2
7 Los Bucares de Mérida B6	17 Posada Guamanchi &	7 Chipen B2
8 Luxemburgo C2	Guamanchi Tours D2	8 El Museo A6
9 Mintoy D2	18 Posada Luz Caraballo A6	9 El Reencuentro B1
10 Montecarlo C2		10 El Sabor de los Quesos A6
11 Nevada Palace B2	**Eating** 🍴	11 El Sano Glotón B4
12 Posada Alemania A5	1 Buona Pizza C2	12 El Tinajero B1
13 Posada Casa	2 Buona Pizza Express C2	13 Federico's D2
Alemana-Suiza A1	3 Café Atico D2	14 Heladería La Coromoto B1

Sleeping 🛏
1 Apart Hotel Central B5
2 El Escalador C2
3 El Tisure B5
4 Encanto Andino C2

Café Calypso, C 26, in Centro Comercial El Viaducto. Pop/rock music, a bit more pricey.
The Clover, Av 4 entre C 14 y 15. Irish bar with live music at weekends.

El Hoyo del Queque, Av 4 across the road from *Alfredo's*. Open 1200-2400, usually packed, good meeting place. The best local bands play here, some nights free, sometimes cover can go up to US$8.50 with one drink, good food. Recommended.
Kontiki, Av 3 y C 19. Mérida's oldest club.

15 La Abadía *B5*
16 La Abadía del Angel *B3*
17 La Astilla *A6*
18 La Esquina de Pajarito *C2*
19 La Mamma *B4*
20 T-Café *B1*

Bars & clubs
21 Alfredo's *B4*
22 Birosco Carioca *A2*
23 El Hoyo del Queque *B4*
24 Kontiki *A4*
25 The Clover *B6*

❀ Festivals and events

Mérida *p64, map p68*
For 2 weeks leading up to Christmas there are daily song contests between local students on Plaza Bolívar, 1700-2200. **Feria del Sol**, held on the week preceding Ash Wednesday. This is also the peak bullfighting season. **1-2 Jan**, Paradura del Niño; **15 May**, San Isidro Labrador, a popular festival nationwide, but especially in Mérida.

◎ Shopping

Mérida *p64, map p68*
Bookshops Fundación Librerías del Sur, on Plaza Bolívar. State-run, good for subsidized books, including national, Latin American and world poets. **Librería Ifigenia**, next door, is also very good. **Temas**, Av 3, entre C31 y 32, No 31-24, T252 6068. Very good, amazing stock.
Camping shops 5007, Av 5 entre C 19 y 20, CC Mediterráneo, T252 6806.
Recommended. **Cumbre Azul**, C 24 opposite Plaza Las Heroínas, T416 3231, cumbreazul@hotmail.com. Rents and sells mountaineering equipment (also sells some fishing tackle). **Eco Bike**, Av 7 No 16-34. For mountain bikes and equipment. Many tour operators rent equipment.
Handicrafts Handicraft market on La Plaza de Las Heroínas, opposite *teleférico*. **Mercado Principal** on Av las Américas (buses for bus station pass by), has many small shops, top floor restaurant has regional *comida típica*, bargaining possible.

Mérida *p64, map p68*

Parapenting All agencies offer jumps. Conditions in Mérida are suitable for flying almost all year round. It takes on average 50 mins to get to a launch site and tandem jumps last 25 mins. There are 7 main sites. Price US$60. Can take own equipment and hire a guide. An experienced pilot is Oswaldo, T0414-717 5953.

Xtreme Adventours, Av 8, C24, Plaza Las Heroínas, T252 7241. Specializes in parapenting (latest equipment, safety) and many other adventure options, plus tours in the region. Also offers tours from Mérida to Canaima, Margarita and Los Roques.

Tour operators
Arassari Trek, C 24 No 8-301 (beside the teleférico), T252 5879, www.arassari.com. Run by Tom and Raquel Evenou (based in Switzerland), for rafting tours.
Cocolight, T0414-756 2575, www.cocolight.com. Alan Highton and his team specialise in 2-day trips to Catatumbo to see the lightning, visit the communities of the region and experience the variety of habitats between the Andes and the delta. They have a camp at Ologa lagoon. Naturalist tours to other parts of the country offered. Very experienced, several languages spoken.
Fanny Tours, C 24, No 8-30, T252 2952, 0414-747 1349, www.fanny-tours.com. Patrizia Rossi, José Albarrán for parapenting (the first to do it), reliable. Apart from parapenting, specializes in mountain biking, US$30 half-day pp for 2, US$40 whole day without jeep support, US$58 with jeep, all inclusive; bike hire US$16. Also rafting US$140 pp for 4; Llanos, Catatumbo, canyoning, trekking to mountains and some climbing; also tours combining all types of sport; book and money exchange. Recommended.

Gravity Tours, C 24 entre Av 7 y 8, 1 block from cable car, T251 1279, 0424-760 8327, www.gravity-tours.com.ve. Bilingual guides, natural history and adventure tours, some extreme, including rock climbing, rafting, biking, Llanos trips and Gran Sabana.
Guamanchi Tours, C 24, No 8-86, T252 2080, www.guamanchi.com. Owned by John and Joëlle Peña, with Volker on the team. German, French, Italian and English spoken, recommended for hiking, paragliding, horse riding, biking, bird-watching, equipment hire, exchange, information, mountain climbing, also tours to Llanos, Amazonia and Angel Falls, email service for customers, new 4WD jeeps, have a posada in town (see above) and at Los Nevados (see below). Recommended.
Natoura Travel and Adventure Tours, C 31 entre Av Don Tulio y prol Av 6 No 5-27 (Diagonal Bomberos ULA), Mérida 5101, T252 4216, in US 303-800 4639, in Germany 05906-303364, in France 0970-449206, www.natoura.com. Open daily 0900-1700, friendly company organizing tours throughout Venezuela, run by Jose Luis Troconis and Renate Reiners, English, French, German and Italian spoken, climbing, trekking, rafting, horse riding, mountain biking, birdwatching and equipment hire. Their self-drive option allows you to rent a car and they will reserve accommodation for your route. Repeatedly recommended.
Drivers Lucio (T252 8416) and Nicolás Savedra (T271 2618) and Juan Medina Yagrumo, C 24, mostalla@hotmail.com.

⊖ Transport

Mérida *p64, map p68*
Air Mérida's airport is closed (2011). Flights to **Caracas** from nearest airports at San Antonio (3-5 hrs by road), or El Vigía (2½ hrs away); both are served by several airlines.
Bus The terminal has 2 levels, the upper one for small buses, minivans and cars to nearby places, the lower for interstate buses. Taxis

line up outside the main entrance. A small exit tax of US$0.35 is charged for journeys in the the state, US$0.50 for long-distance, payable at one of 2 kiosks leading to buses. Make sure you pay, officials check buses before departure. On interstate buses, it is essential to book in advance; for buses within the state you pay on board. The terminal has a tourist office, phones, toilets, luggage store and places to eat. Fares: **Caracas**, US$15.50 (*normal*) to US$25 (*bus-cama*); **Maracay**, US$14-22; **Valencia**, US$13-22; **Coro**, US$11.50-22; **Maracaibo**, US$11; **Barquisimeto**, US$18.50; **Puerto La Cruz**, US$26.70.

Bus companies: Expresos Occidente, T263 5844, daily direct to **Caracas**, 12 hrs, or via Valencia and Maracay; to **Coro/ Punto Fijo**, 12-14 hrs. Expresos San Cristóbal (T263 1881), daily direct to Caracas, 14 hrs, or via Valencia and Maracay; to **Maracaibo**, 8 hrs. Expresos Mérida (T263 3430), to Caracas hourly from 1800, some direct others via Valencia and Maracay; also to **Barquisimeto**, 8 hrs, **Maracaibo**, **Coro** and **Punto Fijo**. Transportes Barinas (T263 4651), **Barinas** (US$5.80) via **Apartaderos** (US$2.75), to **Guanare** (US$8.50) and **Valera** (US$8.50). Expresos Los Llanos (T265 5927), to Caracas at 1900. Expresos Coromoto, T417 1722, to **Maracaibo** 0845, 1345. From upper level of terminal: Táchira Mérida, to **San Cristóbal** (US$9.25, 6 hrs) and **San Antonio**. Also to Jají, Chiguará, Apartaderos, Barinas (US$8.75, 4 hrs), El Vigía, Valera. Líneas Unidas, T263 8472, *por puesto* microbus with TV, and car, to **Maracaibo**, 1000, 2130; also **Fraternidad del Transporte**, T263 1187, 1000, 1400, 2145. If heading for **Ciudad Bolívar**, change buses in Valencia or Maracay.
Taxi In town US$2.75-4.

① Directory

Mérida *p64, map p68*
Banks See also Money, page 11. **Banco Mercantil**, Av 5 y C 18. ATM takes Cirrus (commission lower than Visa). **BBVA Banco Provincial**, Av 4 y C 25, and **Banco de Venezuela**, Av 4 entre C 23 y 24, both ATM and cash advance on Visa and Mastercard. *Italcambio* at airport; this is often the easiest place to change cash and TCs. **Car hire** Several companies at the airport, including **Alquil Auto**, T263 1440, or **Dávila Tours**, Av Los Próceres opposite Urb la Trinidad, T266 0711, or airport T263 4510. **Consulates** Colombia, Av Andrés Bello, CC San Antonio, T266 2646, consulbia merida@yahoo.com, open 0800-1400. Visas take 10 min. **UK**, Professor Robert Kirby, honorary vice-Consul, Finca La Trinitaria, Santa Rosa, 10 mins from the town centre towards La Hechicera, T416 8496.
Internet Places all over town, most with broadband, US$0.40-0.80 per hr. **CANTV Centro de Comunicaciones**, Av 7 entre C 25 y 26. Also at Av 6 y C 21, open Sun, has internet next to *Ipostel*. **Language schools** Iowa Institute, Av 4 y C 18, T252 6404, cathy@iowainstitute.com. Run by Cathy Jensen de Sánchez, competitive prices, fully qualified teachers, homestays arranged. Recommended. **Latinoamericano de Idiomas**, CC Mamayeya, p 4, of C-5-38, T/F244 7808. Contact Marinés Asprino, Conjunto Residencial Andrés Bello, Torre C, p 5, Apt 6-1, T271 1209 for private lessons and cheap accommodation. Recommended. **Carolina Tenías**, 17 years' experience in private lessons for travellers, grammar and conversation, T252 4875, or T0416-971 1445. **Medical services** Doctors: Dr Aldo Olivieri, Av Principal La Llanita, La Otra Banda, Centro Profesional El Buho, 09, T244 0805, T0414-374 0356, aldrolia250@ cantv.net, very good, gastroenterologist, speaks English and Italian. **Dr Giotto Guillén Echeverria**, Centro Médico

La Trinidad, C 42 entre Avs Urdaneta y Gonzalo Picón, T263 9685, T0416-674 0707. Specialist in infections, speaks French. **Post office Ipostel**, C 21 entre Avs 4 y 5, 0800-1900 daily. Post office also in bus terminal, 0800-1200, 1400-1700, weekdays only. **Telephone CANTV**, C 21 y Av 5, Mon-Sat 0800-1930. **Useful addresses Immigration office:** SAIME, Av 4 y C 6, quinta San Isidro, Parroquia Sagrario, T252 9754, Mon-Sat 0800-1700. **Tourist police:** The **CICPC** will provide a *constancia* reporting the crime and listing the losses. Their office is on Av Las Américas, at Viaducto Miranda, T262 0343. Open daily but they won't issue a *constancia* on Sun. To get there, take any bus marked 'Terminal Sur' or 'Mercado' leaving from C 25. You can also get a *constancia* from the *Prefectura Civil del Municipio Libertador*, but it can take all day and is only valid for a limited period; at Av 4 No 21-69, just off Plaza Bolívar; opening hours variable. Tourist offices may be better than police if you need to register a theft for insurance purposes.

Sierra Nevada de Mérida

The Sierra is a mixture of the wild and isolated and the very touristy. In the latter group fall the cable car up Pico Espejo and villages designed to lure the shopper, but it is not difficult to escape the tour groups. There are routes from the mountains to the Llanos and to Colombia.

Parque Nacional Sierra Nevada (South)

Close to Mérida is the popular hiking area around Los Nevados, with the added attraction of the highest cable car in the world (if it's running). The further you go from Mérida, the greater the off-the-beaten-track possibilities for hiking and exploration that arise.

Since this is a national park, you need a permit from the *Inparques* (National Parks) offices in Mérida (see Ins and outs) to hike and camp overnight. Permits are not given to single hikers (except to Los Nevados), a minimum of two people is needed. Have your passport ready. Return permit after your hike; park guards will radio the start of trek to say you've reached the end. If camping, remember that the area is 3500-4200 m so acclimatization is necessary. The night temperatures can fall below freezing so a -12°C sleeping bag is necessary, plus good waterproofs. Conditions are much more severe than you'd think after balmy Mérida. Don't leave litter. Some treks are very difficult so check with the tourist office before leaving. Water purification is also recommended. See Mérida Tour operators and Parque Nacional Sierra Nevada (North) below.

Pico Espejo The world's highest and longest aerial cableway (built by the French in 1957-1960) runs to Pico Espejo (4765 m) in four stages ① *T252 5080/1997. The teleférico was closed in late 2008 and is scheduled to reopen in 2012. A new system is under construction.* When operating, its final station is at Pico Espejo, with a change of car at every station, all of which have cafés, toilets and advice. Beware altitude sickness: there is oxygen and a nursing station at higher points. Barinas is the ground level station, Plaza de las Heroínas; you can hire, or buy, hats, gloves and scarves here, the Venezuelans all do. La Montaña (2442 m) is the second station with a small Museo del Montañismo. You pass over various levels of forest. Next is La Aguada (3452 m), then Loma Redonda (4045 m). From here you can start the trek to Los Nevados (see below); you must inform Inparques if trekking to Los Nevados. Pause for 10 minutes at Loma Redonda before the last stage to Pico Espejo, where there is a statue of Nuestra Señora de las Nieves. As the car nears its final destination, you are welcomed by enormous graffiti of Hugo Chávez waving and smiling from the platform. Next door to Pico Espejo is Pico Bolívar (Mucumbari, where the sun sleeps) with Humboldt behind. It has remnants of a glacier. In the other direction, closest is La Silla del Toro and you can see a statue of Francisco Miranda with the Venezuelan flag on an outcrop. On a clear day you can see the blue haze of the Llanos to the east and, west, as far as Sierra de Cocuy and Guicán in Colombia. Across Río Chama you can see Sierra de la Culata. It is advisable to spend only 30 minutes at Pico Espejo. Apart from Los Nevados trek, the only safe part to walk down is Loma Redonda to La Aguada; a rough but clear trail, two hours; wear boots, not for children or the elderly, take water.

Los Nevados Los Nevados (*Altitude: 2711 m*) is a colonial town with cobbled streets, an ancient chapel and a famous fiesta on 2 May. From here, it is a very testing two-day trek to **Pico Espejo**, with a strong chance of altitude sickness as the ascent is more than 1600 m. It is best done November- June early in the morning (before 0830 ideally), before the clouds spoil the view. In summer the summit is clouded and covered with snow and there is no view. **Do not attempt Pico Espejo alone; go with a guide, it is easy to get lost.** Reputable trekking companies provide suitable clothing; temperatures can be 0° C. August is the coldest month.

From Los Nevados to **Loma Redonda** takes five to seven hours, four hours with mules (14 km). The hike is not too difficult; breathtaking views; be prepared for cold rain in the afternoon, start very early. The walk from Los Nevados to the village of **El Morro** (24 km) takes seven to nine hours (very steep in parts). (It's 47 km to Mérida; jeeps do the trip daily.) Sr Oviller Ruiz provides information on the history of the church of San Jacinto (the patron saint, whose fiesta is on 16 August) and the indigenous cemetery. The town, with its red tiled roofs is an interesting blend of the colonial and the indigenous.

It is possible to hike from Pico Espejo to the cloud forest at La Mucuy (see below), two to three days walking at over 4000 m altitude, passing spectacular snow peaks and Lagos Verde and Coromoto. A tent and a warm sleeping bag are essential, as is a good map (local guides may lend theirs to photocopy). If you start at Pico Espejo you will be at the highest point first, so although you will be descending, you may have altitude sickness from the word go.

Parque Nacional Sierra Nevada (North) and Sierra de La Culata

The Transandean highway snakes its way through the rugged mountain landscape, past neat, little towns of red-tiled roofs, steep fields and terraces of maize and potatoes. Just outside Mérida a side road goes to El Valle, known for *pasteles de trucha*, *vino de mora* and handicraft shops. The snow-tipped peaks of the high sierras watch over this bucolic scene, with Pico Bolívar lording it over them all. Throughout the park you will see a plant with felt-like leaves of pale grey-green, the *frailejón* (or great friar, *espeletia*), which blooms with yellow flowers from September to December. There are more than 130 species; tall ones grow at less than 1 cm a year.

Tabay At 12 km from Mérida, Tabay (*30 minutes; Altitude 1708 m; Population 17,000*) is named after an indigenous tribe. Its Plaza Bolívar has an attractive church, trees and plants. Around it are two minimercados, telecommunications, **Pizzería Valentina** (best in town), **Pastelitos** (at bus stop from Mérida, for empanadas in morning), all other transport stops, and other services. Jeeps run a regular service to **La Mucuy** cloud forest, 0600-2200, they are labelled (US$1.50 one way if five passengers, negotiate hard). They drop you at the Guardaparques. There is nothing to pay for a day visit, but you pay per night if making the Travesía to Pico Espejo and the Teleférico (or alternative route) down to Mérida. The distances on the park signs to Lagos Coromoto and Verde would appear to be very ambitious (eg Coromoto is not three hours, but an overnight trip if not continuing). When going back to Tabay, you may have to wait for a jeep; the driver will charge extra for backpacks. Jeeps also go to the **Aguas Termales** (from a different stop, just off Plaza Bolívar, US$1). It is possible to walk and there are signs. The man-made pool has 38°C water. The area is also good for walking and horse riding (see **Mano Poderosa**, Sleeping), all Mérida agencies go here.

Beyond Tabay the road goes through **Mucurubá** (2400m) with a pleasant Plaza Bolívar and blue and white church, colonial buildings, handicrafts and Hospedaje Mococón, and passes the **Monumento al Perro Nevado**. It depicts Simón Bolívar, the Indian boy, Tinjaca, the Mucuchíes dog, Snowy, and the father and son who gave Bolívar the dog in

1813. According to legend, both Tinjaca and Nevado were devoted to Bolívar until their death on the same day at the Battle of Carabobo, 1821. At Mucuchíes (*Phone code: 0274; Population: 9175; Altitude: 2983 m*) the statue of the Liberator on Plaza Bolívar also features Tinjaca and Snowy. Also on the Plaza is a wooden statue of San Isidro, patron saint of farmers; all rural communities honour him on 15 May. The patron saint of Mucuchíes is San Benito; this festival (and several others) on 27-30 December is celebrated by participants wearing flower-decorated hats and firing blunderbusses. Tourist office on C 9 as you enter from Mérida, internet at C 9 Independencia.

The road leads up from Mucuchíes to **San Rafael de Mucuchíes** (*Altitude: 3140 m; Fiesta 24 October*). You should visit the remarkable church, pieced together from thousands of stones, by the late Juan Félix Sánchez (born 1900), nationally renowned as a sculptor, philosopher and clown. The chapel is dedicated to the Virgen de Coromoto; it was blessed by Pope John Paul II. The tombs of Sánchez and his companion of 50 years, Epifania Gil, are inside. Next door is his house, now a museum with photos, weavings and sculptures. Opposite is the library given by him to the community. He built a similar chapel at El Tisure. The picturesque road continues to Apartaderos (two hours from Mérida). It follows the Río Chama valley in the heart of the cultivated highlands and the fields extend up to the edge of the *páramo*, clinging to the steep slopes. Main crops are potatoes (four harvests a year) onions, garlic and carrots. East of the Río Chama is the Sierra Nevada; to the west is the Sierra de La Culata. There are handicrafts, *posadas* and eateries.

Apartaderos (*Phone code: 0274; Altitude: 3342 m*) is at the junction of Route 7 and the road over the Sierra Nevada to Barinas. About 3 km above Apartaderos, a narrow paved road (signposted) turns west off the highway at Escuela Estatal 121 and winds its way to **Llano del Hato** (3510 m) and on to the Centro de Investigaciones de Astronomía (3600 m) ① *the 4 telescopes and modern facilities are open Wed-Sat 1500-1900, but Mon only Aug-Sep (check website for details), US$1.85 for adults, US$1.15 under-18s, students with card US$0.70, seniors and under-8s free, www.cida.ve*. At least two view-points on the way in give great views of the Lake Mucubají plateau. A good paved road descends 7 km from Llano del Hato to the Mérida highway at La Toma, just above Mucuchíes. Many prehispanic terraces and irrigation systems, adobe houses and ox-ploughed fields (*poyos*) are visible from the road.

Three kilometres beyond the junction of the roads from Barinas and Valera is the entrance to the **Parque Nacional Sierra Nevada** (*Línea Cultura* bus from Mérida ends at the junction, two hours; taxis run from bus stop to Park, US$2.75). At the turn-off to the park is a motel and restaurant. Near the entrance is **Laguna Mucubají**, at 3600 m, with free campsite; visitors' centre, bookshop, good maps, interesting museum. A 2-2½-hour walk takes you to Laguna Negra and back (1½ hours on horseback, US$2-3 to hire a horse, guide US$2.50). A further 1½-hour walk from Laguna Negra is the beautiful Laguna Los Patos. There are many *frailejón* plants here. Guides (not always necessary) are at Laguna Mucubají or the hotels in Santo Domingo. *Páramo* tours to this area usually include Pico El Aguila (see Road to the high Andes, page 61).

From Mérida to the Panamericana

There are three routes from Mérida to the Panamericana which runs at the foot of the Andes near the border with Zulia state. The most northerly of them is the most interesting. This beautiful journey, starting in the highlands from Mérida, heads west. It passes La Chorrera waterfall on the way to La Encrucijada (restaurant and Trébol service station), where a side road leads to **Jají** (*Phone code: 0274*), a pretty, restored colonial village with white-washed houses, cobbled streets, arches on the exits to the plaza and a white and blue church. Most houses are given over to handicrafts shops. There are a few hotels and others in the hills, where there is good walking. *Buseta* from Mérida bus terminal, hourly, 50 minutes, US$1. From La Encrujidada the road passes dairy farms before its descent through cloud forest. Towns passed on the way are San Eusebio and Mirabel. This is prime birdwatching territory as the road, paved but rough in parts, twists down through several habitats. **La Azulita**, 73 km, four hours from Mérida, is the base for birdwatching tours, with several lodges nearby. A modern cathedral stands on the Plaza and, overall, it's a modern town. From La Azulita, the road meets the Panamericana at Caño Zancudo, passing en route the Cascada Palmita. Turn south for El Vigía, one of the hottest zones in South America, and routes to Lago de Maracaibo and Catatumbo.

El Vigía is where the second route from Mérida meets the Panamericana. Transandean Route 7 leaves Mérida and passes through El Ejido, originally known as Las Guayabas, or 'the city of honey and flowers'. El Ejido and surrounding villages in the sugar cane zone are known for handicrafts and ceramics. One such historic town is **Mesa de los Indios** (www.andes.net/ mesadelosindios), where sugarcane is produced, 5 km from El Ejido towards Jají, 1¼ hours from Mérida. It is famous for its musical traditions and for its artists. Among the latter is the sculptor Daniel Camara. Every Saturday *La Retreta*, Antonio Valero's youth group band, plays wind and percussion instruments in the plaza at 2000. Travellers may donate a wind instrument to the youngsters. Buses to La Mesa leave the plaza in El Ejido. The main road follows the Chama valley, to Lagunillas and Tovar.

Lagunillas was founded in the 16th century by Spaniard Juan Rodríguez Suárez on the site of a pre-hispanic ceremonial centre. Its elaborately choreographed dances honouring a beautiful indigenous princess can be seen at festivities taking place on 15 May. More can be learned at **Museo Arqueológico Julio César Salas** ① *on Parque Sucre*. Nearby is Laguna de Urao, whose natural soda crystals have been mined since pre-hispanic times. **San Juan de Lagunillas**, 2 km away, is where Mérida was originally supposed to be built. Locals (and allegedly doctors) say that the climate is one of the healthiest in the world. There are botanical gardens and a colourful fiesta on 24 June.

Near Estanques, a winding road leads towards **Chiguará**, one of the best-preserved coffee towns in Venezuela. Bizarrely, it contains **La Montaña de los Sueños** theme park ① *1700-2400, daily, ticket office open 1700-2000, T0274-245 0053, US$20, children and senior citizens US$15, food available*, devoted to the history of the Venezuelan film industry (1950s to 1970s), complete with sets, old aeroplanes, limousines, cameras and posters. There are also displays of local television, commercial music and theatre. Chiguará is 45 km from Mérida: take bus or por puesto towards El Vigía and ask to be dropped at junction for Chiguará, from where you have to hitch or wait for infrequent bus or por puesto (**$$ Posada Turística La Peña de Lolito**, Vía La Peña, T0275-836 1109, 0414-532 1334, Mexican-style, 8 rooms with bath and hot water, TV).

Beyond Estanques the main highway for bus and heavy traffic turns off Route 7. Near the intersection on the right is 19th-century **Hacienda La Victoria** with an interesting coffee museum. The highway descends from the grey, scarred mountains before the thickly wooded tropical hillsides above the plains. Buses between Mérida and San Cristóbal then belt along the Pan- americana to La Fría. The third route leaves the Transandean road at

Tovar (*Phone code: 0275, 96 km from Mérida*), passing through Zea, a pleasant town in the foothills. A four-lane motorway between San Cristóbal and La Fría is nearly finished and will cut travel by at least one hour.

From Mérida to Táchira

From Tovar the road continues to **Bailadores** (fiesta from Christmas to Candlemas, 2 February), and **La Grita**, a pleasant town in Táchira state (Sunday market, fiesta 6 August). Near Bailadores is the pleasant Parque La Cascada India Carú, named after a legendary princess whose tears at the death of her warrior lover created the waterfall. Cheap posadas include **$$** Posada Santa Eduvigis, C 10 entre Cras 3 y 4, T0275-857 0651, 50 m east of the church, parking, restaurant. This route takes the wild and beautiful old mountain road over Páramo de La Negra to San Cristóbal. Mérida-San Cristóbal buses go via La Fría, not this road; by public transport change in Tovar and La Grita.

San Cristóbal → *Phone code: 0276. Population: 297,620. Altitude: 830 m.*

The capital of Táchira State was founded in 1561. Today it's a large, busy, but friendly place built over hills and ravines, although a few blocks in historic centre, around the cathedral, retain a colonial air. You need to know which district you are in for orientation, eg La Concordia for the bus station. The **Fiesta de San Sebastián** in second half of January is a major international event, with parades, trade shows, and much more; book ahead, prices rise. **Tourist office**: Cotatur, ⓘ *Av España con Av Carabobo, T357 9655, www.cotatur.gob.ve*. Helpful. **Inparques** ⓘ *Parque Metropolitano, Av 19 de Abril, T346 6544*.

On Sunday, take a taxi to **Peribeca** (US$11 one way), a tiny colonial village with handicraft shops, restaurants and sellers of dairy products, fruit desserts and bewildering variety of liqueurs and infusions. The pretty handicraft alley is next to the modern church. There are two posadas, **La Posada de la Abuela** on the Plaza, and **Posada Turística Doña Meche**, just outside the village. Many restaurants open for Sunday lunch, the best is **El Solar de Juancho**. Alternatively, on Monday, go to the wholesale vegetable market of **Táriba**, just off highway going north. The town's huge white Basílica de la Virgen de la Consolación (1959) can be seen from the highway. Stained glass tells the story of the image. Her fiesta in August attracts great numbers of devotees. The market place is reached by a pedestrian suspension bridge from the plaza in front of the basilica. There are longer trips to colonial villages and handicraft-making communities, but public transport is poor.

San Cristóbal to San Antonio → *Phone code: 0276. Population: 38,000.*

The border town of San Antonio is 55 km from San Cristóbal by a paved, congested road. At **Capacho** (25 km from San Antonio) is an interesting old Municipal Market building, with lions at the four corners. If travelling light and in no hurry, you can go via **Rubio** (45 minutes from San Cristóbal, US$1.40, Líneas Unidas). In the coffee zone, it has a pleasant colonial centre, with an enormous brick church, Santa Bárbara, in neo-Gothic style (1934-1971). It's a busy town with extensive modern outskirts. The roads to it are paved and quieter than the main road, with better scenery, too. Buses congregate around the market. Expreso La Moderna to San Antonio (70 minutes, US$1.15, to/from Av Venezuela in San Antonio) continues to Cúcuta (US$1).

San Antonio is connected by international bridge with Cúcuta on the Colombian side (16 km); continue by road or air to Bogotá. San Antonio has a colonial cathedral and some parks, but is not tourist-oriented. Avenida Venezuela leads to Venezuelan customs. You can catch most transport here, to Cúcuta, San Cristóbal, Rubio, even to Caracas, but the bus terminal is off the road to the airport: at the roundabout at end of Avenida Venezuela, turn left (C 11), take a Circunvalación combi marked Terminal (US$0.50). Also buses to airport. There is a festival on 13-20 May.

Border with Colombia This is the main crossing point between the two countries and the border formalities are geared towards locals. Few foreigners travel overland here. Get a Venezuelan exit stamp at **SAIME** ① *Cra 9 entre 6 y 7, Antiguo Hospital San Vicente, T771 2282.* You will have to fill out a departure card and pay US$9.50 (BsF 40) departure tax across the street. The Colombian consulate is at Centro Cívico San Antonio, loc 1-8, T771 5890, open 0800-1400; better to get a visa in Mérida. The border is open 24 hours but **note** Venezuelan time is 30 minutes ahead of Colombian. Colombian formalities are taken care of right after the bridge: DAS procedures are straightforward with only a passport check and stamp. Colombian and Venezuelan citizens do not need any immigration formalities. Foreigners can arrange exit and entry stamps 0800-1800, often much later. If you only travel to Cúcuta (even to spend the night), no immigration formalities are needed. Just cross the bridge by bus, taxi or por puesto and return the same way. If you plan to travel further to Colombia, however, you will need both Venezuelan exit stamp and Colombian entry stamp.

Entering Venezuela, get your passport stamp at DAS and take bus, por puesto or taxi across the bridge. Ask the driver to take you to Venezuelan immigration, otherwise you will be taken to the centre of San Antonio and will have to backtrack. You can also cross the bridge on foot, but watch out for robberies. Information centre is at the end of the bridge on Venezuelan side. Go to **SAIME** for entry formalities then look for a bus or por puesto to San Cristóbal on Av Venezuela, or go to the bus station (taxi from SAIME US$2). If Venezuelan customs is closed at weekends, it is not possible to cross from Cúcuta. There is a customs and Guardia Nacional post at Peracal outside San Antonio; be prepared for luggage and strip searches. There may be more searches en route, as well as searches between San Cristóbal and Mérida, eg at La Jabonosa on the Panamericana.

If crossing by private vehicle, car documents must be stamped at the SENIAT office at the Puente Internacional, just before San Antonio. Two different stamps are needed at separate SENIAT buildings ① *Mon-Fri 0800-1200, 1330-1700, Sat 0800-1200, T771 5411.* It's essential to have proof of car/motorbike ownership. You must check in advance if you need a visa and a *carnet de passages*. Once in Venezuela, you may find police are ignorant of requirements for foreign cars.

Sierra Nevada de Mérida listings

For Sleeping and Eating price codes and other relevant information, see Essentials, pages 9-11.

⊜ Sleeping

Los Nevados *p73*
$ pp El Buen Jesús, T252 5696. Hot water, Meals.

$ Posada run by Doña Chepa, as you enter from Los Nevados, warm. Recommended.
$ pp Posada Bella Vista, behind church. Hot water, hammocks, great views, restaurant. Recommended.
$ pp Posada El Orégano, including meals, basic, good food. Recommended.

$ pp **Posada Guamanchi**, T252 2080, www.guamanchi.com. Solar power, great views, cheaper without bath, 2 meals included. Recommended.

Tabay *p74*
$$ Casa Vieja, Transandina via Páramo, San Rafael de Tabay, inside the Parador Turístico El Paramito, T0274-417 1489, www.casa-vieja-merida.com. Plant-filled colonial house, German and Peruvian owners, good doubles, hot water, breakfast and dinner available, good food, relaxing, very helpful, information on independent trips from Tabay and transport, English, French and German spoken. Travel agency, **Caiman Tours**, for Llanos, wildlife and adventure tours, see also www.birds-venezuela.de. From the bus terminal in Mérida take a bus via Mucuchíes or Apartaderos, 30 mins to Tabay, get off exactly 1.5 km after the gas station in Tabay village (just after you pass Plaza Bolívar); the bus stop is called El Paramito. There is a sign on the road pointing left. Free pick-up from the airport or terminal with reservation. They also have a second *posada* in the village of Altamira de Cáceres. Warmly recommended.
$$ La Casona de Tabay, on the Mérida road 1.5 km from the plaza, T0274-283 0089, posadala casona@cantv.net. A beautiful colonial-style hotel, surrounded by mountains, comfortable, home cooking, family-run. Take *por puesto*, 2 signposts.
$ pp **Posada de la Mano Poderosa**, beyond San Rafael de Tabay on road to Mucuchíes, T0414-742 2862. Dorms, lovely, quiet, hot showers, good food, great value, get off at La Plazuela then walk 15 mins towards Vivero Fruti Flor.

Mucuchíes
$$ Los Conquistadores, Av Carabobo 14, T872 0350. Nice decor, modern, breakfast, TV, heating, lots of facilities like pool tables and other games, garden, parking, restaurant

0800-2200, tasca, and bike hire. Arranges transport for tours, BBV Provincial and ATM.
$ Posada Los Andes, Independencia 25, T872 0151, 0414-717 2313. Old house on street above plaza, run by Las Hermanas Pironi Belli, 5 cosy rooms, hot water, shared bathrooms, TV in living room, excellent restaurant (breakfast extra, criollo and Italian food, 0800-2030). Internet available. Highly recommended.
Mucuposadas is a network of basic lodgings, see www.andestropicales.org/Andes_Vzla.html.

San Rafael de Mucuchíes
$$ Posada San Rafael del Páramo, just outside San Rafael, 500m from the Capilla de Piedra, on road to Apartaderos, T872 0938. With breakfast or **$** without breakfast in low season. Charming converted house with lots of interesting sculpture and paintings, hot water, heating, TV, also cabin with kitchenette, walking and riding tours (guide extra). Recommended.
$ Casa Sur, Independencia 72, T872 0342, 0416-275 1684, njespindola@yahoo.com. Hot water, heating, TV, breakfast extra, other meals on request.
$ El Rosal, Bolívar 37, T872 0331, T0416-275 3254. Hot water, TV, good, also cabins with kitchenette (**$$**), no breakfast, café nearby, restaurant for groups, tasca at weekends.

Apartaderos *p75*
$$$ Hotel Parque Turístico, main road, T888 0094. Cheaper in low season. Attractive modern chalet- style building, heating, very hot showers, helpful owner, expensive restaurant. Recommended.
$$ Hotel y Restaurante Mifafí, on main road, T888 0131, refugioturisticomifafi@hotmail.com. Cheaper without heating, pleasant rooms and cabins, hot water, TV, good food. A welcoming, reliable choice.

$ Posada y Restaurant Juan Hilario,
Mucuchíes side of town, T888 0145,
T0414-747 3779 (mob). 9 big rooms with hot
water, double bed and bunks, TV, cold but
looks OK, all meals extra, parking.

$ Posada Viejo Apartaderos, outside town,
coming from Mucuchíes, T888 0003,
posadaviejoapartaderos@cantv.net. Next to
bomba, with **La Matica de Rosa** restaurant,
T271 2209, Sra Marbeles. Open only in high
season. Good value, good restaurant with
reasonable prices.

From Mérida to the Panamericana *p75*
Jají

$$$ pp Estancia La Bravera, 18 km from Jají
towards La Azulita, T0212-978 2627, 414-293
3306, www.estancialabravera.com. Cabins in
beautiful flower gardens in the cloud forest,
great for bird- watching and for relaxing, hot
water, includes breakfast and dinner, lunch
US$35, uses home produce, holds an annual
Estancia Musical (Aug). Recommended.

$$ Hacienda Santa Filomena, 5 mins from
Jají, T0212-573 1519, 0414-247 9020,
santafilomena@hotmail.com. Stay and dine
on a 19th-century coffee farm. Used by
birders.

$$ Posada Restaurant Aldea Vieja, C
Principal, just off Plaza, T414 6128, or
T414-717 3137, http://aldeavieja.com.
Colonial style main building, also cabins for
4-8, lovely views, simple rooms, TV, hot water,
meals extra (breakfast US$3.40), playground
(watch out for the slides).

$$–$ Hacienda El Carmen, Aldea La Playa, 2
km from Jají (there is public transport),
T414-639 2701, 0414-630 9562,
www.haciendaelcarmen.com.ve. On a
working dairy and coffee-processing farm,
built 1863, fascinating buildings, lovely
rooms, one with jacuzzi (**$$**), some simpler
rooms, breakfast included, coffee tours,
owner Andrés Monzón.

$ Posada Turística Jají, beside the Prefectura,
on the plaza, T416 6333. 4 rooms with hot

water, no TV, historic, 2 fountains, restaurant
0800-2100, breakfast included if staying a few
days.

La Azulita

3 km before town is a turning left to San Luis
and Saysayal Bajo. The sign mentions various
posadas, but most not working.
Recommended are:

$$ El Tao, on a side road beyond Remanso,
4-5 km, 6 mins in car from La Azulita,
T0274-511 3088, 0416-175 0011,
www.eltaomerida.com. Taoist owners and
oriental- style spa with saunas, and natural
therapies, many birds, favoured by birders
and other groups, lovely gardens, very safe
and peaceful, nice public areas. Cabins for
2-4, with breakfast, TV, hot water. Restaurant,
boxed lunches and early breakfast for birding
groups.

$$ Remanso del Quebradón, close to
junction, T0416-775 7573,
www.remanso.com.ve. 4 rooms with bath, on
a small coffee farm with fruit trees in the
gardens, restaurant, breakfast included,
popular with birdwatchers.

$ Posada Turística La Azulita, on Plaza
Bolívar. Rooms around restaurant in
courtyard, OK food. Some other lodgings in
town.

Mesa de los Indios

$$ Posada Papá Miguel, C Piñango 1,
T0274-417 4315/252 2529, 0414-747 9953,
www.andes.net/papamiguel. Rustic and
characterful, a good place to stay if staying to
hear the music on Sat night.

San Cristóbal *p77*

Cheapest hotels around the bus station (ugly
area), **$$$–$$** business hotels in the centre
(**El Faraón**, **Dinastía**) and more upmarket
place in the north- western suburbs (eg
Castillo de la Fantasía, **Los Pirineos**, **Posada
Remanso de Pueblo Nuevo**).

$$$ Lidotel, Sambil San Cristóbal Mall, Autopista Antonio José de Sucre, Las Lomas, T510 3333, www.lidotelhotelboutique.com. Attached to an enormous, posh shopping mall, with all the luxuries of 4-star hotel, pool, very well run. Recommended.

$$$ Posada Rincón Tachirense, Av Ferrero Tamayo con C 3, N Ft-19, La Popita, T341 8573, www.posadarincontachirense.com. Not central, down hill from **Del Rey**, cheaper with shared bath, comfortable, a/c, TV, Wi-Fi and internet, breakfast and will ring out for pizza. Recommended.

$$$-$$ Del Rey, Av Ferrero Tamayo, Edif El Rey, T343 0561. Good showers, fridge, TV, Wi-Fi, kitchenette, laundry, no breakfast but *panadería* in building, pizzas. Recommended.

$$-$ Posada Turística Don Manuel, Cra 10 No 1-104, just off Av 19 de Abril, Urb La Concordia, T347 8082. Rooms are across street; Sra Carmen will direct you. Hot water, family run, TV, fridge, fan, limited kitchen facilities, no breakfast, parking. Sleeps 8, always book in advance, convenient.

$ Río de Janeiro, C 1, No 7-27, Urb Juan Maldonado, La Concordia, by bus station, T347 7666. Big rooms, fan, hot shower, no breakfast.

$ Tropical, Prol 5ta Av No 7472, opposite bus station, T347 2932. Basic. Other cheapies nearby.

San Cristóbal to San Antonio *p77*
Capacho
$$ La Molinera, 20 mins from San Cristóbal at Capacho, municipalidad de Independencia, T788 3117. Rooms and suites in a beautiful, traditional posada with swimming pool and hand-made furniture. Good Tachirense food in its restaurant.

San Antonio
Many hotels near town centre.
$$ Adriático, C6 y Cra 6, T771 3896. Not far from Av Venezuela, 3-star, functional.

$ Neveri, C 3, No 3-13, esq Carrera 3, T771 5702. A/c, TV, safe, parking nearby, 1 block from Customs, opposite Guardia Nacional barracks. No food, dated. Internet next door.

🍴 Eating

San Cristóbal *p77*
El Barrio Obrero has the main concentration of eateries, bars and discos. Try **Rocamar**, Cra 20 y C 14, for seafood. Also pizza places and *pastelerías*.

¶¶¶-¶¶ La Olleta, Cra 21, no 10-171, just off plaza, Barrio Obrero, T356 6944. Smart, simple décor, Venezuelan and international with creative touches, well presented.

Around town there are many *panaderías* and *pastelerías* for snacks as well as bread and cakes, coffee and other drinks, eg **América**, Cra 8, Edif La Concordia, no 4-113, La Concordia (several on Cra 8 y C 4, La Concordia); also **Táchira** branches.

San Antonio *p77*
¶ Rosmar, Cra 6 y C 6, opposite Hotel Adriático. Very popular for lunch, several choices, OK food.

🚌 Transport

Los Nevados *p73*
Jeep Los Nevados-**Mérida**, late afternoon (depart 0700 from Plaza Las Heroínas in Mérida), 5-6 hrs, US$11 pp, US$48 per jeep, very rough and narrow but spectacular.

Tabay *p74*
Regular bus service from **Mérida** C 19 entre Avs 3 y 4, every 10 mins, US$0.40; taxi US$4-8 (more at night). Gasoline in Tabay.

Apartaderos *p75*
Bus To **Mérida** from turn-off to Barinas; bus to **Barinas** on the road over the Sierra Nevada is unreliable, best to catch it in Mérida.

San Cristóbal *p77*

Air Airport at Santo Domingo, 40 km away. Helpful tourist kiosk with leaflets, map of San Cristóbal US$0.50. Taxi to San Cristóbal US$22, can take as little as 35 mins, but normally much more, lots of traffic, nice scenery (tourist office says no other option). The highway is 30 mins' walk away; it may be possible to catch a bus, 1 hr, US$1.50. Daily flights to/from **Caracas** with Aserca, **Aeropostal** and **Rutaca**. Alternatively fly to San Antonio (see below) for better public transport links.

Bus Local: buses cost US$0.35. 'Intercomunal' goes from Av Ferrero Tamayo (northwest) to Bus Terminal. 'Tusca' from Av Ferrero Tamayo to centre. Taxis US$3.50 for a short run. **Línea Pirineos**, T355 1717/355 0405 recommended.

The **bus station** is in La Concordia, in the southeast. It is a bus terminal, shopping mall, market, phone exchange and food court all lumped together. Terminal tax US$0.10, paid on bus before departure. Company offices are grouped together: **Expresos Mérida** (not to Mérida), **Aerobuses, Expresos Los Llanos** (to San Fernando), **Expresos Barinas** (direct to San Fernando at 1700, and to Puerto Ayacucho, T0276-414 6950), many others. **Expresos Occidente** have their own terminal nearby. To **Mérida**, US$9.25, 5 hrs, with **Táchira-Mérida** (buy ticket on bus); **Expreso Unido** to Mérida, 0530, 0830, plus *ejecutivos* 1130, 1430, 1730; also to Tovar 0930, 1430, 4 hrs, US$9.50. Buses to Mérida go via the Panamericana, not over the Páramo. National Guard Control at La Jabonesa, just before San Juan de Colón, be prepared for luggage search. To **Maracaibo**, 6-8 hrs, US$18.50-20. To **Caracas**, US$18-23, 15 hrs; **Valencia**, US$14.25-23. To **Barinas**, US$8.60. To **San Fernando de Apure** via **Guasdualito**, US$19-23. To **San Antonio**, 1¼ hrs (but San Cristóbal rush hour can add lots of time), US$1.50, **Línea San Antonio**,

T347 0976 (San Antonio 771 2966) and **Unión de Conductores**, T346 0691 (San Antonio 771 1364). To **Cúcuta**, **Línea Venezuela**, T347 3086 (Cúcuta T0270-583 6413) and **Fronteras Unidas**, T347 7446 (Cúcuta T0270 583 5445) , US$2.75, Mon-Fri 0800-1200, 1400-1800. Opposite terminal on Rugeles, **Coop de Conductores Fronterizos** cars, T611 2256, to **San Antonio**.

San Antonio *p77*

Air The airport has exchange facilities (mainly for Colombian pesos). Taxis run to SAIME (immigration) in town, and on to Cúcuta airport. Flights to **Caracas** with **Aeropostal** and **Rutaca**.

Bus From terminal several companies to **Caracas**, via the Llanos, Valencia and Maracay. All *bus-cama*: Caracas US$27, Valencia US$22, Maracay US$22. **Expresos San Cristóbal** have office on Av Venezuela, close to Customs, 1800 to Caracas, 13-14 hrs; **Expresos Mérida**, Av Venezuala, No 6-17, at 1900. **Táchira-Mérida** to **Mérida** and **Barquisimeto**, 1600; Expresos Unidos to Mérida 1200, 1700. To **San Cristóbal**, catch a bus on Av Venezuela. Taxi from SAIME area to San Cristóbal, 40 mins, they try to charge US$40 but will negotiate down to US$18.

Border with Colombia *p78*

Air It is cheaper, but slower, to fly **Caracas**-San Antonio, take a taxi to Cúcuta, then take an internal Colombian flight, than to fly direct Caracas- Colombia. The airport transfer at San Antonio is well-organized and taxi drivers make the 25-min trip with all stops. Air tickets out of Cúcuta can be reserved in a Venezuelan travel agency.

Bus On Av Venezuela por puestos/colectivos to **Cúcuta** charge US$1, and buses US$0.70 payable in bolívares or pesos, 30 mins. Some say to terminal, others to centre. Taxi to Cúcuta, US$11. On any transport that crosses the border, make sure the driver knows you need to stop to obtain stamps. *Por puesto* drivers may refuse to wait. Taxi drivers will stop at all the offices. Just to visit Cúcuta, no documents are needed.

Directory

San Cristóbal *p77*

Banks Plenty of ATMs in town. Major banks on Av 7 between Cs 9 and 10. Mon-Fri 0830-1530. TCs are difficult to change.
Consulates **German**, Cra 3 con C 4,CC Dr Toto Gonzáles, p 1, of 7, T343 6218, kmargeit@ hotmail.com. **UK**, CC El Tama, loc 49, Altos de Pirineos, T356 6732, britcon-sc@cantv.net. **Telephones** Many **CANTV** offices and phones; also independent phone tables, with land lines and mobiles, everywhere.

San Antonio *p77*

Banks Many *casas de cambio* on Av Venezuela near the international bridge will change Colombian pesos, but not all change cheques or even US$ cash. The exchange rate for bolívares to pesos is the same in San Antonio as in Cúcuta.

Los Llanos and Amazonas

A spectacular route descends from the Sierra Nevada to the flat llanos, one of the best places in the world to see birds and animals. This vast, sparsely populated wilderness of 300,000 sq km – one third of the country's area – lies between the Andes to the west and the Orinoco to the south and east. Southwest of the Guayana region, on the banks of the Orinoco, Puerto Ayacucho is the gateway to the jungles of Venezuela. Although it takes up about a fifth of the country, Amazonas and its tropical forests is for the most part unexplored and unspoilt.

Los Llanos

The *llanos* are veined by numerous slow-running rivers, forested along their banks. The flat plain is only varied here and there by *mesas*, or slight upthrusts of the land. About five million of the country's 6.4 million cattle are in the *llanos*, but only around 10% of the human population. When the whole plain is periodically under water, the *llaneros* drive their cattle into the hills or through the flood from one *mesa* to another. When the plain is parched by the sun and the savanna grasses become inedible they herd the cattle down to the damper region of the Apure and Orinoco. Finally they drive them into the valley of Valencia to be fattened.

In October and November, when the vast plains are still partially flooded, wildlife abounds. Animals include capybara, caiman, monkeys, anacondas, river dolphins, pumas and many bird species. Though it's possible to explore this region independently, towns are few and far between and distances are great. It's better to visit the *llanos* as part of a tour from Mérida (see Tour operators, page 70), or stay at one of the ecotourism *hatos*, or ranches (see below).

Guanare → *Phone code: 0257. Population: 32,500.*

An excellent road goes to the western *llanos* of Barinas from Valencia. It goes through San Carlos, Acarigua (an agricultural centre and the largest city in Portuguesa state) and Guanare, a national place of pilgrimage with a cathedral containing the much venerated relic of the Virgin of Coromoto. The **Santuario Nacional Nuestra Señora de Coromoto** on the spot where the Virgin appeared to Cacique Coromoto in 1652 ① *25 km frm Guanare on road to Barinas, open 0800-1700, bus from C 20 y Cra 9, Guanare, every 15 mins, US$0.35* is an imposing modern basilica dedicated to the Virgin. It was inaugurated by Pope John II in 1996. Pilgrimages to Coromoto are 2 January and 11 September and Candlemas is 2 February. There is also a large park devoted to María, 4 km from Coromoto. For tourist information: fondomixtoportuguesa@hotmail.com.

Barinas ➔ *Phone code: 0273. Population: 240,000.*

The road continues to Barinas, the hot, sticky capital of the cattle-raising and oil-rich state of Barinas. A couple of colonial buildings remain: the Palacio del Marqués on the west side of the plaza and the Casa de la Cultura on the north side. On the south side of the plaza is the beautifully restored, 19th-century Escuela de Música; the cathedral is to the east. The shady Parque Universitario, just outside the city on Avenida 23 de Enero, has a botanical garden.
Tourist office ⓘ *Av Insauste con Av Adonay Parra Jiménez, at entrance to La Ciudad Deportiva, T552 7091, www.corbatur.org.ve.* Helpful, maps, no English spoken; kiosks at airport and bus station.

San Fernando de Apure ➔ *Phone code: 0247. Population: 135,000.*

At Lagua, 16 km east of Maracay, a good road leads south to San Fernando de Apure. It passes through San Juan de los Morros, with natural hot springs; Ortiz, near the crossroads with the San Carlos-El Tigre road; the Guárico lake and Calabozo. Some 132 km south of Calabozo, San Fernando is the hot and sticky capital of the state of Apure and a fast-growing trade and transport hub for the region. There is *Corp Banca* for American Express, Avenida Miranda, Edif Chang, PB, and *Bancos Mercantil* (Paseo Libertador) and *Provincial* (Plaza Páez) with Visa and Mastercard ATM and cash advance. From San Fernando you can travel east to Ciudad Bolívar (see page 120) or south to Puerto Ayacucho (see below).

San Fernando to Barinas

From San Fernando a road heads to head west to Barinas (468 km). It's a beautiful journey, but the road can be in terrible condition, eg between Mantecal, La Ye junction and Bruzual, a town just south of the Puente Nutrias on the Río Apure. In the early morning, many animals and birds can be seen, and in the wet season caiman (alligators) cross the road. **Mantecal** is a friendly cattle-ranching town with hotels and restaurants. *Fiesta*, 23-26 February.

Los Llanos listings

For Sleeping and Eating price codes and other relevant information, see Essentials, pages 9-11.

⊜ Sleeping

Guanare *p84*
Hotels include:
$ Italia, Carrera 5, No 19-60, T253 1213. A/c, bar and restaurant, off-street parking.

Barinas *p85*
$$ Internacional, C Arzobispo Méndez on Plaza Zamora, T552 2343, hotelinternacional_3@ hotmail.com. A/c, safe, cable TV, good restaurant.

$$ Varyná, Av 23 de Enero, near the airport, T533 2477. A/c, cable TV, hot water, restaurant, parking. Recommended.
$ El Palacio, Av Elías Cordero con C 5, T552 6947. A/c, good value, parking, near bus terminal so front rooms are noisy.
$ Mónaco, Av Elías Cordero, T533 2096. A/c, cable TV, hot water, parking.
$ Motel Don Ripoli, Av 23 de Enero, near the airport, T552 2829. Cold showers, a/c, pool, basic, parking.

Staying at a tourist ranch
An alternative to travelling independently or arranging a tour from Mérida is to stay at one

of the tourist ranches. Most of these are in Apure state and can be reached from Barinas or San Fernando de Apure.

$$$$ pp Hato Piñero, T0212-991 8935. A safari-type lodge at a working ranch near El Baúl (turn off Tinaco-El Sombrero road at El Cantón). Inclusive price, per day, packages can include return overland or air transport from Caracas. Bird- and animal-watching trips. Since its nationalization by the government it is unclear what services are offered her, or what their standards are. From Caracas, 6 hrs; from Ciudad Bolívar, 9 hrs.

$$$ Hato Chinea Arriba, the closest *hato* to Caracas, is a 5 mins' drive from Calabozo, T0212-781 4241 or 0414-322 0785, www.haciendachineaarriba.com. Prices all-inclusive. Owner Francisco Leitz speaks French, German and English.

$$$ pp Hato El Cedral, about 30 mins by bus from Mantecal (see above). Address: Av La Salle, edif Pancho p 5, of 33, Los Caobos, Caracas, T0212- 781 8995, www.elcedral.com. A 53,000-ha ranch, where hunting is banned. Fully inclusive price, tax extra (high season Dec to Apr), a/c, hot water, land and river safaris, guides, pool. Special offers at certain times of year. Can also rent a room without tour or food.

$$$ Hato La Fe, halfway between Calabozo and San Fernando de Apure in Guárico state, T0414- 325 4188/468 8749, www.hatolafe.com. All-inclusive tours include animal-watching trips and horse riding. 8 bedrooms in a colonial-style house, pool, camping available.

$$ pp Rancho Grande, close to Mantecal, T0240-808 7434. Run by very friendly and knowledgeable Ramón González. All inclusive, good wildlife spotting and horse riding trips.

$$ pp Reserva Privada de Flora y Fauna Mataclara, on road to El Baúl at Km 93 (next to Hato Piñero turn off). Address: Prof Antonio González-Fernández, Universidad de Los Llanos 'Unellez', Mesa de Caracas, Guanare 3323, Estado de Portuguesa, T0241-867 7254. Full board, fishing with own equipment and animal watching trips.

San Fernando de Apure *p85*
Most hotels are within 1 block of the intersection of Paseo Libertador and Av Miranda.

$$ Gran Hotel Plaza, C Bolívar, T342 1746, 2 blocks from the bus terminal, www.granhotelplaza.com/index.htm. A/c, cable TV, safe, good, Wi-Fi, parking.

$$ Trinacria, Av Miranda, near bus terminal, T342 3778. Huge rooms, a/c, cable TV, fridge.

$ El Río, Av María Nieves, near the bus terminal, T341 1928. With a/c, cable TV, good value.

$ La Fuente, Miranda y Libertador, T342 3233. A/c, TV, phone, safe.

$ La Torraca, Av Boulevard y Paseo Libertador by Plaza Bolívar, T342 2777. Excellent rooms, a/c, balcony overlooking centre of town. Recommended.

🍴 Eating

Barinas *p85*
🍴 **El Estribo**, C Apure entre Av Garguera y Andrés Varela. Roast and barbecue meat, good, open 1100-2400.

🍴 **Sol Llanero**, facing **Hotel Palacio**. Good, cheap.

🍴 **Restaurant Pizzería El Budare**, Av 23 de Energo y Mérida. Good pizza, local dishes. 3 restaurants across the street serve similar fare.

🔺 Activities and tours

Barinas *p85*
Grados Alta Aventura, Altamira de Cáceres, T0416-877 4540, http://www.grados.com.ve/2011. Manager, Gregorio Montilla Valero. For rafting trips, kayaking, birdwatching and other adventures, based in the historic town of Altamira de Cáceres. Recommended.

Barinas *p85*

Air Aeropuerto Nacional, Av 23 de Enero. Flights to **Caracas**.

Bus To **Mérida**, 6 a day with **Transportes Barinas**, US$5.80, spectacular ride through the mountains, 5-7 hrs (sit on right for best views); also to **Valera** at 0730, 1130, US$7.40, 7 hrs. To **Caracas**, US$16.30, 8 hrs, several companies go direct or via **Maracay** and **Valencia**, regularly 0730-2300. To **San Cristóbal**, several daily, US$8.60, 5 hrs; to **San Fernando de Apure**, US$12, 9 hrs with **Expresos Los Llanos** at 0900, 2300; the same company also goes to **Maracaibo** (at 2000 and 2200, US$16.30, 8 hrs) and **Puerto La Cruz** (3 a day, US$23.25, 16 hrs).

From Barinas there is a beautifully scenic road to Apartaderos, in the Sierra Nevada de Mérida (see page 75). Motorists travelling east to Ciudad Bolívar can either go across the *llanos* or via San Carlos, Tinaco, El Sombrero, Chaguaramas, Valle de la Pascua (see below) and El Tigre. The latter route requires no ferry crossings and has more places with accommodation.

San Fernando de Apure *p85*

Air Aeropuerto Las Flecheras, Av 1 de Mayo, T341 0139. Flights to **Caracas**.

Bus Terminal is modern and clean, not far from centre; US$3 taxi. To **Caracas**, US$15.80, 7 hrs; to **Barinas**, Expresos Zamora, 5 daily, 7 hrs (take food and drink), rough ride, day and night bus, US$12; to **Maracay**, US$11.50; to **Puerto Ayacucho**, US$17.75, 8 hrs; to **Calabozo**, 1½ hrs, US$3.75.

San Fernando to Barinas *p85*

Bus San Fernando de Apure-Mantecal 3½ hrs, US$6.80; Mantecal-Barinas, 4 hrs, US$8.50.

Barinas *p85*

Banks **Banco Mercantil**, Av Marqués del Pumar y Bolívar, and **Banco Provincial**, Av Marqués del Pumar y Carvajal, for Mastercard or Visa cash withdrawals.

Amazonas

Much of Amazonas is stunningly beautiful and untouched, but access is only by river. The more easily accessible places lie on the course of the Orinoco and its tributaries. The best time to visit is October to December after the rains, but at any season, this is a remote part of the country.

San Fernando to Puerto Ayacucho

Due south of San Fernando de Apure is **Puerto Páez** (*Phone code: 0247; Population: 2600*) at the confluence of the Meta and Orinoco rivers; here there is a crossing to El Burro west of the Caicara-Puerto Ayacucho road. Route 2 runs south from San Fernando to Puerto Páez, crossing several major rivers. Between the Capanaparo and Cinaruco rivers is the **Parque Nacional Cinaruco- Capanaparo** (also called **Santos Luzardo**), reached only from this road. If this road is closed, to get to Puerto Ayacucho from San Fernando involves a minimum 15-hour detour via the Caicara ferry.

From Caicara a new paved road runs 370 km southwest to Puerto Ayacucho. The turn off to **El Burro**, where the boat crosses the Orinoco to Puerto Páez (ferry US$1), is 88 km north of Puerto Ayacucho (*taxi* El Burro-Puerto Ayacucho, two hours US$8.50).

Puerto Ayacucho → *Phone code: 0248. Population: 41,240.*

The capital of the State of Amazonas is 800 km via the Orinoco from Ciudad Bolívar. At the end of the dry season (April), it is very hot and sticky. It is deep in the wild, but no direct boats do the five day journey up river. **Museo Etnológico Monseñor Enzo Ceccarelli** ① *Av Río Negro, Tue-Sat 0830-1200, 1430-1830, Sun 0900-1300, US$1*, has a library and collection of regional exhibits, recommended. In front of the museum is a market, open every day, where *indígenas* sell handicrafts. One block away is the cathedral. The Salesian Mission House and boys' school on Plaza Bolívar may also be visited. Prices in Puerto Ayacucho are generally higher than north of the Orinoco. **Tourist office** is in the Gobernación building, Av Río Negro, T521 0033, www.amazonas.gob.ve. **Note** Malaria is prevalent in this area; take precautions.

Excursions October to December is the best time, when rivers are high but the worst of the rains has passed. In the low season, May-June, it may be difficult to organize tours for only a few days.

You can walk up **Cerro Perico** for good views of the town, or go to the Mirador, 1 km from centre, for good views of the Ature rapids. A recommended trip is to the village of Pintado (12 km south), where petroglyphs described by Humboldt can be seen on the huge rock **Cerro Pintado**. This is the most accessible petroglyph site of the hundreds scattered throughout Amazonas.

Some 35 km south on the road to Samariapo is the **Parque Tobogán de la Selva**, a pleasant picnic area based around a steeply inclined, smooth rock over which the Río Maripures cascades. This waterslide is great fun in the wet season; crowded on Sunday, take swimsuit and food and drink (stick to the right to avoid crashing into the barrier, few locals slide right from the top; also beware of broken glass). A small trail leads up from the slide to a natural jacuzzi after about 20 minutes. Taxi to Cerro Pintado and Parque Tobogán, US$17 return (organize your return, otherwise you may face a lengthy hike). Agencies in town arrange tours; easier but more expensive.

The well-paved road from Puerto Ayacucho to Samariapo (63 km) was built to bypass the rapids which here interrupt the Orinoco, dividing it into 'Upper' and 'Lower'; the powerful Maripures Rapids are very impressive.

Tours in Amazonas
The best base is Puerto Ayacucho. Do not travel alone. By ascending the Autana or Sipapo rivers, you can see **Autana-tepuy**, a 1200 m-high mass of rock no-one has climbed from the base. Other *tepuis* in the region include the great mass of the Sierra de la Neblina on the Brazilian border.

San Juan de Manapiare (*Population: 3700*) is the regional centre for the middle Ventuari. A beautiful track winds around the Cerro Guanay to get there. The road starts at Caicara and goes through Guaniamo and Sabana de Cardona.

Amazonas listings

For Sleeping and Eating price codes and other relevant information, see Essentials, pages 9-11.

⊜ Sleeping

Puerto Ayacucho *p88*
$$$ Orinoquia Lodge, on the Río Orinoco, 20 mins from airport, book through Cacao Travel, www.cacaotravel.com, or through, T0248-414 3833, www.casatropical.com.ve. Nice setting, comfortable lodgings in thatched huts, full board.
$$ Apure, Av Orinoco 28, T521 0516, less than 1 km from centre. A/c, good restaurant. Recommended.
$$ City Center, Av 23 de Enero, on roundabout at entrance to town, T521 0639. Pleasant, safe parking, takes credit cards.
$ Res Internacional, Av Aguerrevere 18, T521 0242. A/c (cheaper without), comfortable, shower, locked parking, safe but basic, not very clean, good place to find tour information and meet other travellers, if no room available you can sling up your hammock, bus drivers stay here and will drive you to the terminal for early starts.
Private camps in Amazonas There are a number of private river camps on the upper Orinoco but they do not welcome casual guests.

Río Manapiare area
$$$$ Campamento Camani, in a forest clearing on the banks of the Río Alto Ventuari, 2 hrs by launch from San Juan de Manapiare, T521 4865, www.campamentocamani.com. From Puerto Ayacucho daily aerotaxi takes 50 mins. Maximum 26 at any one time, mosquito nets, all amenities, excursions available. Has 2-, 3- and 4-night packages including transport, full board and jungle excursions.
$$$$ Yutajé Camp, on a tributary of Río Manapiare due east of Puerto Ayacucho, T0248-521 6110. Restaurant and bar, full board, fishing, canoes, horses, excursions to indigenous villages, expensive but professional, welcoming. Reached by plane from Puerto Ayacucho or boat up the Ríos Manapiare and Corocoro (take something soft to sit on). Price is for a 3 day/2 night package.

❷ Eating

Puerto Ayacucho *p88*
†† Cherazad, Aguerrevere y Av Orinoco. Arabic food, relatively expensive.
†† El Padrino, in Urb Andrés Eloy Blanco on Av Belisio Pérez off Av 23 de Enero. Good Italian.
††-† El Espagetazo, Av Aguerrevere. Mainly pasta, popular with locals.

♔♔ **Las Palmeras**, Av 23 de Enero, 2 blocks from the Redoma. Pizzas and fast food.
♔ **Capi Fuente de Soda**, on Av Evelio Roa behind *gobernación*. Some vegetarian dishes.

⊙ Shopping

Puerto Ayacucho *p88*
Handicrafts Good *artesanía* in the Plaza del Indio; also in **Artes Amazonas** on Av Evelio Roa, next to **Wayumi**, and in **Topocho** just up from Plaza del Indio. Vicente Barletta, **Típico El Casique**, Av Principal 583, Urb Andrés Eloy Blanco, has a good collection of masks (free); he also works as a guide, recommended, take own food and equipment.

▲ Activities and tours

Tours in Amazonas *p89*
It is strongly recommended to go on tours organized by tour agents or guides registered in the **Asocación de Guías**, in the Cámara de Turismo de Puerto Ayacucho, Casa de la Piedra, on the Arteria Vial de la Av Orinoco with Av Principal (the house on top of the large rock). Some independent guides may not have permission to visit Amazonas. Those listed below will arrange permits and insurance but shop around.
Coyote Expediciones, Av Aguirrevere 75, T521 4582, 0416-448 7125, coyoteexpedition@ cantv.net. Helpful, professional, English spoken, organizes trips staying in indigenous villages.
Expediciones Aguas Bravas Venezuela, Av Río Negro, No 32-2, in front of Plaza Rómulo Betancourt, T521 4458/0541, aguasbravas@ cantv.net. Whitewater rafting, 2 daily 0900-1200 and 1500-1800, 3-13 people per boat, reservations required at peak times, take insect repellent, sun protector, light shoes and swimsuit.

Tobogán Tours, Av 23 de Enero 24, near *Instituto del Menor*, T521 4865, tobogant@cantv.net.
Yutajé Tours, in Urb Monte Bello, 1 block from Av Orinoco, past the Mercadito going out of town, T521 0664, turismoamazona@cantv.net. Good value for money but the organization is erratic.

⊝ Transport

Puerto Ayacucho *p88*
Air Airport 7 km southeast along Av Orinoco.
Bus Expresos del Valle to **Cuidad Bolívar** (US$20, 10 hrs; take something to eat, bus stops once for early lunch), **Caicara, Puerto Ordaz** and **San Félix**; Cooperativa Cacique to **San Fernando de Apure**, US$17.75, 8 hrs; both companies in bus terminal. **Expresos La Prosperidad** to **Caracas** and **Maracay** from Urb Alto Parima. Bus from **Caracas**, 2030, 2230 daily, US$25, 12 hrs (but much longer in wet season). *Por puesto* to Ciudad Bolívar, 3 daily, US$25, 10-12 hrs (Caicara Amazonas).
Ferry Ferry service across the Orinoco, US$0.50. Boat to **Caicara**, 1½ days, US$25 including food, but bargain; repellent and hammock required.

⊙ Directory

Puerto Ayacucho *p88*
Banks Changing dollars is difficult.
Internet El Navegante, CC Maniglia, Av Orinoco, or on top floor of Biblioteca Pública Central, Av Río Negro. **Post offices** Ipostel on Av Aguerrevere 3 blocks up from Av Orinoco. **Telephones** International calls from **CANTV**, on Av Orinoco next to *Hotel Apure*; also from *Las Churuatas* on Av Aguerrevere y C Amazonas, 1 block from Plaza del Indio.

East coast

Beautiful sandy bays, islands, forested slopes and a strong colonial influence all contribute to make this one of the most visited parts of the country. The western part, which is relatively dry, has the two main cities, Puerto La Cruz and Cumaná, which is possibly the oldest Hispanic city on the South American mainland. As you go east, you find some splendid beaches. Off shore are two of Venezuela's prime holiday attractions, Isla de Margarita, a mix of the overdeveloped and the quiet, and the island paradise of the Los Roques archipelago.

Caracas to Puerto La Cruz

Very much a holiday coastline, the first part takes its name from the sweeping Barlovento bay in Miranda state. Onshore trade winds give the seaboard a lusher aspect than the more arid landscape elsewhere.

It is some five hours from Caracas to Puerto La Cruz through Caucagua, from which there is a 58 km road northeast to **Higuerote** (*Phone code: 0234. Population: 13,700*); three basic hotels, the best beaches are out of town. A coastal road from Los Caracas to Higuerote has many beaches and beautiful views.

Parque Nacional Laguna de Tacarigua

At 14 km before Higuerote on the road from Caucagua is Tacarigua de Mamporal, where you can turn off to the **Parque Nacional Laguna de Tacarigua**. The 18,400 ha national park enclosing the lagoon is an important ecological reserve, with mangroves, good fishing and many water birds, including flamingos (usually involving a day-long boat trip to see them, best time to see them 1700-1930; permit required from *Inparques* at the *muelle*, US\$1). Boats leave from *Muelle Ciudad Tablita*; also from Inparques *muelle* (overcharging is common). Agencies have offices in Sector Belén in the fishing village of **Tacarigua de la Laguna**; fixed price of US\$4.60. Boats can be hired to anywhere in the Park and to *Club Miami* beach resort, **\$\$**, on the Caribbean side of the eastern sandspit. Good fish dishes are served at *Bar-Restaurant Poleo Lebranche Asado*. The beaches beyond here are unspoilt and relaxing, but mosquitoes are a problem after sunset.

Puerto La Cruz and around → *Phone code: 0281.*

Originally a fishing village, Puerto La Cruz (*Population: 185,000*) is now a major oil refining town and busy, modern holiday resort. (Tourist facilities are above average, if expensive, and the sea is polluted.) The seafront avenue, Paseo Colón, extends to the eastern extremity of a broad bay. To the west the bay ends at the prominent El Morro headland. Most hotels, restaurants, bars and clubs are along Paseo Colón, with excellent views of Bahía de Pozuelas and the islands of the Parque Nacional Mochima (see below). Vendors of paintings, jewellery, leather and hammocks are on Paseo Colón in the evening. The *Santa Cruz* festival is on 3 May, while 8 September is the *Virgen del Valle*, when boats cruise the harbour clad in palms and balloons; afternoon party at El Faro, Chimana, lots of salsa and beer. The main attractions of Puerto La Cruz lie offshore on the many islands of the beautiful Parque Nacional Mochima and in the surrounding waters. For details of how to get there, see below. The tourist office is **Fondoturismo** ① *C Bolívar, Ed Araya, local 3 PB, T267 1632, Mon-Fri 0800-1300*, very helpful and friendly.

Caracas to Puerto La Cruz listings

For Sleeping and Eating price codes and other relevant information, see Essentials, pages 9-11.

⊜ Sleeping

Parque Nacional Laguna de Tacarigua *p91*
Tacarigua de la Laguna
$$ Villa del Río, about 3 km before the village on the road. Apart-hotel, price for 1-7 persons, bath, kitchen facilities, fan, connected with *Remigios Tours*, transfer to and from Tacarigua for US$25.
$$-$ La Posada de Carlos, C Real, T0234-871 1156. Basic.

Puerto La Cruz *p91, map p93*
Newer, up-market hotels are at Lechería and El Morro; cheaper hotels are concentrated in the centre, though it's not easy to find a cheap hotel.
$$$$ Venetur Puerto La Cruz, Paseo Colón, east edge of the centre, T500 3611, www.venetur.gob.ve. 5-star luxury hotel with all facilities, including gym, spa, marina and beach access.
$$$ Caribbean Inn, Freites, T267 4292, hotelcaribbean@cantv.net. Big rooms, very well kept with quiet a/c, small pool, very good service.
$$$ Rasil, Paseo Colón y Monagas 6, T262 3000, www.hotelrasil.com.ve. Rooms, suites and bungalows, 3 restaurants, bar, pool, tour office, gym, money exchange, car rental, convenient for ferries and buses.
$$$ Riviera, Paseo Colón 33, T267 2111, hotelriviera@cantv.net. Seafront hotel, noisy

a/c, some rooms have balcony, phone, bar, watersports, very good location, restaurant, poor breakfast.
$$ Cristal Park, Buenos Aires y Libertad, T267 0744. Some with a/c, exchange at a good rate.
$$ Gaeta, Paseo Colón y Maneiro, T265 0411, gaeta@telcel.net.ve. Very modern, a/c, good location but very small rooms, restaurant, can change money at good rates.
$$ Senador, Miranda y Bolívar, T267 3522, hotelsenadorplc@cantv.net. A/c, back rooms quieter, phone, restaurant with view, parking.
$$-$ Comercio, Maneiro y Libertad, T265 1429. A/c, hot water, safe, cable TV.
$ Pippo, Freites 66 y Municipal, T268 8810. Cold water, some rooms with TV, very noisy and not very clean.

⊘ Eating

Puerto La Cruz *p91, map p93*
Many on Paseo Colón, eg **Tío Pepe** and **Big Garden**, delicious sea food. **O Sole Mio**, cheap, excellent, wide variety. **Trattoria Dalla Nonna**, Italian food.
ⴊ Celeri, on Av Municipal, 1 block from Guamaché. Vegetarian, weekdays 1130-1530. Recommended.
ⴊ La Colmena, next to **Hotel Riviera**. Vegetarian.
ⴊ La Taberna del Guácharo, C Carabobo, east end of Paseo Colón. Excellent Venezuelan cuisine, good service. Highly recommended.

El Guatacarauzo, Paseo Colón near Pizza Hut. Live music, salsa, good atmosphere and value.

Moroco, Av 5 de Julio 103. Good seafood.

Salmorejo, Miranda y Honduras. For chicken and seafood, with a terrace.

El Farao, east corner of main bus station. Excellent, authentic, spicy Arabic food.

Cafés

Heladería Tropic, Galería Colón on Paseo Colón. Good ice cream.

Sourdough Bakery and Grill, Paseo Colón. Vegetarian options, excellent.

🎵 **Bars and clubs**

Puerto La Cruz *p91, map p93*
Most clubs are in El Morro and Lechería.
Casa Latina Av 5 de Julio. Good 1970s salsa.

⚠️ **Activities and tours**

Puerto La Cruz *p91, map p93*
Diving Several companies, mostly on Paseo Colón, run diving courses. They're a bit more expensive than Santa Fe and Mochima. Hotels and travel agents also organize trips. The nearest recompression chamber is on Isla

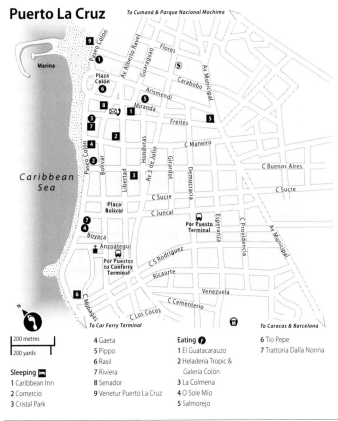

Puerto La Cruz

To Cumaná & Parque Nacional Mochima

Marina

Caribbean Sea

Plaza Colón

Paseo Colón

Av Alberto Ravel
Flores
Guaraguao
Carabobo
Av Municipal
Arismendi
Miranda
Freites
Honduras
Av 5 de Julio
Libertad
Girardot
C Maneiro
Democracia
C Buenos Aires
C Sucre
Bolívar
Plaza Bolívar
C Sucre
C Juncal
Esperanza
Providencia
Por Puesto Terminal
Av Municipal
Boyacá
Anzoátegui
Por Puestos to Conferry Terminal
C S Rodríguez
Ricaurte
Venezuela
C Monagas
C Los Cocos
C Cementerio

To Car Ferry Terminal

To Caracas & Barcelona

200 metres
200 yards

Sleeping 🛏
1 Caribbean Inn
2 Comercio
3 Cristal Park
4 Gaeta
5 Pippo
6 Rasil
7 Riviera
8 Senador
9 Venetur Puerto La Cruz

Eating 🍴
1 El Guatacarauzo
2 Heladería Tropic & Galería Colón
3 La Colmena
4 O Sole Mio
5 Salmorejo
6 Tío Pepe
7 Trattoria Dalla Nonna

Margarita. We've received favourable reports on these:

Aquatic Adventures, at end of Paseo Colón in the Marina, T0414-806 3744, or 0414-820 8758 (mob). Very experienced, English spoken, collect you from hotel and provide lunch, US$55 for 2 dives, 2-3 person minimum, 4-day PADI course US$350, rents snorkelling equipment.

Explosub, *Gran Hotel Puerto La Cruz*, T267 3256, explosub@gmail.com. Efficient, helpful, will dive with 1 person, US$75 for 2 dives, good 4-island tour.

Kayaking Jakera, www.jakera.com. Sea kayaks for rent from their lodge at Playa Colorada (T0293-808 7057), trips to whole country arranged (lodge in Mérida too, office C 24, No 8-205, Plaza Las Heroínas, Mérida, T0274-252 9577, 0416-887 2239 – mob), Chris and Joanna helpful, English spoken.

General tours
Note Do not buy tours from wandering salespeople not affiliated with a registered tour company.

⊖ **Transport**

Puerto La Cruz *p91, map p93*
Bus Bus terminal to the east of town; *por puesto* terminal at Av Juncal y Democracia, many buses also stop here. **Aero- expresos Ejecutivos** to/from **Caracas** 5 a day, 5 hrs, US$13-15 (T267 8855, next to ferry terminal), highly recommended (also to Maracay, Valencia and Barquisimeto). Other cheaper companies to **Caracas** include Expresos Los Llanos (T267 0330, recommended, a/c, movies), **Camargüi** and others. To **Mérida**,

US$26.70, 16 hrs. To **Ciudad Bolívar** US$12; to **Ciudad Guayana** US$18. To **Cumaná**, bus US$4.60, *por puesto* US$9.50, 1½ hrs. To **Carúpano**, US$8, 5 hrs. *Por puesto* to Playa Colorado US$1 and to Santa Fe US$4.60. There are also services to Maracay, Valencia, Barinas, San Cristóbal, Güiria. Along Av 5 de Julio runs a bus marked 'Intercomunal'. It links Puerto La Cruz with the city of Barcelona (which has the nearest airport) and intervening points. Another Barcelona bus is marked 'Ruta Alternativa' and uses the inland highway via the Puerto La Cruz Golf and Country Club and Universidad de Oriente, US$0.35.

Ferry For details of ferries to **Isla Margarita**, see page 115.

⊙ **Directory**

Puerto La Cruz *p91, map p93*
Banks Corp Banca (Amex TCs), Av 5 de Julio y Las Flores, Local No 43. **Banco de Venezuela** and **Banesco** on Av Libertad near Miranda. **Italcambio**, Av Ppal de Lechería, CC Galery Center, Loc 10, T700 0524. Amex representative. **Oficambio**, Maneiro y Honduras, no commission on TCs, open 0800-1645 Mon-Fri. **Internet** In Galería Colón, Paseo Colón, **American Net** and **CANTV Centro de Comunicaciones**. **North American Connection**, CC Paseo Plaza, C Carabobo, ½ block south of **Hotel Puerto La Cruz**. Fax and scanning facility as well as internet. **Puerto Internet**, C Maneiro. **Post offices and telephones** CANTV and Ipostel, Freites y Bolívar, 1 block from Paseo Colón. Telephone office accepts Visa for calls.

Parque Nacional Mochima

Beyond the cities of Barcelona and Puerto La Cruz, the main focus is the Mochima national park, one of the country's most beautiful regions. Hundreds of tiny Caribbean islands, a seemingly endless series of beaches backed by some of Venezuela's most beautiful scenery and tiny coves tucked into bays, all offer excellent snorkelling, fishing and swimming.

Ins and outs Tour companies offer trips to the islands from Puerto La Cruz: for example Passion, Paseo Colón, Edif Araya, pb 4, T268 5684/T0414-822 3200; passiontours@cantv.net, manager Gabriel Laclé, day tour around several islands for snorkelling, diving, fishing. Also **Aquatic Adventures**, see Puerto la Cruz, Activities and tours, above. **Transtupaco**, next to *Gran Hotel Puerto La Cruz*, no tours, they act as a taxi to the islands. Alternatively, you can reach the islands with the *Embarcadero de Peñeros*, on Paseo Colón, behind the *Tejas Restaurant*. Departures from 0900-1000, return at 1600-1630; US$6.50 per person. Tourist office in Puerto La Cruz provides tour operators for day trips to various islands for swimming or snorkelling; six-hour trip to four islands costs US$40 per person, including drinks. The islands to the east (Isla de Plata, Monos, Picuda Grande and Chica and the beaches of Conoma and Conomita) are best reached from the port at **Guanta** (taxi from town, or *por puesto* from C Freites between Avenida 5 de Julio and C Democracia, and ask to be dropped off at the Urb Pamatacualito). **Note** Boat trips to the islands are cheaper from **Santa Fe** or **Mochima** (see below). Bring your own food as the island restaurants are expensive.

When to avoid At Christmas, Carnival and Easter this part of the coast becomes extremely congested so patience is needed as long queues of traffic can develop. Accommodation is very hard to find and prices increase by 20-30%. It can also become littered and polluted, especially on the islands. Robbery may be a problem, but if you take care and use common sense the risk is minimal. Camping on the islands in Parque Nacional Mochima is not advisable.

Around the park Starting east from Puerto La Cruz is the Costa Azul, with the islands of the Parque Nacional Mochima offshore. Highway 9 follows the shore for much of the 85 km to Cumaná. The road is spectacular but if driving take great care between Playa Colorada and Cumaná. It passes the 'paradise-like' beaches of **Conoma** and **Conomita**. Further along is **Playa Arapito** (*posada*, **$**, restaurant, parking extra). Here boats can be hired to **La Piscina**, a beautiful coral reef near some small islands, for good snorkelling (with lots of dolphins); US$15 per boat.

Playa Colorada is a popular beach (Km 32) with beautiful red sands and palm trees (take a *por puesto* from corner of terminal in Puerto La Cruz, US$1). Nearby are **Playa Vallecito** (camping free, security guard, car US$1.50, bar with good food and bottled water on sale, plenty of palm trees for slinging a hammock) and **Playa Santa Cruz**. At **Playa Los Hicacos** is a lovely coral reef. **Note** Robberies have been reported on the empty beach at the west end of Playa Colorada.

In Sucre State 40 km from Puerto La Cruz is **Santa Fe** (*Phone code: 0293*), larger and noisier than Mochima, but a good place to relax. The attractive beach is cleaned daily. It has a market on Saturday. Jeep, boat or diving tours available. Fishermen offer trips but their prices are usually high. Boat trips to Playas Colorada or Blanca cost US$23 per person; better to hire your own boat for half the price, or hitch down the road to Colorada.

The little village of **Mochima** beyond Santa Fe, is 4 km off the main road (hitching difficult). It's busy at weekends but almost deserted through the week. The sea is dirty near the town. Boats take tourists to nearby beaches, such as Playa Marita and Playa Blanca (excellent snorkelling, take own equipment). Both have restaurants, but bring food and water to be safe. Boats to the islands cost US$14-18 (up to six people), depending on distance, eg **Semilla Tours** on the main street. Arrange with the boatman what time he will collect you. The tourist office arranges six hour, four-island trips with snorkelling and swimming, US$16. Canoeing trips are available and walks on local trails and to caves (ask for information, eg from Carlos Hernández, or Rodolfo Plaza – see Diving, below).

Parque Nacional Mochima listings

For Sleeping and Eating price codes and other relevant information, see Essentials, pages 9-11.

● Sleeping

Parque Nacional Mochima *p95*
Playa Colorada
$$$ Sunset Inn, Av Principal, T0416- 887 8156. Clean, comfortable, pool, a/c, hot water.
$ Carmita, Apdo 46/7, on road from beach to village. Excellent breakfast included, very helpful German-speaking owner. Highly recommended.
$ Posada Edgar Lemus, off Av Principal, T0416-795 0574. Very clean, laundry, excellent food. Highly recommended.
$ Quinta Jaly, C Marchán, T808 3246/0416-681 8113. A/c, hot water, very quiet, also one bungalow sleeps 6, family atmosphere, English and French spoken, use of kitchen, laundry facilities, good breakfast extra, multilingual library. Recommended.
$ Villa Nirvana, 6-min walk uphill from beach, opposite *Jaly*, run by Sra Rita who is Swiss, T808 7844. Rooms with fan or a/c, also mini-apartments with kitchen for 2-6 people, hot water, kitchen facilities, English, French and German spoken, book exchange, laundry, breakfast extra.

Santa Fe
$$ Café del Mar, first hotel on beach, T231 0009, rogelioalcaraz@hotmail.com. A/c or cheaper with fan, good restaurant. Rogelio

Alcaraz speaks English and Italian, arranges tours to islands.
$$ La Sierra Inn, near *Café del Mar*, T642 3802. A/c, self-contained garden suite with fridge and cooker, run by Sr José Vivas, English spoken, helpful, tours to islands. Recommended.
$$ Siete Delfines, on beach, T808 8064/T0416-317 9290, lossietedelfinessantafe@ hotmail.com. Cheaper without breakfast, safe, fan, bar, good meals in restaurant, owner speaks English.
$ Bahía del Mar, T231 0073/T0426-481 7242. Pleasant rooms with a/c or fan, upstairs rooms have a cool breeze, owners María and Juan speak French and some English.
$ Cochaima, on beach, T642 07828. Run by Margot, noisy, popular, a/c or fan, safe. Recommended.
$ Las Palmeras, T231 0008/T0426-884 0753. Behind **Cochaima**, fan, room for 5 with fridge and cooker. Price negotiable, ask about light work in exchange for longer stays. English, German, Italian and Portuguese spoken.
$ Playa Santa Fe Resort and Dive Center, T808 8249/T0426-620 7133, stafedive@ cantv.net. Renovated posada with rooms and suites, laundry service, owner Howard Rankell speaks English, can arrange transport to beaches, kitchen.
$ Petit Jardin, behind **Cochaima**, T231 0036/T0416-387 5093. A/c, hot water, fan, kitchen, pool, helpful.

Mochima

Various apartments available for larger groups, look for signs.

$$$ Posada Gaby, at end of road with its own pier next to sea, T431 0842/0414-773 1104. A/c or fan, breakfast available, lovely place.

$$ Posada Doña Cruz, T416 6114. A/c, cable TV. Run by José Cruz, family also rents rooms at **Posada Mama Cruz** on the plaza with a/c, cable TV, living room.

$$ Posada Mochimero, on main street in front of *Restaurant Mochimero*, T0414-773 8782. A/c or fan, rooms with bath.

$$ Villa Vicenta, Av Principal, T414 0868. Basic rooms with cold water and larger rooms with balcony, also cold water, a/c, dining room, owner Otilio is helpful.

❼ Eating

Parque Nacional Mochima *p95*
Playa Colorada
† **Daniel's Barraca**, at east end of the beach, is good for cheap food.

Santa Fe
†† **Club Naútico**, fish and Venezuelan dishes, open for lunch and dinner.
†† **Los Molinos (Julios)**, open from 0800, beach bar serves sandwiches, hamburgers and cocktails.

Mochima
† **El Mochimero**, on waterfront 5 mins from jetty. Highly recommended for lunch and dinner.
† **Il Forno de Mochima**, main street. Run by Roberto Iorio, for those who would like a change from seafood, homemade pastas and pizza.
† **Puerto Viejo**, on the plaza. Good food, if a bit pricey, good views.

▲ Activities and tours

Parque Nacional Mochima *p95*
Mochima
Diving Francisco García, runs a diving school and shop (*Aquatics Diving Center*, T0426-581 0434/0414-777 4894), C La Marina at Plaza Apolinar. Equipment hire, courses, trips.

Rodolfo Plaza runs a diving school (*La Posada de los Buzos*, T416 0856/T0424-807 7647, mochimarafting@hotmail.com) and hires equipment, also walking, rafting, kayaking and canoeing trips; contact him in Caracas (Los Palos Grandes, Av Andrés Bello entre 3a y 4a transversal, T0212-961 2531).

❂ Transport

Parque Nacional Mochima *p95*
Santa Fe
Getting there from **Cumaná**, take *por puesto* 1 block down from the Redonda del Indio, along Av Perimetral, US$4.65. It may be difficult to get a bus from **Puerto La Cruz** to stop at Santa Fe, take a *por puesto* (depart from terminal, US$4.60, 1 hr), or taxi, US$25 including wait.

Mochima
Bus From **Cumaná** to Mochima take a bus from outside the terminal and ask to be let off at the street where the transport goes to Mochima, US$2.40; change here to crowded bus or jeep (US$0.50). No buses between Santa Fe and Mochima, take a *por puesto*, bargain hard on the price, US$11-15 is reasonable. Bus to Cumaná, 1400, US$1.20.

Cumaná → *Phone code: 0293. Population: 343,500.*

Cumaná was founded in 1521 to exploit the nearby pearl fisheries. It straddles both banks of the Río Manzanares. Because of a succession of devastating earthquakes (the last in 1997), only a few historic sites remain. Cumaná is a charming place with its mixture of old and new, but the port area (1.5 km from the centre) is not safe at night. Main festivals are 22 January, Santa Inés, a pre-Lenten carnival throughout the state of Sucre and 2 November, the Santos y Fideles Difuntos festival at El Tacal.

A long public beach, **San Luis**, is a short bus ride from the centre of town; take the 'San Luis/Los Chaimas' bus. The least spoilt part is the end by the *Hotel Los Bordones*.

The **Castillo de San Antonio de la Eminencia** (1686) has 16 mounted cannons, a draw-bridge and dungeons from which there are said to be underground tunnels leading to the Santa Inés church. Restored in 1975, it is flood-lit at night (but don't go there after dark, it's not safe). The **Castillo de Santa María de la Cabeza** (1669) is a rectangular fortress

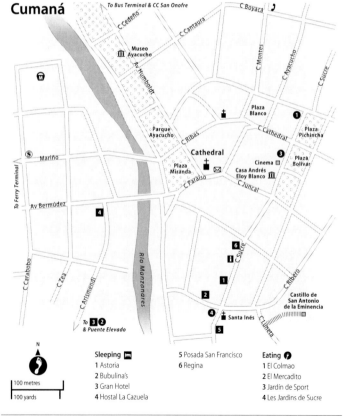

Cumaná

Sleeping
1 Astoria
2 Bubulina's
3 Gran Hotel
4 Hostal La Cazuela
5 Posada San Francisco
6 Regina

Eating
1 El Colmao
2 El Mercadito
3 Jardín de Sport
4 Les Jardins de Sucre

with a panoramic view of San Antonio and the elegant homes below. **Convento de San Francisco**, the original Capuchin mission of 1514, was the first school on the continent; its remains are on the Plaza Badaracco Bermúdez facing the beach. The **Church of Santa Inés** (1637) was the base of the Franciscan missionaries; earthquakes have caused it to be rebuilt five times. A tiny 400-year-old statue of the Virgen de Candelaria is in the garden. The **home of Andrés Eloy Blanco** (1896-1955) ① *0800-1200, 1430-1730, free,* one of Venezuela's greatest poets and politicians, on Plaza Bolívar, has been nicely restored to its turn-of-the-century elegance. On the opposite side of the plaza is **La Gobernación** around a courtyard lined by cannon from Santa María de la Cabeza; note the gargoyles and other colonial features. There are markets selling handicrafts and food on both sides of the river.

The **Museo Gran Mariscal de Ayacucho** ① *Consejo Municipal in Parque Ayacucho, Tue-Fri 0845-1130, 1545-1830; free tours,* commemorates the battle of Ayacucho: with portraits, relics and letters of Bolívar and José Antonio Sucre (Bolívar's first lieutenant). **Museo del Mar** ① *Av Universidad with Av Industrial, Tue-Sun 0830-1130, 1500-1800, US$0.75, getting there: take San Luis minibus from the cathedral,* has exhibits of tropical marine life, at the old airport.

For information contact **Dirección de Turismo** ① *C Sucre 49, T808 7769/T0414-189 2071, open mornings only.* This office is very helpful, English spoken. See also www.sucreturistico.com.

Cumaná listings

For Sleeping and Eating price codes and other relevant information, see Essentials, pages 9-11.

😴 Sleeping

Cumaná *p98, map p*

$$$ Los Bordones, at end of Av Universidad on the beach, T400 0350, www.losbordones.com. A/c, pool, restaurant, another hotel with all-inclusive options.

$$$ Nueva Toledo Suites, end of Av Universidad, close to San Luis beach, T451 8118, www.nueva toledo.com. A/c, hot water, TV, pool, beach bar, good value all-inclusive deals.

$$ Bubulina's, Callejón Santa Inés, ½ a block west of Santa Inés church, T431 4025, bubulinas10@hotmail.com. In the historic centre, beautifully restored colonial building, a/c, TV, hot water, good service, German spoken.

$$ Gran Hotel, Av Universidad near San Luis beach, T451 0671. A/c, pool, restaurant, includes breakfast.

$$ Posada San Francisco, C Sucre 16, near Santa Inés, T431 3926. Renovated colonial house, courtyard, spacious rooms, hot water, a/c (cheaper with fan), very helpful, bar, restaurant. Recommended.

$$ Regina, Arismendi y Av Bermúdez, T432 2581. Hot water, a/c, restaurant, helpful.

$$-$ Hostal La Cazuela, Sucre 63, T432 1401/T0416-090 1388, narart@hotmail.com. A/c, cable TV, pleasant, personable.

$ Astoria, Sucre, T433 2708. A/c, shower, basic, bar, restaurant with good food cooked to order.

🍴 Eating

Cumaná *p98, map p98*
All central restaurants close Sun lunchtime

††† Les Jardins de Sucre, Sucre 27, in front of the Santa Inés church. French food, good service, outdoor seating. Recommended.

†† El Colmao on Plaza Pichincha, C Sucre. Very good fish, charming service, karaoke.

Ali Baba, Av Bermúdez near corner of C Castellón. Excellent middle eastern food. Recommended.
El Mercadito at Puente Elevado. For excellent cheap lunches, fish and seafood.
Jardín de Sport, Plaza Bolívar. Outdoor café, good food, noisy atmosphere. Recommended.
Mi Jardín, on C Humboldt. Cheap, tasty roast chicken.

▲ Activities and tours

Cumaná *p98, map p98*
Rosa Theron, T432 5502, rositatheron@ sucreturistico.com offers tours. **Posadas San Francisco** and **Bubulina's** can also help arrange local tours, sailing, diving.

⊖ Transport

Cumaná *p98, map p98*
Bus Terminal 3 km northwest of the centre on Av Las Palomas, just before the junction with the peripheral road. Local bus into centre US$0.45, taxi US$3.50. *Por puesto* to **Puerto La Cruz**, US$9.30, bus US$4.65, 1½ hrs. To **Güiria**, US$11.60, **Expresos Los Llanos** once a day, *por puesto* US$14 (6-7 hrs), beware of overcharging, often stop in Irapa.

To **Carúpano**, US$4.65, 2-3 hrs. To **Caripe**, you have to go to **Santa María**, south of Cariaco, and change to *por puesto* there. To **Caracas**, US$14 (7-8 hrs), frequent service; many daily to **Ciudad Guayana** and **Ciudad Bolívar**, US$16.30 and 14 respectively. **Caribe** runs all the way to the border with Brazil, US$16.30. Also to Maturín.
Ferry For Ferries to **Araya Peninsula** and **Isla Margarita**, see below and page 115.

⊕ Directory

Cumaná *p98, map p98*
Banks See also Money, page 11. For cash advance on Mastercard **Banco Mercantil**, Av Bermúdez. ATM and cash advance on Visa and Mastercard. Also **Banco Venezuela**, at Mariño y Rojas and **Banesco** at Mariño y Carabobo. **Corp Banca**, Av Bermúdez y Av Perimetral, edif Don Jesús No 21. Amex TCs changed at good rates, no commission. **Internet** Centro de **Comunicaciones CANTV**, CC San Onofre at the end of Av Humboldt. **Comiti**, Edif Arismendi p 2, Av Arismendi. Two internet cafes on C Cedral near Plaza Bolívar. **Post offices** Ipostel, next to Cathedral on C Paraíso. **Telephones** CANTV, on C Montés con Boyacá, 2 blocks from Plaza Blanco.

Araya to Paria

This section is bounded by two peninsulas, Araya, which is an area of desert landscapes and pink salt lakes, and Paria, a finger of land stretching out to the most easterly point on Venezuela's Caribbean coast and a place of peaceful, coastal towns, beaches and forest. The eastern mountains, rising to 2000 m at their highest point, receive abundant rainfall in their tropical forest.

Araya Peninsula

The main settlement is Araya which has an airport and a ferry dock. The major sight is the Fortaleza de Santiago de León, built by Spain to protect the salt mines, but of which very little now remains. Construction began in 1622 and it took 47 years to complete. Entry is free, but the only facilities are a refreshment stand and a picnic area. Today the mines are exploited by a state-owned corporation, ENSAL. Windsurfing is excellent, but only for the experienced.

Carúpano → *Phone code: 0294. Population: 147,000.*

This is a colonial town dating back to 1647, from which 70% of Venezuela's cocoa is shipped. The area around Plaza Santa Rosa has been declared a national and international heritage site by UNESCO. Buildings include the **Museo Histórico**, containing a comprehensive database on the city, and the **Iglesia Santa Rosa**. The **Casa del Cable** ⓘ *T331 3847/0414-780 0060, merle@ telcel.net.ve, www.fundacionthomasmerle.org.ve,* location of the first telecommunications link with Europe, is the headquarters of the Fundación Thomas Merle, run by Wilfried Merle, who has been instrumental in setting up ecotourism and economic development projects in the Paria Peninsula. Carúpano is famous throughout Venezuela as the last place still celebrating a traditional pre-Lenten Carnival: days of dancing, rum drinking, with masked women in black (*negritas*). Book well ahead for places to stay at this time (February). Other local festivals are 3 May, Velorios de la Cruz (street dances); 15 August, Asunción de la Virgen. On the outskirts of Carúpano is **Playa Copey** (ask the *por puesto/* bus to drop you at Playa Copey if arriving from Cumaná or other westerly points, or take a taxi from town, US$7). See www.carupano.org.

Caripe → *Phone code: 0292. Population: 23,880.*

A paved road runs inland from Carúpano to Caripe via Cariaco and Santa María, two hours. Caripe is an attractive town set in gorgeous mountain scenery. There is a lively daily market. It is 12 km from the famous Cueva del Guácharo and a good place to escape from the beaches. It's especially good for walking and biking. At San Francisco, on the Maturín-Cumaná road (212 km, all paved but twisty; beautiful tropical mountain scenery), is a branch road running 22.5 km northeast to Caripe. *Feria de las Flores* is on 2-12 August and *NS del Pilar* is 10-12 October. See http://caripe.net. To get to Caripe from Caracas you must go to **Maturín**, the capital of Monagas state (*Phone code: 0291, relatively expensive accommodation*), then take a *por puesto*. Alternatively go to Cumaná and then to Santa María for *por puesto* services.

Cueva del Guácharo

ⓘ *0800-1600, US$3.50 with compulsory guide in Spanish, speak some English and German. Leave backpacks at the ticket office, photography is not allowed. To go further into the caves permits from Inparques in Caracas are needed.*

This remarkable cave was discovered by Humboldt and has since been penetrated 10.5 km along a small, crystal-clear stream. In the first caves live around 18,000 *guácharos* (oil birds) with an in-built radar system for sightless flight. Their presence supports a variety of wildlife in the cave: blind mice, fish and crabs in the stream, yellow-green plants, crickets and ants. For two hours at dusk (about 1900) the birds pour out of the cave's mouth. Through a very narrow entrance is the *Cueva del Silencio* (Cave of Silence). About 2 km in is the *Pozo del Viento* (Well of the Wind).

Wear old clothes, stout shoes and be prepared to get wet. In the wet season it can be a bit slippery; tours in the cave may be closed in August-September because of rising water level. There is a caving museum with good cafeteria. Opposite the road is a paved path to **Salto Paila**, a 25 m waterfall, about 30 minutes' walk, guides available for US$4.65. A beautiful path, built by Inparqes, starts at the caving museum, with some nice shelters for picnics. Camping is allowed by the cave for US$2.30, or you can sleep without a tent under the roof by the café for free.

Between Cariaco and Casanay, **Las Aguas de Moisés** ⓘ *open 0800-1700, US$11.45, half price for seniors and children, T0414-780 2013, www.lasaguasdemoises.com, ask to be let off from bus or por puesto on Cariaco-Carúpano route* is a tourist park containing eleven large thermal pools. The waters are said to be curative and there are lots of sporting and other activities. Camping (**$**) is available, or **Hotel San Remo Suites** (T555 1036).

Paria Peninsula

Río Caribe This lovely fishing village (*Phone code: 0294; Population: 51,100; 20 km east of Carúpano*) used to be a major cacao-exporting port. It is a good jumping-off point for the beautiful beaches of **Playa Medina** (in an old coconut plantation, 25 km east) and Pui Puy, both famous for their crystal-clear water and golden sands. Playa Medina is safe, has shade for rent and stalls selling food and drink; it is crowded at weekends and holidays. Cabins at the beach are very expensive (**$$$** per person). To get to Playa Medina, take a taxi, US$35 return trip per car, US$40 to Pui Puy. There are *camionetas* which go quite close to Medina and one which departs from opposite petrol station at exit to village (US$1, one hour), which drops you at entrance to beaches, but it's two hours' walk from there (further to Pui Puy – take great care, armed robberies have been reported). Surfing at Playas Pui Puy and Querepare; visit **Querepare** between May and August to watch sea turtles laying their eggs. Ask at **Posada Shalimar** (see Sleeping, below) about boat trips to Santa Isabel, a small village near a waterfall (stay at **$$ Posada de Cucha**). There is a Banco Venezuela in Río Caribe for exchange.

Further east is the delightful village of **San Juan de las Galdonas** and some great beaches. Near Chacaracual, 15 minutes' drive from Río Caribe is **Paria Shakti** *T611 8767/T0416-517 9676*, a 4-acre cacao plantation and holistic health centre that offers factory tours and massages. Next door, visit **Aguasana**, a *hacienda* with mineral-rich hot springs and mud pools (see Sleeping, below). Recommended guide: Eli Monroy (T0426-985 7670 or through **Posada Shalimar**). Near Bohordal is **Hacienda Rio de Agua**, a buffalo ranch available for day visits and milk factory tours; many species of birds can be seen (also see Sleeping). Day trips are also available to **Caño de Ajíes** with a visit to a waterfall and the estuary which flows into the Golfo de Paria; you can see crocodiles, birds and snakes. It is part of the Parque Nacional Turuépano. A trip by car and boat costs US$130.

Güiria At Bohordal, the paved road from Río Caribe across the mountains meets Route 9, which continues to the pleasant town of Irapa (*Population: 23,710; hotels, bus connections*). The paved highway continues 42 km to Güiria (*Phone code: 0294; Population: 36,860*), a friendly, peaceful town and a badly littered beach. Feria de la Pesca, 14 July. Gasoline is available.

Macuro A quiet town on the tip of the Peninsula, Macuro (*Population: 1500*) is accessible by boat (two hours from Güiria) and by a new road from Güiria (20 km paved, the remainder passable by 4WD). It was around here Columbus made the first recorded European landing on the continent on 5 August 1498. Locals like to believe the landing took place at Macuro, and the town's official new name is Puerto Colón. A big party is held here every year on 12 October to mark the official 'discovery' of America. Restaurants only open at weekends (good food at Sra Mercedes, on C Carabobo, round corner from *Posada Beatriz*, blue house). There are also a few basic shops and a pharmacy. The boat to Güiria leaves at 0500, arrive early, US$5 per person.

The beach is unattractive but the coast on the north side of the peninsula is truly wonderful; crystal-clear water and dazzling sands backed by dense jungle. A highly recommended trip for the adventurous is the hike to **Uquire** and **Don Pedro** on the north coast; 4-6 hours' walk, places to hang a hammock or pitch a tent. In Uquire ask for Nestor Mata, the Inparques guard, very helpful. **Note** This part of the peninsula is a national park; you need a permit from Inparques in Caracas.

Araya to Paria listings

For Sleeping and Eating price codes and other relevant information, see Essentials, pages 9-11.

◉ Sleeping

Araya *p101*
$ Araya Mar, El Castillo, T437 1382/T0414-777 3682. A/c, hot water, good restaurant, arranges car and boat tours to the Salinas and around Araya, parking. Good restaurant serves Venezuelan food. Recommended.
$ Araya's Wind, beside the Fortaleza in front of beach, T0414-189 0717. A/c, some rooms with bath, cold water, cable TV.
$ Lagunasal, C El Progreso ½ block from El Timonel de Fabi, T437 1290/T0414-778 2533. New posada, no sign as yet, a/c, cable TV.

$ Posada Helen, behind *Araya's Wind*, T437 1101/T0414- 189 3867. A/c, cold water, cable TV.

Carúpano *p101*
$$$ Hotel Euro Caribe Internacional, Av Perimetral Rómulo Gallegos, T331 3911. A/c, cable TV, hot water, breakfast included, parking, good Italian restaurant.
$$ La Colina, Av Rómulo Gallegos 33, behind *Hotel Victoria*, T332 2915. A/c, cable TV, hot water, includes breakfast, restaurant and bar, beautiful view. Recommended.
$$ Lilma, Av Independencia, 3 blocks from Plaza Colón, T331 1361, hotellilma@hotmail.com. A/c, hot water, TV, restaurant, *tasca*, cinema.

$$ Paradise, Av Independencia, T331 1007/T0416-387 7576. A/c, cable TV, hot water.

$$ San Francisco, Av Juncal 87A y Las Margaritas, T331 1074. A/c, no hot water, TV, parking, restaurant, *tasca*.

$$ Victoria, Av Perimetral Rómulo Gallegos, T331 1554, hotelvictoria@hotmail.com. Safe but basic, a/c, hot water.

$ Bologna, Av Independencia, 1 block from Plaza Santa Rosa, T331 1241. Basic but clean, a/c.

$ El Centro, Carabobo 71, close to Iglesia Santa Catalina, T331 3673. A/c, cable TV.

Playa Copey

$$ Posada Casa Blanca, Av Principal, 5 mins from *Posada Nena*, T331 6896. A/c, hot water, safe, good family atmosphere, private stretch of beach illuminated at night, Spanish restaurant, German spoken, discounts for long stays.

$$ Posada Nena, 1 block from the beach, T331 7297, www.posadanena.de. A/c, hot water, games room, good restaurant, public phone, good service, German spoken, owner Volker Alsen offers day trips to Cueva del Guácharo, Mochima, Medina and other Venezuelan destinations. Recommended.

Caripe *p101*

$$ Finca Agroturística Campo Claro, at Teresén, T555 1013/0414 770 8043 (mob), www.haciendacampoclaro.com. Cabins for 4-15 people with cooking facilities and hot water, also rooms (**C**), restaurant for residents, horse riding.

$$ Samán, Enrique Chaumer 29, T545 1183, www.hotelsaman.com. Also has more expensive suites, comfortable, pool, parking, not so welcoming to backpackers.

$ Caripe Plaza, opposite church on Plaza Bolívar, T744 9185. Hot water, cable TV, parking.

$ La Perla, Av Enrique Chaumer 118, 5 mins from centre, T0424-921 1007. Very basic.

Río Caribe *p102*

As well as those listed, there are other *posadas* and private, unmarked pensions; ask around.

$$ La Posada de Arlet, 24 de Julio 22, T/F646 1290. Price includes breakfast, a/c, laundry service, English and German spoken, bar, arranges day trips to local beaches. Recommended.

$$ Posada Caribana, Av Bermúdez 25, T646 1242. Beautifully restored colonial house, tastefully decorated, a/c or fan, with breakfast, restaurant, bar, excursions. Ask about *posada* at Playa Uva.

$$ Posada de Angel, 2 km away from the beach at **Playa Medina**, T0414-100 7247. Nice place, private bathrooms, fan, mosquito netting on windows.

$$ Posada Shalimar, Av Bermúdez 54, T646 1135, www.posada-shalimar.com. Francisco González speaks English, very helpful, can arrange tours to and provide information about local beaches and other areas. Beautiful rooms situated around pool have a/c, cable TV. Recommended.

$ Pensión Papagayo, 14 de Febrero, 1 block from police station, opposite *liceo*, T646 1868. Charming house and garden, a/c, shared bath with hot water (single sex), use of kitchen, nice atmosphere, owner Cristina Castillo.

San Juan de las Galdonas

$$ pp Habitat Paria, T511 9571. With breakfast and supper, huge, splendid, zodiac theme, fan, bar/restaurant, terraces, garden. The posada is right behind Barlovento beach on the right hand side of San Juan. Can arrange boat tours. Recommended.

$$ Posada Las Tres Carabelas, T0416-894 0914 (mob), carabelas3@hotmail.com. Fans and mosquito nets, restaurant, wonderful view, owner Javier knowledgeable about local area. Ask about new *posada* at Guariquen, as yet untouched by tourism.

$$ Posada Playa Galdonas, T889 1892. 4-star, overlooking the main beach, a/c, hot water, bar/restaurant, swimming pool, English and French spoken, arranges boat tours to Santa Isabel and beaches.

Outside Río Caribe
$$ Hato Río de Agua, T332 0527. Rustic cabins with fans, private bathrooms, restaurant on a buffalo ranch (see above), price includes breakfast and tours of dairy factory.
$ Hacienda Posada Aguasana, T416 2944/T0414-304 5687, www.posadaaguasana.com. Attractive rooms with fans near hot springs, **$$** with meals.

Güiria *p103*
$$ Timón de Máximo, C Bideau, 2 blocks from plaza, T982 1535. A/c, cable TV, fridge, good créole restaurant. Recommended.
$$ Vista Mar, Valdez y Trincheras, T982 1055. A/c, hot water, fridge, cable TV, restaurant.
$ Plaza, esq Plaza Bolívar, T982 0022. Basic, restaurant, luggage store, a/c.

Macuro *p103*
$ Posada Beatriz, C Mariño y Carabobo. Basic, clean, with bath, fan.

🍴 Eating

Araya *p101*
Eat early as most places close before 2000. Hamburger stalls around the dock and 2 *panaderías*.
🍴 **El Timonel de Fabi**. *Tasca* across from dock, Venezuelan food, karaoke.
🍴 **Las Churuatas de Miguel**, on the beach near dock. Fish and typical food.
🍴 **Eugenía**, in front of *Posada Helen*. For good value meals.

Carúpano *p101*
🍴🍴-🍴 **El Fogón de La Petaca**, Av Perimetral on the seafront. Traditional Venezuelan dishes, fish.
🍴🍴-🍴 **La Madriguera**, Av Perimetral Rómulo Gallegos, in Hotel Eurocaribe. Good Italian

food, some vegetarian dishes, Italian and English spoken.
🍴 **Bam Bam**, kiosk at the end of Plaza Miranda, close to seafront. Tasty hotdogs and hamburgers.
🍴 **El Oasis**, Juncal in front of Plaza Bolívar. Open from 1700, best Arabic food in Carúpano.
🍴 **La Flor de Oriente**, Av Libertad y Victoria, 4 blocks from Plaza Colón. Open from 0800, arepas, fruit juice and main meals, good, large portions, good, food, reasonable prices, very busy at lunchtime.
   Other options include the **food stalls** in the market, especially the one next to the car park, and the *empanadas* in the Plaza Santa Rosa.

Caripe *p101*
🍴🍴 **Tasca Mogambo**, next to **Hotel Saman**. Good, local food.
🍴🍴 **La Trattoria**, C Cabello. Wide variety of good food, popular with locals and tourists.

Río Caribe *p102*
🍴🍴 **Mi Cocina**, on the road parallel to Av Bermúdez, 3 mins' walk from Plaza Bolívar. Very good food, large portions.
🍴🍴 **Mis Manos Benditos**, near the beach.

Güiria *p103*
Everywhere is closed Sun, except for kiosks on Plaza Bolívar. Restaurants include:
🍴🍴 **El Limón**, C Trinchera near C Concepcion, good value, outdoor seating.
🍴🍴 **El Milagro**, corner of Plaza Bolívar. OK.
🍴🍴 **Rincón Güireño**, corner of Plaza Sucre. Good for breakfast (also rents rooms, **$**).

⛰ Activities and tours

Carúpano *p101*
Corpomedina, T331 5241, F331 3021, at the airport, associated with Fundación Thomas Merle (see Casa del Cable, page 101), reservations for cabins at Medina or Pui Puy beach: at Medina **$$$$-$$$** depending on

numbers, including meals, but not alcoholic drinks or transport; at Pui Puy **$$$-$$**, including breakfast. Transport from the airport to Medina and Pui Puy can be arranged.

Mar y Luna, T/F332 2668, louisa@cantv.net. Offer day trips to Medina, Pui Puy, Caripe, El Pilar, Los Pozos, specialist surfing and diving packages, walking and hiking in the Paria Peninsula, reconfirmation of international flights, reservations for *posadas*, reception of fax and email, information and advice, English, French, Portuguese and a little Italian spoken, very helpful.

Macuro *p103*

A highly recommended **guide** is Eduardo Rothe, who put together, and lives at, the Museo de Macuro on Calle Bolívar, 1 block from *Posada Beatriz*. He'll take you on walking tours to the north coast, US$4-7 pp per day, or boat trips (US$40 per boat) or fishing trips (US$30 pp per day, including mangroves).

⊖ Transport

Araya *p101*

Ferry Cumaná-Araya ferry with **Naviarca** car ferry, T/F0293-433 5577, www.grancacique. com.ve, shuttles back and forth 24 hrs a day, US$1.40 pp, US$14-18 per car. At weekends it usually makes only 1 trip each way. To get to ferry terminal take taxi in Cumaná, US$3.50 (avoid walking; it can be dangerous). Alternatively, take a *tapadito* (passenger ferry in a converted fishing boat, leave when full, crowded, stuffy, US$1.15) to Manicuare and *camioneta* from there to Araya (15 mins). Return ferries from Araya depart from main wharf at end of Av Bermúdez. Ferries to **Isla de Margarita**, *tapaditos* depart from **Chacopata** (1 hr, US$10.50 one way). To get to Chacopata from Carúpano, take a *por puesto* at the stop diagonal to the market entrance (where the fish is unloaded), US$4.65, 1½ hrs.

Carúpano *p101*

Air The airport is 15 mins' walk from the centre, US$3.50 by taxi. Check with **Rutaca** (T0212-355 1838), which occasionally offers flights to Caracas through Porlamar.
Bus To **Caracas**, US$16.30-19.75, 9 hrs, to Terminal de Oriente. To **Maracay, Valencia**, US$20, 10 hrs. For other destinations such as **Cumaná**, US$4.65, 2 hrs, **Puerto La Cruz**, US$7, 4 hrs (Mochima/Santa Fé), **Güiria**, US$7, 3 hrs *por puestos* are a better option. They run more frequently and make fewer stops. Buses do not go from Carúpano to Caripe, you have to take a *por puesto* to **Cariaco**, US$2.50, then another to **Santa María**, US$3.50, then another to Caripe, US$3.

Caripe *p101*

Bus Terminal 1 block south of main plaza. For **Carúpano**, take *por puestos* to Santa María and Cariaco (see above), similarly for **Río Caribe** and **Las Aguas de Moisés**. To get to **Cumaná**, go to Santa María and catch transport from there. Bus to **Maturín** several daily, 2½ hrs, US$6; Maturín-**Caracas** costs US$14-20 (bus cama), 7½ hrs. *Por puestos* run from Maturín to Ciudad Bolívar.

Cueva del Guácharo *p102*

Bus Frequent from **Caripe** to the caves. If staying in Caripe, take a *por puesto* (a jeep marked Santa María-Muelle), at 0800, see the caves and waterfall and catch the Cumaná bus which goes past the caves between 1200 and 1230. Taxis from Caripe US$3.50, hitching possible. *Por puesto* from Cumaná US$11.60, 2 hrs. Private tours can be organized from Cumaná for about US$21 per person, with guide.

Río Caribe and San Juan de las Galdonas *p102*

Bus Direct from **Caracas** (Terminal del Oriente) to Río Caribe with **Cruceros Oriente Sur**, 10 hrs, and from **Maturín** with **Expresos Maturín**. *Por puesto* Carúpano-Río Caribe,

US$2.80, or taxi US$9.30. Buses depart Río Caribe from the other Plaza Bolívar, 7 blocks up from pier. Jeep Carúpano-San Juan de las Galdonas 1100, 1½ hrs; *camioneta* from Río Caribe from stop near petrol station, 0600 till 1300, US$3.50.

Güiria *p103*

Bus Depart Plaza Sucre, at top end of C Bolívar: **Expresos Maturín** to **Maturín** (0400, US$10.50, 6 hrs), **Caripito**, **San Félix**, **Cumaná** (*por puesto*, US$9.30), Puerto La Cruz and **Caracas**; also **Expresos Los Llanos** (recommended).

Ferry To **Macuro**: daily 1100-1200 from the Playita, US$4-7, return 0500, 2 hrs. To **Trinidad** A ferry leaves every Wed at 1700 for Chaguaramas, Trinidad (leaves Trinidad at 0900, Wed), 3½ hrs, US$92 one way (plus tax), operated by **Pier 1 Cruises**. There is a US$23 exit tax from Venezuela (US$13 from Trinidad). Talk to Siciliano Bottini at the *Agencia Naviera* for other ships to Trinidad. Don't take any old boat that's going; however safe it may appear, you may come under suspicion for drug running.

⊙ Directory

Carúpano *p101*

Banks It is not easy to change foreign currency in Carúpano. American Express TCs can be changed until 1400 at **Corp Banca**, C Güiria y C Carabobo. Cash advance on Visa or Mastercard at **Banco Caribe**, Av Independencia, 4 blocks from Plaza Santa Rosa. ATMs are unreliable for European cards. Good rate at the casino on the waterfront near the bus station. It may be possible to change dollars in *Hotels Lilma, San Francisco* or *Victoria*, but rates are not good.
Internet Centro de Comunicaciones **CANTV**, C Juncal, opposite *Hotel San Francisco*, 0800-2000. **Cybercafé**, C Las Margaritas entre Juncal y Carabobo, same hours. **Ebenezer**, CC Sahara, C San Félix. **Post offices and telephones** Both **Ipostel** and **CANTV** are at the end of Carabobo, 1 block up from Plaza Santa Rosa.

Güiria *p103*

Useful services Immigration: visas can't be arranged in Güiria, should you need one; maximum length of stay 14 days (but check). For more than 14 days, get visa in Caracas. Remember to get exit stamp before leaving Venezuela. Officially, to enter Trinidad and Tobago you need a ticket to your home country, but a return to Venezuela is usually enough.

Isla de Margarita

Margarita is the country's main Caribbean holiday destination and is popular with both Venezuelans and foreign tourists. The island's reputation for picture-postcard, white-sand beaches is well-deserved. Some parts are crowded but there are undeveloped beaches and colonial villages. Porlamar is the most built up and commercial part of the island while Juan Griego and La Restinga are much quieter.

If you book a place to stay in advance, it is possible to enjoy the island even on a budget during high season. If you don't reserve ahead, it is almost impossible to find accommodation for under US$25-30 per person a night. Despite the property boom and the frenetic building on much of the coast and in Porlamar, much of the island has been given over to natural parks. Of these the most striking is the Laguna La Restinga.

The western part, the Peninsula de Macanao, is hotter and more barren, with scrub, sand dunes and marshes. Wild deer, goats and hares roam the interior, but 4WDs are needed to penetrate it. The entrance to the Peninsula de Macanao is a pair of hills known as **Las Tetas de María Guevara**, a national monument covering 1670 ha. There are mangroves in the **Laguna de las Marites** natural monument, west of Porlamar.

Isla de Margarita

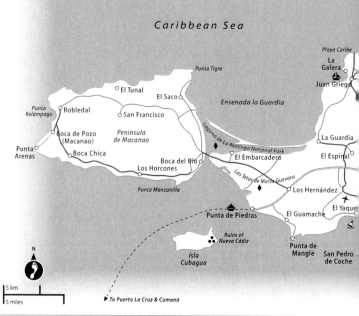

Other parks are **Cerro El Copey**, 7130 ha, and **Cerro Matasiete y Guayamurí**, 1672 ha (both reached from La Asunción). The climate is exceptionally good and dry. Roads are good and a bridge links the two parts. Nueva Esparta's population is over 377,700, of whom 85,000 live in Porlamar. The capital is La Asunción.

Ins and outs

Getting there and around There are many national, international and charter flights to Isla de Margarita. There also ferries from La Guaira (Caracas), Puerto La Cruz and Cumaná. Car hire is a good way of getting around (see Directory, below). Women should avoid walking alone at night on the island. ›› *See also Transport, page 115.*

Information Isla de Margarita: The private Cámara de Turismo is at Av Virgen del Valle in the Jorge Coll sector of Porlamar, T262 0683. They have free maps and are very helpful. The **state tourism department** can be contacted on T262 2322. Travel agencies can also provide a tourist guide to Margarita. *MultiGuía de Margarita* (US$4) is published yearly and is a useful directory of tourist information and can be found in kiosks, *panaderías*, cafés and bookshops. The best map is available from *Corpoven*. See also the websites www.islamargarita.com and www.margarita online.com. Many offices close for lunch.

Porlamar → *Phone code: 0295.*

Most of the island's high-rise hotels are at Porlamar which is 20 km from airport and 28 km from Punta de Piedra, where ferries dock. If you're seeking sun and sand, then head for the north coast towns where the beaches tend to be lined with low-rise hotels and thatched restaurants. Porlamar's beaches are nothing special, but it makes up for what it lacks in this department with its shops (see Shopping below). At Igualdad y Díaz is the **Museo de Arte Francisco Narváez**, which has some good displays of the work of this local sculptor. At night everything closes by 2300.

The **Bella Vista** beach is busy but clean and has lots of restaurants lining the seafront. **Playa Concorde** is small, sheltered and tucked by the marina. **Playa Morena** is a long, barren strip of sand for the Costa Azul hotel zone east of the city. **La Caracola** is a popular beach for a young crowd.

Boats go from Punta de Piedra, El Yaque and La Isleta to the **Isla de Coche** (11 km by 6), which has 4500 inhabitants and one of the richest salt mines in the country (see Transport below). They also go, on hire only, to **Isla de Cubagua**, which is totally deserted, but you can visit the **ruins of Nueva Cádiz** (which have been excavated). Large private yachts and catamarans take tourists on day trips to Coche.

La Asunción → *Population: 27,500.*

The capital of La Asunción located a few kilometres inland from Porlamar. It has several **colonial buildings**, a **cathedral**, and the **fort of Santa Rosa** ① *Mon 0800-1500, the rest of the week 0800-1800*, which features a famous bottle dungeon. There is a **museum** in the Casa Capitular, and a good local **market**, worth browsing for handicrafts. Nearby is the **Cerro Matasiete** historical site, where the defeat of the Spanish on 31 July 1817 led to their evacuation of the island.

Pampatar → *Population: 25,000.*

For a more Venezuelan atmosphere go northeast to Pampatar, which is set around a bay favoured by yachtsmen as a summer anchorage. Pampatar has the island's largest fort, **San Carlos de Borromeo**, which was built in 1662 after the Dutch destroyed the original. It's worth visiting the church of **Cristo del Buen Viaje**, the **Library/Museum** and the **customs house**. Jet skis can be hired on the clean and pretty beach. A fishing boat can be hired for US$20 for 2½ hours, 4-6 passengers; shop around for best price; it's good fun and makes for a worthwhile fishing trip. There is a *casa de cambio* in the Centro Comercial Sambil.

Eastern and northern beaches

Playa Guacuco, reached from La Asunción by a road through the Guayamurí reserve, is a popular local beach with a lot of surf, fairly shallow, palm trees, restaurants and car park; excellent horseriding here or up into the hills, US$30 for two hours, contact Harry Padrón at the ranch in Agua de Vaca, or phone travel agent on T261 1311. Playa Parguito further up the east coast is best for surfing (strong waves; full public services).

Playa El Agua has 4 km of white sand with many kiosks and shady restaurants. The sea is very rough in winter (dangerous for children), but fairly shallow; beware the strong cross current when you are about waist deep. This beach gets overcrowded at Venezuelan holiday times. The fashionable part is at the south end. The beach is 45 minutes by bus from Porlamar (US$0.80). See also www.playaelagua.info.

Manzanillo (*population: 2000*) is a picturesque bay between the mountains on the northeast point of the island with apartments (**$$$-$$**), beach houses and good places to eat (cheaper than Playa El Agua). Playa Escondida is at the far end. Puerto Fermín/ El Tirano is where Lope de Aguirre, the infamous conquistador, landed in 1561 on his flight from Peru.

The coast road is interesting, with glimpses of the sea and beaches to one side. There are a number of clifftop look-out points. The road improves radically beyond Manzanillo, winding from one beach to the next. **Playa Puerto la Cruz** (wide and windy) adjoins **Pedro González** (*Population: 3700*), with a broad sweeping beach, running from a promontory (easy to climb) to scrub and brush that reach down almost to the water's edge. **Playa Caribe** is a fantastic curve of white sand with moderate surf. Chairs and umbrellas can be hired from the many beach bars.

Juan Griego (*Population: 25,500*) is further west, a fast-expanding town whose pretty bay is full of fishing boats. The little fort of La Galera is on a promontory at the northern side, beyond which is a bay of the same name with a narrow strip of beach lined with many seafront restaurants.

Playa El Yaque

Playa El Yaque on the south coast, near the airport, is a Mecca for wind- and kitesurfers. The winds are perfect from mid-June to mid-October and the water is shallow enough to stand when you fall off (see Activities and tours, below). Most visitors come on package deals and therefore accommodation is expensive, but cheaper places to stay can be found. There is no public transport; a taxi from Porlamar costs US$14. **Cholymar** travel agency will change money and there is a *casa de cambio* in the Hotel California. A certified Spanish teacher, Mary Luz Jinete, offers lessons, T0412-094 1651 (mob), spanishwith maryluz@yahoo.com, which cost US$28 an hour depending on the size of the group.

La Restinga and around

This is the 22-km sandbar of broken seashells that joins the eastern and western parts of Margarita. Behind the *restinga* is the eponymous **national park**, designated a wetland of international importance. More than 100 species of birds live here, including the blue-crowned parakeet, which is endemic to Margarita. There are also marine turtles and other reptiles, dolphins, deer, ocelots, seahorses and oysters. *Lanchas* can be taken into the fascinating lagoon and mangrove swamps to the beach from landing stages at the eastern end (US$4.60 for 30 minutes, US$25 for an hour trip in a boat taking five, plus US$2.50 entrance fee to park). Bus from Porlamar US$1.60. On La Restinga beach you can look for shellfish in the shallows (sun protection is essential) and the delicious oysters can be bought here for around US$1 a dozen.

The **Peninsula de Macanao**, over the road bridge from La Restinga, is mountainous, arid, barely populated and a peaceful place to get away from the holidaymakers on the main part of Isla Margarita. It also has some good beaches that are often deserted and is a good place for horse riding. Punta Arenas is a very pleasant beach with calm water and is the most popular. It has some restaurants, chairs and sunshades. Further on is the wilder Playa Manzanillo. It's best visited in a hire car as public transport is scarce. **Boca del Río**, near the road bridge, has a **Museo Marino** ⓘ *T291-3231, daily 0900-1630, open until 1730 in the high season, US$1, US$0.50 children*, which has interesting collections of marine life, organized by ecosystem, and also features a small aquarium.

Isla de Margarita listings

For Sleeping and Eating price codes and other relevant information, see Essentials, pages 9-11.

😑 Sleeping

Porlamar *p109*

Many luxury hotels are grouped in the Costa Azul suburb east of Porlamar, but they now pepper most of the northeast coast of the island. Most hotels and tour operators work on a high season/ low season price system. High season prices (Christmas, Easter and Jun-Aug) can be up to 35% higher. Flights and hotels are usually fully booked at this time. In low season, bargaining is possible. **$$$ Bella Vista**, Av Santiago Mariño, T261 7222, www.hbellavista.com. Large, luxury hotel with all services (but not overly helpful), good pool with sea views, beach, car hire, travel agency, French restaurant, and restaurant serving *comida criolla*.

$$$ Margarita Princess, Av 4 de Mayo, T263 6777, hotelprincess@cantv.net. Large, comfortable rooms, balcony, restaurant, small pool.

$$ For You, Av Santiago Mariño, T263 8635. Modern, bland, large rooms, good service and roof restaurant, bar.

$$ Imperial, Av Raul Leoni, via El Morro, T261 6420, www.hotelimperial.com.ve. Modern, best rooms have sea view, parking, balcony, safe, a/c, TV, restaurant, hot water, parking, English spoken.

$$ María Luisa, Av Raúl Leoni entre Campos y Fermín, T263 7940. A/c, pool, some beach views.

$$-$ Posada Casa Lutecia, Final C Campos Cedeño y Marcano, T263 8526. Lovely bright rooms with personal touch, a/c, hot water, TV, French- owned, café with outdoor seating near beach.

La Asunción *p110*
$$ Ciudad Colonial, C La Margarita, T416 7647. Upmarket apartments minimum 4 people, swimming pool, a/c, accepts credit cards, restaurant.

$$ Posada Restaurant Ticino Da´Rocco, Crucero de Guacuco, vía Playa El Agua, C San Onofre, sector Camoruco, T242 2727. Pool, a/c, restaurant, accepts credit cards.

Playa Guacuco *p110*
$$$ Guacuco Resort, Vía Playa Guacuco, T242 3040, www.guacucoresort.com. Stylish, comfortable apartments for up to 4 people with balcony or terrace, 1 km from the beach and 300 m off the road, a/c, self-catering, tranquil, beautiful tropical gardens with birds, spa, pool and bar.

Playa El Agua *p110*
Most *posadas* are on C Miragua, near the beach.

$$$ Coco Paraíso, Av Principal, T0414-320 5859 (Caracas 0212-578 3922). Pleasant, large rooms, a/c, pool, 3 mins from beach, English and German spoken.

$$$ Costa Linda, C Miragua, T249 1303, www.hotel costalinda.com. Lovely rooms in colonial-style house with a/c, relaxing, TV, safe, pool, restaurant and bar, includes breakfast, accepts credit cards, changes TCs and US$, English and German spoken.

$$$ Costa Linda Beach, C Miragua. T415 9961, hotelcostalinda@cantv.net. Comfortable rooms, pool, bar and restaurant, gym, a/c, TV.

$$$ Doña Romelia, Av 31 de Julio (1 km before Playa Manzanillo), 10 min walk to Playa El Agua, T249 0238, yoya37@cantv.net. Very attractive rustic style hotel, bright rooms with balconies and hammocks, nice pool area and garden. Well-run, helpful staff. Parking, breakfast included. Recommended.

$$ Chalets de Belén, Miragua 3, T249 1707. 2 chalets for 4 and 6, kitchen, good value, parking TV, no hot water, also 2 double rooms, **$** (discounts in low season).

$$ Margarita Tropical Villa, C Díaz Ordaz, T249 0558, www.casatrudel.com. Canadian run (formerly Casa Trudel), small place, patio with hammocks, includes breakfast, 5 mins from beach, Wi-Fi, king size beds, hot water shower.

$ Hostería El Agua, Av 31 de Julio vía Manzanillo, T249 1297, hosteriaelagua@ hotmail.com. Simple, a/c, hot water, safe, restaurant/bar, on roadside 4 mins' walk from beach, English spoken.

Juan Griego *p111*
$$ Hostel El Caney, Giulliana Torrico 17, Rue Guevara, T253 5059, elcaney1@hotmail.com. A/c, TV, shared kitchen, small pool, Engish and French spoken.

$$ Patrick's, El Fuerte, T/F253 6218, www.hotel patrick.com. Good travellers hostel, a/c rooms with fine sunset views, excellent restaurant and bar, near beach, internet access. English spoken, will arrange salsa and Spanish lessons. Recommended.
$ The Sunset Posada Turística, T253 2168, www.sunsetposada.com. Spartan, single rooms with a/c, no TV. Apartments sleep 4-8, good value, some with beachfront balconies.

Playa El Yaque p111
$$ Hotel El Yaque Paradise, T263 9810, yaque@ grupoparadise.com. Upmarket, pleasant, good rooms, a/c, safety deposit box, bar, restaurant, English spoken, includes breakfast.
$ El Yaque Motion, T263 9742, www.elyaque motion.com. 400 m from beach. German run, popular with wind- and kitesurfers (lessons and equipment hire available), well-established, a/c, kitchen, laundry, free internet and Wi-Fi, roof terrace, cheaper with shared bath, rents 3 apartments for 4-8 people, English spoken, good.
$ Sail Fast Shop, T263 3449, herbert@ sail-fast.com. Basic rooms 300 m from the beach, ask for Herbert Novak at the Sail Fast Shop opposite Hotel Yaque Paradise. Rooms with private bath, some with a/c, kitchen facilities.

La Restinga and around: Peninsula de Macanao p111
$$$ Makatao, T0412-092 7187, www.makatao.com. Run by Dr Alexis Vásquez, price includes transfer, food, some therapies, natural drinks and lodging in the singular rooms. The doctor runs health, 'eco-relax' and therapy programs, and there are mud baths at the *campamento*.
$$$ Posada Río Grande, at *Cabatucan Ranch*, 2 km from Guayacancito on the road to Punta Arenas, T416 8349. Attractive rooms with a/c, hot water, full board available,

charming, includes breakfast. Also offer horse riding tours twice a day, T416 3584.
$$ L'Oasis Posada, Robledal, T291 5339. A/c or fan, hot water, TV, sea view, garden, restaurant. Arrange tours including jeep tours, windsurfing and horse riding.

Eating

Porlamar p109
The upmarket dining, such as Japanese food, is in Urb Costa Azul on Av Bolívar. Plenty of eating places on Campos and 4 de Mayo.
♥♥-♥ **La Casa del Mero**, Av Raúl Leoni. Good place for a cocktail on the water, serves seafood, steaks and chicken.
♥♥-♥ **La Pimienta**, Cedeño entre Campos y Fermín. Good seafood.
♥♥-♥ **Rancho Grande**, C Guevara, near Playa El Agua bus stop. Colombian, good value.
♥ **Dino's Grill**, Igualdad y Martínez. Open 0700-1400, buffet lunch, indoor/outdoor seating, grill, home-made sausages, cheap, good service.
♥ **Dragón Chino**, 4 de Mayo. Great Chinese.
♥ **El Pollo de Carlitos**, Marcano y Martínez. Pleasant location, good food.
♥ **El Punto Criollo**, Igualdad near **Hotel Porlamar**. Excellent value *comida margariteña*.

Playa El Agua p110
Several restaurants along C Miragua. 2 good restaurants on beach in Playa Agua, ♥♥ **El Pacífico**, thatched roof, popular, good fish. Another beach restaurant ♥ **La Isla** owned by friendly Italian, serves good, fresh Mediterranean-style food, pleasant terrace area and good service.
♥♥ **Marlín**, with beach view. Serves seafood.

Juan Griego p111
Several restaurants along the beach. **La Calera de mi Caribina** recommended.

🎵 Bars and clubs

Porlamar p109
Several bars in the Centro Comercial Costal Azul. **Señor Frog's** is popular.
El Remo, Av 4 de Mayo. Seafood restaurant with disco upstairs, open until 0300, no cover.
Tasca Gaita, C Marcano. Loud music, wood-panelled ceilings.
Many hotels in Urb Costa Azul have relatively inexpensive **casinos**; the best are **Casino del Sol** at the *Hotel Marina Bay*, and **Hilton Margarita**.

Playa El Yaque p111
Several beach bars; best bar is **Los Surf Piratas**, drinks and dancing from 2130.

Juan Griego p111
Los Tucanes for eating and drinking. **Rose's Place** for late-night partying.

❀ Festivals and events

Isla de Margarita p108
Many religious festivals, including **19 Mar** at Paraguachí (*Feria de San José*, 10 days); **26 Jul** at Punta de Piedras; **31 Jul** (Batalla de Matasiete) and **15 Aug** (Asunción de la Virgen) at La Asunción; **1-8 Sep** at El Valle; **4-11 Nov** at Boca del Río, **4-30 Nov** at Boca del Pozo; **5-6 Dec** at Porlamar; **27 Dec-3 Jan** at Juan Griego See map for locations.

○ Shopping

Porlamar p109
Margarita's status as a duty-free zone attracts Venezuelan shoppers, who go in droves for clothing, electronic goods and other items. Street sellers lay out their handicrafts on Av Santiago Mariño in the afternoon. When buying jewellery, bargain, don't pay by credit card (surcharges are imposed) and get a detailed guarantee of the item. Av Santiago Mariño and surroundings are the place for designer labels, but decent copies can be found on Blvds Guevara and Gómez and around Plaza Bolívar in the centre. For bargains on denims, T-shirts, shorts, swimming gear and bikinis, take a bus to Conejeros market (from Fraternidad, Igualdad a Velásquez).

⛰ Activities and tours

Porlamar p109
Aquanauts Diving, Urb Costa Azul, C Los Almendrones, Centro Comercial Bayside, local No 1-47, PB, T267 1645. PADI school, snorkelling and fishing trips.
Natura Raid, Av 4 de Mayo con Av Santiago Mariño, Edif Silcat p 4, of 4-1, T261 4419, www.naturaraid.com. Eco-tourism and adventure trips across Venezuela, including diving in Los Roques and sailing (also has an office in Caracas).
Sailing The private yacht **Viola Festival** can be hired for mini cruises to the island of Coche, contact **Festival Tours**, Calle Los Uveros, Caribbean Center Mall, PB, Local 82, Costa Azul, T264 9554, www.violafestival.com. There are other yachts offering island cruises, fishing trips, etc.

Playa El Agua p110
Tour shops in Playa El Agua are the best places to book scuba diving and snorkelling trips: most go to Los Frailes, a small group of islands to the north of Playa Agua, and reputedly the best diving and snorkelling in Margarita, but it's also possible to dive at Parque Nacional La Restinga and Isla Cubagua. Prices from US$75 pp for an all-inclusive full day (2 dives), but bargaining is possible if you have a group of 4 or more. Snorkelling is always about half the price of scuba diving.
Enomis Divers, Av 31 de Julio, CC Turístico, Playa El Agua, loc 2, sector La Mira, T249 0366, www.divemargarita.com. PADI school, diving trips. Open water certification US$250.

Playa El Yaque *p111*
Sailboards, **kite surf** and **kayaks** can be hired on the beach from at least 5 well-equipped companies, who also offer lessons. Half day including lesson costs US$70 for wind/kite surfing; US14 per hr for kayak. English, German, French and Portuguese spoken. Enquire at **El Yaque Motion** (see Sleeping, above) for more information about wind and kite surfing. See also www.velawind surf.com. A 20-min boat ride to Isla Coche leaves from next door to **El Yaque Motion**, a recommended spot for advanced kiters. Rescue service available at the beach.

La Restinga and around: Peninsula de Macanao *p111*
Horse riding You can ride on the peninsula at **Ranch Cabatucan**, T416 3584, www.cabatucan.com. Prices start at US$93 pp for 2 hrs.

⊘ Transport

Porlamar *p109*
Air There are too many flight options to list here: check with local offices for details. **Gen Santiago Mariño Airport**, between Porlamar and Punta de Piedras, has the international and national terminals at either end. Airport tax US$12.80. Taxi from Porlamar US$28, 20-30 mins. There are scheduled flights to **Frankfurt** and internal flights to almost all Venezuela's airports. All national airlines have routes to **Margarita**. Many daily flights to/from **Caracas**, with **Aeropostal**, and **Aserca**, 45 mins flight; tickets are much cheaper if purchased in Venezuela. Reservations made from outside Venezuela are not always honoured. To **Canaima** and to **Los Roques** with **Aereotuy** and **Rutaca**.
Bus Local: *Por Puestos* serve most of the island, minimum fare US$1, few services at night and in low season: Airport, from Centro Comercial AB, Av Bolívar; La Asunción, from Fajardo, Igualdad a Marcano; Pampatar, from Fajardo y La Marina; La Restinga, from Mariño,

La Marina a Maneiro; Playa El Agua, from Guevara, Marcano a Cedeño; Juan Griego, from Av Miranda, Igualdad a Marcano; Playa Guacuco, from Fraternidad, La Marina a Mérito (mornings), from Fajardo, Igualdad a Velásquez (afternoons).
Long distance: Several bus companies in Caracas sell through tickets from Caracas to Porlamar, arriving about midday. Buses return to Caracas from La Paralela bus station in Porlamar.
Ferry From **Puerto La Cruz** to Margarita (**Punta de Piedras**): **Conferry**, Los Cocos terminal, Puerto La Cruz, freephone T0501-2663 3779, www.conferry.com. Terminal has restaurant, CANTV and internet services. Price varies according to speed of ferry and class of seat, 2½-4½ hrs, 4-6 a day, night departures too (check times, extra ferries during high season). Fast ferry, passengers US$17 one way, over-60s and children 2-7 half price (proof of age required), cars US$23. Slow ferries US$10 one way. **Conferry** office in **Porlamar**, Av Terranova con Av Llano Adentro, Mon-Fri 0800-1200, 1400-1730, Sat 0800-1200. **Gran Cacique**, 2-3 fast ferries a day Puerto la Cruz-Punta de Piedras, US$13.25-19 one way, T0281-263 0935 (Puerto La Cruz ferry terminal), T0295-239 8339 (Punta de Piedras, or Av Santiago Mariño, Edif Blue Sky, loc 3, Porlamar, T0295-264 2945). Ferries not always punctual. It is not uncommon for delays up to 6 hours in high season. It is most advisable to book in advance, especially if travelling with a car or motorbike during high season. Insist on a ticket even when you are told it is full. Don't believe taxi drivers at bus terminal who may tell you there's a ferry about to leave. To get to terminal in Puerto La Cruz, take 'Bello Monte' *por puesto* from Libertad y Anzoátegui, 2 blocks from Plaza Bolívar. From **Cumaná** ferry terminal, El Salado, **Gran Cacique**, T0293-432 0011, 2-3 a day, US$14-19 one way (children 3-7 and over-60s cheaper), and **Naviarca**, T0293-433 5577,

continuous service, US$9.30 one way for passengers (children 3-7 and over-60s half price), vehicles US$17-19.50. **Note** Ferries are very busy at weekends and Mon.

Taxi Taxi for a day is US$23 per hr. Always fix fare in advance; 30% extra after 2100. Taxi from Playa El Agua to airport, US$28, from Restinga, US$33.

Directory

Porlamar *p109*

Airline offices **Aeropostal**, Sambil Margarita, local Mn17, T262 2179. **Aereotuy**, T415 5778, sramirez@tuy.com. **Aserca**, Av Bolívar, CC Provemed, PB, local 5, Pampatar, T0800-648 8356. **Rutaca**, Centro Comercial Jumbo, T263 9936, 0501-788 2221.

Banks Banks on Avs Santiago Mariño and 4 de Mayo, open 0830-1130, 1400-1630. **Casas de cambio: Cambio Cussco** at Velásquez y Av Santiago Mariño. **Italcambio**, CC Jumbo, Av 4 de Mayo, Nivel Ciudad, T265 9392. **Car hire** Several offices at the airport and at the entrance to *Hotel Bella Vista*, others on Av Santiago Mariño. **Ramcar II**, at airport and *Hotel Bella Vista*, cheap and reliable. Check the brakes, bodywork and terms and conditions of hire thoroughly. Scooters can also be hired. Motor bikes may not be ridden 2000-0500. **Note** Fill up before leaving Porlamar as service stations are scarce. Roads are generally good and most are paved. Signposts are often nonexistent. Free maps are confusing, but it's worth having one with you. Avoid driving outside Porlamar after dark. Beware of robbery; park in private car parks. **Internet** Several on Av Santiago Mariño. **Post offices** On Maneiro. **Telephones** Several on Av Santiago Mariño.

Pampatar *p110*

Language school **Centro de Lingüistica Aplicada**, Corocoro Qta, Cela Urb, Playa El Angel between Porlamar and Pampatar, T/F262 8198, http://cela-ve.com (useful website).

Los Roques

→ *Phone code: 0237. National park entry US$12, Venezuelans and children 5-12 years half price.*

The turquoise and emerald lagoons and dazzling white sands of the Archipelago de Los Roques make up one of Venezuela's loveliest national parks. For lazing on an untouched beach, or for snorkelling and diving amid schools of fish and coral reefs, these islands cannot be beaten. Diving and snorkelling are best to the south of the archipelago. The islands tend to be very busy in July-August and at Christmas. See www.los-roques.com. Also look out for the excellent *Guía del Parque Nacional Archipiélago Los Roques* (Ecograph, 2004).

The islands of Los Roques, with long stretches of white beaches and over 20 km of coral reef in crystal-clear water, lie 166 km due north of La Guaira; the atoll, of about 340 islets and reefs, constitutes a national park of 225,153 ha. There are many bird nesting sites (eg the huge gull colonies on Francisqui and the pelicans, boobies and frigates on Selenqui); May is nesting time at the gull colonies. For more information visit www.fundacionlosroques.org. This is one of the least visited diving spots in the Caribbean; best visited midweek as Venezuelans swarm here on long weekends and at school holidays, after which there is litter on every island. (Low season is Easter to July.) There are at least seven main dive sites offering caves, cliffs, coral and, at Nordesqui, shipwrecks. There are many fish to be seen, including sharks at the caves of Olapa de Bavusqui. Prices are higher than the mainland and infrastructure is limited but the islands are beautiful and unspoiled. Camping is free, but campers need a permit from Inparques ① *T0212-273 2811 in Caracas, or the office on Plaza Bolívar, Gran Roque, Mon-Fri 0830-1200 and 1400-1800, weekends and holidays 0830-1200 and 1430-1730, another small office by the runway.* Average temperature 29°C with coolish nights. You will need strong sunblock as there is no shade and an umbrella is recommended.

Gran Roque (*Population: 900*) is the main and only permanently inhabited island. The airport is here, as is the national guard, a few small grocery stores and souvenir shops, public phones (expensive internet), a bank with an ATM, medical facilities, dive shops, a few restaurants and accommodation. There is nowhere to change traveller's cheques. Park Headquarters are in the scattered fishing village. Tourist information is available free of charge from the very helpful *Oscar Shop*, directly in front as you leave the airstrip. Boat trips to other islands can be arranged here (round trip fares US$7-US$42, depending on distance, more for a tour), which are worthwhile as you can not swim off Gran Roque.

You can negotiate with local fishermen for transport to other islands: you will need to take your own tent, food and (especially) water. **Madrisqui** has a good shallow beach and joins Pirata Cay by a sandspit. **Francisqui** is three islands joined by sandspits, with calm lagoon waters to the south and rolling surf to the north. You can walk with care from one cay to the other, maybe swimming at times. There's some shade in the mangrove near the bar at La Cueva. **Crasqui** has a 3-km beach with beautiful water and white sand. **Cayo de Agua** (one hour by fast boat from Gran Roque) has an amazing sandspit joining its two parts and a nice walk to the lighthouse where you'll find two natural pools.

Los Roques listings

For Sleeping and Eating price codes and other relevant information, see Essentials, pages 9-11.

😴 Sleeping

In most places on Islas Los Roques, breakfast and dinner are included in the price.

Los Roques: Gran Roque *p117*
posadas on Gran Roque (some bookable through **Aereotuy**), from **$$$$-$** pp. In high season, Jul-Aug, Dec, prices are very high. Bargaining is advisable (especially in low season) for stays of more than 2 nights.

$$$$ pp **Piano y Papaya**, near Plaza Bolívar towards seafront, T0414-281 0104. Very tasteful, run by Italian artist, with fan, **$$$** pp for bed and breakfast, credit cards and TCs accepted, Italian and English spoken, laundry service.

$$$$-$$ pp **El Botuto**, on seafront near *Supermercado W Salazar*, T0416-621 0381 (mob), www.posadael botuto.com. Price depends on season and if half board or full board, reservations must be made 50% in advance. Nice airy rooms with fan, good simple food, locally owned. Trips to other islands and watersports arranged.

$$$ Posada Acquamarina, C 2 No 149, T0412-310 1962, www.posada-acquamarina.com. All-inclusive, rooms have a/c, cable TV, private bathrooms with hot water, terrace. Owner Giorgio very helpful, speaks Italian and some French, can arrange flights from Caracas. Also operates the **Rasqui Island Chalet** (**$$$** 3 rooms), the only posada on that island.

$$$ pp **Posada Caracol**, on seafront near airstrip, T414 5525, www.caracolgroup.com. Delightful, half-board and bed and breakfast options available, **$$$** pp, credit cards and TCs accepted, Italian and English spoken, good boats.

$$$ Posada Doña Magalis, Plaza Bolívar 46, T0414-287 7554, www.magalis.com.

Simple place, locally owned, with fan, cheaper with shared bath, includes soft drinks, breakfast and dinner, delicious food, mostly fish and rice.

$$ pp **Roquelusa**, C 3 No 214, behind *Supermercado W Salazar*, T0414-369 6401 (mob). Probably the cheapest option on Gran Roque, basic, with cold water, a/c.

⚠️ Activities and tours

Los Roques *p117*
Diving Note For health reasons you must allow 12 hrs to elapse between diving and flying back to the mainland. Companies charge US$70 for 2 dives including equipment and US$95 for an introductory course; lots of courses and packages available.
Cayo de Agua and **Francisqui** recommended for **snorkelling**. Boats and equipment rentals can be arranged.
Ecobuzos, 3 blocks from the airstrip, T0295-262 9811/0414-791 9380, www.ecobuzos.com. Very good, new equipment, modern boats, experienced dive masters. PADI courses (US$350) and beginner dives available.
Recife Divers, past Inparques at the far end of town. PADI courses and beginner dives available.
Sailing Fully equipped yachts can be chartered for US$300-500 per night for 2 people, all inclusive, highly recommended as a worthwhile way of getting some shade on the treeless beaches. Ask at **Angel & Oscar Shop**, or **Posada Pez Ratón**, T0414-257 1067, info@pezraton.com.
Windsurfing and kitesurfing On Francisqui, ask for Elías.

🚌 Transport

Los Roques *p117*
Air Flights from Maiquetía or Porlamar. **Aereotuy, Chapi Air, Transaven** (T0212-355 1965) and **Los Roques Airlines** (T0212 6352166, www.losroques-airlines.com) all fly

from Maiquetía (Aeropuerto Auxiliar) once a day, 40 mins, US$130-150 round trip, more expensive if booked outside of Venezuela. Some carriers charge more at weekends. Remember that small planes usually restrict luggage to 10 kg. They offer full-day packages (return flight, meals and activities), and Aerotuy offers overnight packages as well (see www.tuy.com for details), recommended. It's best to buy a return to the mainland as buying and confirming tickets and finding offices open on the islands is difficult

O Directory

Los Roques *p117*
Banks Banesco, Plaza Bolívar, Mon-Fri 0830-1230, 1430-1700. Cash advances on Visa.
Internet Many posadas have computers. If not, **Posada Acquamarina** (see Sleeping) has a service for the public. **Public telephones** Plaza Bolívar and Guardia National on seafront.

Canaima and the Orinoco Delta

In Parque Nacional Canaima, one of the largest national parks in the world, you'll find the spectacular Angel Falls, the highest in the world, and the mysterious "Lost World" of Roraima (described under South to Brazil). Canaima is the tourist centre for the park, but indigenous communities are now accepting tourists. The historic Ciudad Bolívar on the Río Orinoco is a good starting place for the superb landscapes further south. Further east, beyond the industrial city of Ciudad Guayana, the Orinoco Delta is developing as a tourist destination.

Guayana, south of the Orinoco River, constitutes half of Venezuela, comprising rounded forested hills and narrow valleys, rising to ancient flat-topped tablelands on the borders of Brazil. These savannahs interspersed with semi-deciduous forest are sparsely populated. So far, communications have been the main difficulty, but a road that leads to Manaus has now been opened to Santa Elena de Uairén on the Brazilian frontier (see page 138). The area is Venezuela's largest gold and diamond source, but its immense reserves of iron ore, manganese and bauxite are of far greater economic importance.

Ciudad Bolívar → *Phone code: 0285. Population: 300,000.*

Ciudad Bolívar is on the narrows of the Orinoco, some 300 m wide, which gave the town its old name of Angostura, 'The Narrows'. It is 400 km from the Orinoco delta. It was here that Bolívar came after defeat to reorganize his forces, and the British Legionnaires joined him. At Angostura he was declared President of the Gran Colombia he had yet to build and which was to fragment before his death. With its cobbled streets, pastel buildings and setting on the Orinoco, it is one of Venezuela's most beautiful colonial towns and its status as a UNESCO World Heritage Site is under consideration.

At the Congress of Angostura, 15 February 1819, the representatives of the present day Venezuela, Colombia, Panama and Ecuador met to proclaim Gran Colombia. The building, on **Plaza Bolívar**, built 1766-1776 by Manuel Centurión, the provincial governor, houses a museum, the **Casa del Congreso de Angostura**, with an ethnographic museum in the basement. Guides give tours in Spanish only. Also on this plaza is the **Cathedral** (which was completed in 1840), the **Casa de Los Gobernadores de la Colonia** (also built by Centurión in 1766), the **Real Intendencia**, and the **Casa de la Cultura**. Also here, at Bolívar 33, is the house where Gen Manuel Piar, the Liberator of Guayana from the Spanish, was held prisoner before being executed by Bolívar on 16 October 1817, for refusing to put himself under Bolívar's command. The restored **Plaza Miranda**, up C Carabobo, has an art centre. The present legislative assembly and **Consejo Municipal** are between Plaza Bolívar and Plaza Miranda. In 1824, when the town was still known as Angostura a Prussian physician to Bolívar's troops invented the bitters; the factory moved to Port of Spain in 1875.

Museum at **Casa del Correo del Orinoco** ① *Paseo Orinoco y Carabobo, Mon-Fri 0930-1200, 1430-1700*, houses modern art and some exhibits of history of the city. **Museo Casa San Isidro** ① *Av Táchira, Tue-Sun 0900-1700, free, knowledgeable guides*, a colonial mansion where Simón Bolívar stayed for two weeks. It has antique furniture and an old garden. **Museo de Arte Moderno Jesús Soto** ① *Av Germania, 0930-1730, weekends and holidays 1000-1700, free, guide in Spanish only*, is located some distance from the centre in pleasant gardens. It has works by Venezuela's celebrated Jesús Rafael Soto and other modern artists from around the world. Recommended. The best views of the city are from **Fortín El Zamuro** ① *C 28 de Octubre y Av 5 de Julio, open daily except Mon, free, guides available*, dating from 1902, strategically located at one of the tallest points of the city.

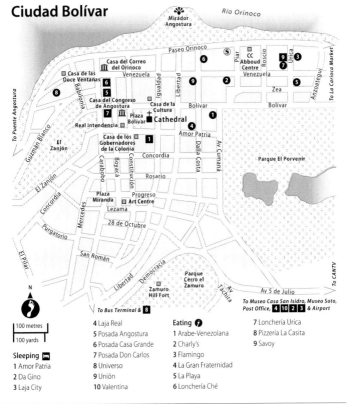

Ciudad Bolívar

Sleeping 🛏	4 Laja Real
1 Amor Patria	5 Posada Angostura
2 Da Gino	6 Posada Casa Grande
3 Laja City	7 Posada Don Carlos
	8 Universo
	9 Unión
	10 Valentina

Eating 🍴	
1 Arabe-Venezolana	7 Lonchería Urica
2 Charly's	8 Pizzería La Casita
3 Flamingo	9 Savoy
4 La Gran Fraternidad	
5 La Playa	
6 Lonchería Ché	

Speedboats take passengers across the river to the small, picturesque town of **Soledad** (US$0.50 one way, five minutes) on a journey that offers great views of colonial centre, the bridge and the river itself. Security can be an issue at either end; don't cross at night. There are no other passenger boat services. The Paseo Orinoco leading west out of town goes to the **Angostura Bridge**, which can be seen from town. This is the first bridge across the Orinoco, 1668 m long, opened in 1967, again with great views (cyclists and walkers are not allowed to cross, you must flag down a car or truck).

West of the centre is **El Zanjón**, an area of vegetation typical of the region. East is **Parque El Porvenir**, with botanical gardens (entrance on C Bolívar). Outside the airport is the *Río Caroní* aeroplane, which Jimmy Angel landed on top of Auyán Tepuy (see page 127).

The **tourist office** is Dirección de Turismo ① *Av Bolívar, Quinta Yeita 59, T632 2362, Mon-Fri 0800-1200, 1400-1730*. Helpful, English spoken. State website: www.e-bolivar.gov.ve.

To Ciudad Bolívar from the coast and the llanos Ciudad Bolívar can be reached easily by roads south from Caracas and Puerto La Cruz. The Caracas route, via Valle de la Pascua, and the Puerto La Cruz route, via Anaco, meet at El Tigre (*Population: 122,000*), which has good hotels and services. From the *llanos*, from **Chaguaramas** turn south through Las Mercedes (hotel **$**) to **Cabruta** (*Population: 4300*), 179 km, road in very bad shape, daily bus to Caracas, US$11, basic hotel. Then take a ferry from opposite the airport to **Caicara** (car ferry 1½ hours, *lanchas* for pedestrians 25 minutes). An 11.2 km bridge across the Orinoco is being built between Cabruta and Caicara (due to open in 2012). Alternatively, from San Fernando de Apure take a bus to Calabozo (*Population: 108,000*) and *por puesto* from there to El Sombrero (*Population: 23,000; US$2.25*), where you can catch the Ciudad Bolívar bus.

Tours can be made into the area south of the Río Orinoco from **Maripa**, travelling on the Río Caura. These include visits to indigenous villages, river bathing, jungle treks to waterfalls with explanations of wildlife and vegetation, usually starting from Ciudad Bolívar (see Activities and tours, below).

Ciudad Bolívar listings

For Sleeping and Eating price codes and other relevant information, see Essentials, pages 9-11.

● Sleeping

Ciudad Bolívar *p120, map p121*
Near airport
$$$ Laja Real, Av Andrés Bello y Jesús Soto, opposite airport (take your life in your hands if you walk across), T617 0100, www.hotellajareal.com. 1980s hotel, rooms with a/c, hot water, TV, fridge, pool open to non-residents for US$5 per day, Wi-Fi, overpriced restaurant, sauna, gym, parking.
$$ Valentina, Av Maracay 55, T632 2145. Quiet, a/c, hot water, TV, comfortable, very good restaurant.

$ Da Gino, Av Jesús Soto, opposite airport, T632 0313. A/c, hot water, TV, good service and restaurant, changes US$ cash.

In the centre
$$$$ Posada Casa Grande. C Boyacá 8, T632 4639, angostura@cacaotravel.com. A beautiful hotel in colonial style, with breakfast, cable TV, a/c, hot water, restaurant, pool on the roof.
$$ Posada Angostura, same contact details as *Posada Casa Grande* above, also on C Boyacá. Handsome rooms in old colonial house, some rooms have river view, a/c, fan, hot water, travel agency, unwelcoming service. A chef prepares some of the best food in Venezuela for guests.

$$-$ Laja City, Av Táchira y Av Bolívar, T/F632 9919, hotellajacity@cantv.net. Quiet, a/c, hot water, TV, restaurant.

$$-$ Posada Don Carlos, C Boyacá 26 y Amor Patrio, just 30m from Plaza Bolívar, T632 6017, www.hosteltrail.com/posadadoncarlos. Stunning old house, could be museum. Double rooms with a/c and bath, cheaper with fan, hammock and shared facilities **$**, breakfast and dinner available, free internet, lovely patio, bar. Very popular with travellers. Recommended.

$ Amor Patria, Amor Patria 30, T632 8819, plazabolivar@hotmail.com. Renovated colonial house, fan, shared bathrooms, kitchen, hammocks for hire (**$**). Run by Gerd Altmann, German and English spoken. Recommended.

$ Unión, Calle Urica, T632 3374. Clean, basic with fan, cable TV, helpful, filtered water, good value.

Near the bus terminal

$ Universo, Av República, 2 blocks left out of terminal, T654 3732. A/c, hot water, TV, restaurant, accepts credit cards.

Outside town

$ Posada La Casita, Av Ligia Pulido, Urb 24 de Julio, PO Box 118, T617 0832, T0414-854 5146, www.posada-la-casita.com. Very nice rooms, with cold water, fan (a/c extra), hammock with mosquito net can be rented, **$**. Beautiful gardens (with small zoo), pool, laundry service, good food and drinks available, German and English spoken, helpful. Free pick up from airport or bus terminal (ring in advance). Free shuttle service into town. The owner runs **Gekko Tours** (see below).

◉ Eating

Ciudad Bolívar *p120, map p121*
Many restaurants close at 1700.

👄👄-👄 Mercado La Carioca, Octava Estrella y Paseo Orinoco, on the banks of the river. The best place for eating tasty local food, open daily from 0600-1500. Great view. Various stalls and

excellent local food with a range of prices. The municipality is providing daily security.

👄 Arabe-Venezolano, on Cumaná near Bolívar. Clean, a/c, good Arabic food, not cheap.

👄 Mirador Paseo Orinoco. *Comida criolla* with views over the river.

👄-👄 La Playa, C Urica entre Venezuela y Zea. Good for fish, reasonable prices.

👄 Charly's, Venezuela. Good *fuente de soda*, cheap, fast service.

👄 Flamingo, C Urica opposite Hotel Unión. Peruvian dishes, good value if they don't overcharge.

👄 Lonchería Ché, Dalla Cosat y Paseo Orinoco. Good breakfast.

👄 Lonchería Urica, Urica, next to *Hotel Unión*. Good lunch for US$1.25, get there early.

👄 Pizzería La Casita Venezuela, opposite *La Casa de las Doce Ventanas*. Good value pizza and ice cream, views over Puente Angostura.

👄 Restaurant Vegetariano La Gran Fraternidad Amor Patria y Dalla Costa. Lunch only.

👄 Savoy, Venezuela y Dalla Costa. Good value breakfast.

Cafés and fast food

Café Estilo, Av Andrés Bello, opposite **Laja Real Hotel** and very near airport. Open 0900-1200, 1500-1900. Boutique and café with homemade sweets, comfortable, spotless. Run by very nice elderly couple. Recommended.

Several fast food restaurants around **Museo de Arte Moderno Jesús Soto**, including **McDonalds. Café Park**, great ice cream parlour with coffee and simple but decent food, playground for children.

◉ Shopping

Ciudad Bolívar *p120, map p121*
Camping equipment White gas (stove fuel) is available at **Lubriven**, Av República 16, near the bus terminal.

Handicrafts Arts and crafts from Bolívar state, basketry from the Orinoco Delta can be found in **La Carioca** market, at the end of Paseo Orinoco and **Tienda Artesanía Guayanesa** at the airport.

Jewellery There are many jewellers on Pasaje Guayana, which runs off Paseo Orinoco.

Supermarket Close to the Museo Soto on Av Germania, large and well-stocked.

▲ Activities and tours

Ciudad Bolívar *p120, map p121*
Competition is stiff in Ciudad Bolívar, and among the genuine companies roam phoney salesmen. You are more than likely to have someone attempt to sell you a tour at the bus station. Do not pay any money to anyone in the bus station or on the street. Always ask to be taken to the office. Always ask for a receipt (and make sure that it comes on paper bearing the company logo). Be suspicious of people offering tours that start in another town or city. If you are unfortunate enough to fall prey to a con artist, be sure to make a *denuncio* at the police station and inform genuine travel agents.

Ciudad Bolívar is the best place to book a tour to Canaima, but you may pick up cheaper deals for trips to Roraima and the Gran Sabana from Santa Elena. The main tour operators in Canaima offering tours at backpacker prices are *Bernal Tours*, *Express Dorado*, *Kawi Travel Adventure* and *Tiuna Tours*. Most other agents in Ciudad Bolívar sell tours run by these operators, but sometimes add commission. Always ask who will be running the actual tour; it may be cheaper to book from the tour operator directly. Service seems to change with the seasons and year-on-year: get independent recommendations on standards of guiding, food, time-keeping, etc. For 3 days/2 nights tours to Canaima expect to pay around US$350 pp (official exchange rate), or US$310 for 1-day tour that includes flights to Canaima, flight near the Angel Falls, boat ride across Canaima lagoon (just a few minutes) and food (see page 130 for flights to Canaima). A 4 day/3 night tour to Gran Sabana costs about US$250; 5 days/4 nights; Río Caura US$245.

Asociación Cooperativa Yajimadu, Servicios y Excursiones Ecoturísticas, T615 2354, dichenedu@hotmail.com, or Miguel Estaba, T0414-099 0568. 5-day trip to Río Caura, 10 and 15-day trips also available, small groups catered for, guides are Ye'kwana from villages on the river, knowledgeable, Spanish spoken (some guides learning English), sleep in hammocks, very good.

Bernal Tours/Sapito Tours, at airport, T632 6890, 0414-854 8234 (mob in Spanish), 414-899 7162 (in English), www.bernaltours.com. They use *indígena* guides and their own eco lodge at Canaima lagoon overlooking the falls. Canaima tours are slightly more expensive, and inconsistent, than others. Sapito Tours is the only agent authorized to issue domestic and international tickets at the airport. Also offer day tours to Kavác caves, Gran Sabana, Río Caura, Roraima (6 days/5 nights), Orinoco Delta (3 days/2 nights), Los Roques, Puerto Ordaz and city tours. Agency is run by descendents of Peruvian adventurer Tomás Bernal from Arequipa (see page 126).

Di Blasio, Av Cumaná 12, T632 1931. Very helpful for domestic and international air tickets, reconfirmations, hotel bookings in Caracas and other Venezuelan cities.

Expediciones Dearuna, C Libertad 16 (above Inversiones Ruiz), T632 4635. All usual tours at competitive prices.

Gekko Tours, run by Pieter Rothfuss at airport (also *Posada La Casita*), T632 3223, T0414-854 5146, www.gekkotours-venezuela.de. Gran Sabana, Canaima, Roraima, Orinoco Delta, rafting and river trips.

Kawi Travel Adventure, at the airport, T511 4581, 0414-899 6399 (mob). Offers usual routes in the area, plus US$16.25 for night in hammock in the countryside, 10 mins from the airport, with pool (discount or even free if tour is booked with them).

Miguel Gasca, T0414-923 5210/0166-629 4600 (mob), or find him at *Hotel Italia*. Recommended for tours to Roraima, Gran Sabana and Canaima.

Soana Travel, run by Martin Haars at *Posada Don Carlos*, Boyacá 26, T632 6017, T0414-864 6616 (mob), soanatravel@gmx.de. Tours to Río Caura, Canaima and Gran Sabana, English and German spoken.

Tiuna Tours, at airport, T632 8697. Cheapest option for Canaima, have a camp that takes 180 people. Guides speak English, German and Italian.

Turi Express, at airport, T652 9764, T0414-893 9078 (mob), turiexpress@cantv.net. Range of tours plus Guri dam and fishing tours, good English.

⊖ Transport

Ciudad Bolívar *p120, map p121*
Air Minibuses and buses marked Terminal to town centre. Taxi to Paseo Orinoco US$3. To **Caracas** 5-6 a week, 1 hr, **Aserca** and **Rutaca**. Transmandú (T0285-632 1462, www.transmandu.com) and **Rutaca** (recommended for views) fly daily to **Canaima**. Transmandú also flies to **Kamarata, Kavác** and **Santa Elena**. There are international phones at the airport, excellent café with runway view and some food, and car hire. Check where tours start from as some fly from Ciudad Guayana (**Turi Tours**), and charge passengers for taxi transfers. Taxi to Ciudad Guayana or its airport for daily flights to Caracas about US$35.

Bus Terminal at junction of Av República and Av Sucre. Left luggage. To get there take bus marked Terminal going west along Paseo Orinoco (US$0.35). Buy bus tickets in advance. 10 daily to **Caracas** US$17, 8-9 hrs with **Aeroexpresos Ejecutivos**; also **Camargüi, Expresos Los Llanos**; *por puesto*

US$40. 10 daily to **Puerto La Cruz**, US$8, 5 hrs, with **Caribe** and **Expresos San Cristóbal**, *por puesto*, US$16. 1 daily to **Cumaná**, US$11.50, 7 hrs with **Caribe**. Several daily to **Maracay**, US$14, and **Valencia**, via Maracay, US$14, 8-9 hrs, with **Expresos Los Llanos**. **Tumeremo** US$8.50; Tumeremo bus through to El Dorado US$9.50, 3 daily. To **Santa Elena de Uairén** direct with **Caribe** US$26.50 (3 daily), **Expresos San Cristóbal**, US$21.50 (2 daily), stopping en route with **Línea Orinoco, Transportes Mundial** (5 daily), spectacular views of Gran Sabana, 12-13 hrs. 1 daily to **Boa Vista** with **Caribe**, US$34, 20 hrs. To **Ciudad Guayana** hourly from 0700, US$1.75, 1½ hrs, *por puesto*, US$5.75, 1½ hrs. To **Ciudad Piar**, US$5.75, 3 hrs, and **La Paragua**, US$8.25, 4 hrs, with **Coop Gran Mcal Sucre**. 2 daily to **Caicara**, US$13.50 (including 2 ferry crossings), 7-8 hrs, with **Coop Gran Mcal Sucre**. To **Maturín** with **Unión Maturín**. 2 daily to **Puerto Ayacucho**, US$16, 10-12 hrs with **Coop Gran Mcal Sucre**, take food.

Taxi US$2 to virtually anywhere in town. US$1.75 from bus station to town centre.

❶ Directory

Ciudad Bolívar *p120, map p121*
Banks See also Money, page 11. TCs difficult to change. ATMs open only in banking hours. **Corp Banca**, Paseo Meneses, Edif Johanna. Amex TCs. **Banco de Venezuela**, Paseo Orinoco near Piar. Cash on Visa, ATM. **Banco Mercantil**, east end of Paseo Orinoco. Changes TCs, has ATM. **BBVA Banco Provincial**, west end of Av Jesús Soto, opposite Mobil petrol station. Cash on Visa, ATM. **Internet** Places in the centre. **Galaxia.com**, C C Abboud Centre, Paseo Orinoco. **Galaxy Computer**, Av República y Jesús Soto, behind Mobil petrol station. **Post offices** Av Táchira, 15 mins walk from centre. **Telephones** *CANTV*, Av 5 de Julio, 100 m from Av Táchira (closed Sun).

Canaima and Angel Falls → *Park entry US$16 pp paid to Inparques on arrival in Canaima.*

Canaima National Park, a UNESCO World Heritage Site since 1994, is one of the most unspoilt places on earth. At over 3 million ha, it is the second largest national park in Venezuela, the 6th largest on the planet. It is a world apart, with its fantastic table mountains, waterfalls which include the world's highest (Angel Falls), caves, deep forests and indigenous cultures.

At Canaima camp, the Río Carrao tumbles spectacularly over Ucaima, Golondrina and Hacha Falls into the lagoon, which has beautiful tannin-stained water with soft beige beaches. It's a lovely spot, but it also has the air strip and is the centre of operations for river trips to indigenous areas and to Angel Falls. The Falls are named after Jimmie Angel, the US airman who first reported their existence in 1935. Two years later he returned and crash landed his plane, the *Río Caroní*, on top of Auyán Tepuy. The site is marked with a plaque. The sheer rock face was climbed in 1971 by three Americans and an Englishman, David Nott, who recounted the 10-day adventure in his book *Angels Four* (Prentice-Hall). Hugo Chávez has said that the falls should be called by an indigenous name: Kerepakupai Merú.

There is a famous 'tunnel' between Sapo and Sapito Falls (where Río Carrao passes behind Isla Anatoliy), where one can walk behind the huge waterfall – a must for any visitor. It is essential to be accompanied by guide. The easiest way to get there is from

Parque Nacional Canaima

Tomás Bernal Camp on Isla Anatoliy (five minutes boat ride from Canaima Camp). It's a 25-minute walk from there. Plastic raincoats are usually provided by the guide, or wear a swim suit. Wrap your camera and other belongings in a plastic bag. No matter what, you will get completely soaked in the middle of the tunnel. The path behind the waterfall is extremely slippery and should be taken only by the reasonably fit. Wrap your hand in an extra plastic bag, otherwise it will be cut by the rough rope. When taking photos from behind the wall of water, experiment with camera speeds for the best effects.

Warning There is one more, invisible, waterfall on Canaima Lagoon, at the opposite end from Canaima Camp. It is called Salto Ara. The lagoon is a terrace and at Salto Ara all the water goes down one step. It is invisible from the surface, the only indicator is foam rising as if from nowhere. This fall is extremely dangerous: do not swim or take a boat near it. This is where Tomás Bernal, the Peruvian discoverer of the above tunnel, lost his life in 1998 after the engine of his boat broke down. He is buried on Isla Anatoliy.

Canaima

There are several tourist lodges at Canaima and some package tours now visit on day trips. Do not forget swimwear, insect repellent and sun cream; waterproof clothing may be advisable. Do not walk barefoot as there are chiggers, or *niguas*, in the lagoon's sand beaches.

Trips to the Angel Falls

The Angel Falls, the highest in the world (979 m – its longest single drop is 807 m), 70 km downriver from Canaima, are best reached by plane to Canaima from Caracas, Ciudad Bolívar or Ciudad Guayana. Trips by boat upriver to the Angel Falls operate May-January, depending on the level of the water in the rivers. Boats literally fly up and down river over the bolders (not for faint-hearted), but even during the rainy season you may have to get out and push in places. Most trips make an overnight stop on one of the islands, continuing to the Falls the next day. There are also bottom-numbing, 12-hour day trips which cost around US$80. More relaxing, with more stops at beauty spots, are 44-hour, 'three day' trips, US$140. **Inparques** is in Ciudad Guayana ① *Av Guayana, Edif Centro Empresarial Alta Vista, p 8, Puerto Ordaz, T0286- 966 2033*. Ask here if you need a *permiso de excursionistas* to go on one tour and come back with another, giving yourself more time at the Falls. You may have to pay extra to do this, up to US$30 (take all food and gear). Trips can be arranged with agencies in Ciudad Bolívar (see above) or at Canaima airport. All *curiaras* (dugouts) must carry first aid, life jackets, etc. Take wet weather gear, swimwear, mosquito net for hammock and insect repellent, lots of film and a plastic bag to protect your camera/day bag. The light is best on the falls in the morning.

The cheapest way to fly over the falls is on scheduled flights from Ciudad Bolívar. From Canaima a 45-minute flight costs US$60 per person (black market rates) and does some circuits over and alongside the falls; departures only if enough passengers.

Kamarata

The largest of the tepuis, **Auyán Tepuy** (700 sq km) is also one of the more accessible. **Kamarata** is a friendly indigenous settlement with a Capuchin mission on the plain at the east foot of the tepuy. It has a well-stocked shop but no real hotels; basic rooms can be found for about US$4 per person, camping also possible at the mission (mosquito nets necessary and anti-malarial pills advised). Take food, although there is one place to eat, and locals may sell you dinner. The whole area is within the Parque Nacional Canaima.

Pemón families in Kamarata have formed co-operatives and can arrange *curiaras*, tents and porters for various excursions: see Activities and tours, below.

Kavác

About a two-hour walk northwest of Kamarata, this is a new indigenous-run resort consisting of a dozen thatched huts (*churuatas*) for guests, a small shop, and an excitingly short airstrip serviced by Cessnas from Ciudad Bolívar, Santa Elena, and Isla Margarita; flights from the north provide excellent views of Angel Falls and Auyán Tepuy. There is a vehicle connection with Kamarata but it is expensive because all fuel has to be flown in.

The prime local excursion is to **Kavác Canyon** and its waterfall known as La Cueva, which can be reached by joining a group or by setting out early west up the Río Kavác. A natural jacuzzi is encountered after a 30-minute wade along the sparkling stream, after which the gorge narrows dramatically until the falls are reached. Go in the morning to avoid groups of day-trippers from Porlamar. The sun's rays illuminate the vertical walls of the canyon only for a short time around 1100. Be prepared to get wet; swimwear and shoes with good grip, plus a dry change of clothing are recommended; also insect repellent, as there is a mosquito and midge invasion around dusk. Late afternoon winds off the savannah can make conditions chilly. It costs US$10 per person to stay at the camp (cheaper in hammocks), including a canyon tour. Take food with you.

Uruyén

South of Auyán Tepuy and west of Kamarata, **Uruyén** is similar to Kavác, only smaller and more intimate. It also has a beautiful canyon and is the starting point for treks up Auyán Tepuy. The camp is run by the Carvallo family. For more information, see www.angel conservation.org/lodges.html.

Canaima and Angel Falls listings

For Sleeping and Eating price codes and other relevant information, see Essentials, pages 9-11.

🛏 Sleeping

Canaima *p126*
$$$$ Camp Wey Tüpü, in the village, T0416-185 7231 (mob). Ring direct to the camp if reserving lodgings only, *Roymar* in Caracas handle reservations of all-inclusive packages run from the camp, T/F0212- 576 5655, roymar@ cantv.net. Fan, shower, bar, price includes meals and flight over Falls.
$$$$ Campamiento Canaima, T0289-540 1239, www.venetur.gob.ve. Taken over by Venetur in 2007, it has been rebuilt as a luxury resort with 109 cabins.

$$$$ Campamiento Ucaima Jungle Rudy, T0289- 808 9241, 0286-952 1529 in Puerto Ordaz, 0212- 754 0244 in Caracas, www.junglerudy.com. Run by daughters of the late 'Jungle' Rudy Truffino, full board, 1 hr walk from Canaima above Hacha Falls, local transfers included, bilingual guides.
$$$$ pp Parakaupa Lodge, 5 mins from airport, on southwestern side of lagoon, T Caracas 0212-287 0517, parakaupa@etheron.net. Attractive rooms with bath, hammocks outside rooms, views over the lagoon and falls, restaurant, full board.
$$$$ Wakü Lodge (Canaima Tours), T0286-962 0559, www.wakulodge.com. The

best option in Canaima, 4-star luxury, romantic, comfortable, a/c, good food, right on lagoon, free satellite/ WiFi internet for guests. Specializes mainly in all-inclusive packages. Recommended.

$$$ Kusary, close to *Parakaupa Lodge*, near airport, T0286-962 0443. Basic but clean, with bath, fan, food available, ask for Claudio at *Tienda Canaima*.

$ pp Kaikusé, next to *Kusary*, T0414-884 9031. Basic, clean with bath, hammocks.

Best place to rent a hammock or camp is at **Campamento Tomás Bernal** (*Bernal Tours*) on Isla Anatoliy, T0414-854-8234 Spanish, T0414-899 7162 English (mob), www.bernal tours.com. Camp has capacity for 60 hammocks. Also 4 beds in open for elderly travelers, 4 rooms with private bath. Clean bathrooms. Package (**$$$$**) includes flight, bilingual guide, hammock, mosquito repellent, all meals, boat trip across lagoon, raincoat. Bernal Tours also has a camp on Ratoncito Island by Angel Falls.

Campamento Tiuna (*Tiuna Tours*) may have camping space. Some families in the village rent hammocks for US$7-10 per person.

Camping Camp for free, but only around the *fuente de soda*; fires are not permitted. No tents available for hire.

Eating

Canaima *p126*
Food is expensive at the *Campamiento Canaima* restaurant. A cheaper option is **Simon's** restaurant in the village which is used by many agencies. It is advisable to take food, though there are various stores, both on the west side, **Tienda Canaima**, or in the indian village, selling mainly canned foods. A *fuente de soda* overlooks the lagoon. There is an expensive snack bar at the airport selling basic food, soft drinks and coffee; also souvenir shop.

▲ Activities and tours

Canaima *p126*
You can do walking expeditions into the jungle to indigenous villages with a guide, but bargain hard on the price. Other excursions are to the Mayupa Falls, including a canoe ride on the Río Carrao (US$30, half day), to Yuri Falls by jeep and boat (US$20, half day); to Isla Orquídea (US$45, full day, good boat ride, beach barbecue); to Saltos de Sapo and Sapito (3 hrs, US$18).

Guides in Canaima Fierce competition at the airport but agencies pretty much offer the same thing at the same price. Some package tours to Canaima are listed under Caracas and Ciudad Bolívar Tour operators. Agents may tell you that guides speak English: some do, but many don't.

Bernal Tours (see above).

Kamaracoto Tours and **Tiuna Tours** for trips to Salto Sapo, Kavác, Salto Angel; they will also help with finding accommodation.

Kamarata *p127*
Macunaima Tours (Tito Abati), **Excursiones Pemón** (Marino Sandoval), and **Jorge and Antonio Calcaño II** run local tours.

For details on climbing Auyán Tepuy, contact **Kamadac** in Santa Elena, run by Andreas Hauer (T0289-995 1408, T0414-886 6526, www.abenteuer-venezuela.de).

Alechiven and Pemón co-operatives run 6-day river trips from Kamarata to Angel Falls (May-Dec), descending the **Río Akanán** to the Carrao by motorized dugout then turning south up the 'Devil's Canyon' to the Falls; the tours continue downriver to Canaima. Cost is US$240 for the *curiara* (minimum 4), not including flights to Kamarata or food – supply your own food. River trips in this area are easier in the rainy season. Guides for Auyán Tepuy can be hired here for about US$18 per day, if you have your own equipment. Contact Andreas Hauer at *Kamadac*.

Canaima *p126*

Air There are no flights from Caracas to Canaima. **Aereotuy** runs 1 day excursions out of **Isla Margarita**, to Canaima, with a possible stopover in Ciudad Bolívar or Puerto Ordaz and overflight of Angel Falls if conditions permit, US$798.14. They also have a camp, Arekuna, near the foot of Nonoy Tepuy, visits to which can be direct from Margarita or with an extension to Canaima; bookable only through **Aereotuy**, recommended (T0212-212 3110, www.tuy.com).

The flight to Canaima from **Ciudad Bolívar** is spectacular and takes approximately 1 hr each way, overflying mining towns of San Isidro and Los Barrancos, as well as the vast artificial lake at Guri and the Yuri Falls. For flights in 5-seater Cessnas to Canaima from Ciudad Bolívar, go to the airport early, 0600-0700. Several companies operate flights: **Rutaca, Sundance, Transmandú, La Montaña**. The first plane leaves at about 0800, and all run on a first- come, first-served basis. The less passengers, the fewer the flights. A one-way ticket costs US$140 pp, flight only. Tickets can also be bought from **Bernal Tours, Kawi Travel, Express Dorado** or **Tiuna Tours**; prices are the same. Bigger groups can negotiate slightly better rates on 19-seater Jetstream if it is available. For tours that include flight over Angel Falls, boat across lagoon, lunch and trip to Salto Sapo, etc, see Ciudad Bolívar and Canaima Tour operators, above.

Kamarata *p127*

Air Transmandú from **Ciudad Bolívar** (2 hrs).

Kavác *p128*

Air A day excursion by light plane to Kavác from **Canaima** (45 mins' flight) can be made with any of the tour operators at the airport. There are also flights from **Ciudad Bolívar** with **Transmandú**. Trips from Ciudad Bolívar can be arranged with tour agencies in town or at airport, including flight via Angel Falls, meals, and 1 night's accommodation.

Ciudad Guayana and the Orinoco Delta

Ciudad Guayana → *Phone code: 0286. Population: 700,000.*
In an area rich in natural resources 105 km downriver from Ciudad Bolívar, Ciudad Guayana was founded in 1961 by merging two towns, San Félix and Puerto Ordaz, on either bank of the Río Caroní where it spills into the Orinoco. Now a single city, it is hot, humid and futuristic. Its wide avenues, lack of sidewalks and public transport reflect the influence of the US-owned Orinoco Mining Company, which had its headquarters here and was nationalized in 1976. East of the Caroní is the commercial port of **San Félix** and the Palúa iron-ore terminal. Across the Caroní by the 470 m concrete bridge is **Puerto Ordaz** (airport), the iron-ore port connected by rail with the Cerro Bolívar open-cast iron mine. The second bridge across the Río Orinoco, Puente Orinoquia, 3156 m long, was opened in Ciudad Guayana in 2006.

Visitors should be particularly careful while exploring Ciudad Guyana: it is surrounded by some desperately poor neighbourhoods. Violent crime, including rape, is unfortunately very common. And so is police unwillingness to answer 171 calls, let alone to investigate.

Excursions Unlike elsewhere in Venezuela, there is little emphasis on arts and culture. However, you can get beyond the urban functionality into some pleasant parks, all well kept and free to enter. Just up the Caroní at Macagua, some truly beautiful cataracts called Salto Llovizna are in the **Parque Nacional La Llovizna** ① *open from early morning till 1630, taxi, US$8.50,* which covers 26 islands separated by narrow waterways and connected by 36 footbridges. Also in the park are hydroelectric plants, but these do not spoil the views of the larger and smaller falls, diverse fauna, including monkeys, and magnificent plants growing from the falling water. There are several trails. A facility on the **hydroelectric dam** ① *Tue-Sun 0900-2100,* houses an ecological museum, art exhibitions and displays on the dam's construction, and a café. Near La Llovizna, the iron-tinted waterfall in the pretty **Parque Cachamay** (about 8 km from centre, near the Guayana Hotel; closes 1700) is worth a visit. A third park, adjoining Cachamay, is **Loefling Wildlife Park**, with tapirs, capybaras and capuchin monkeys.

Higher up the Caroní is the massive **Guri dam** ① *daily 0900-1030, 1415-1515,* take your passport; the area gets busy during holidays, Easter or carnival, powered by the world's second-largest reservoir, which is filled by the Paragua and Caroní rivers. The trip to Guri takes 90 minutes by taxi.

Los Castillos, supposedly where Sir Walter Raleigh's son was killed in the search for El Dorado, are two old forts down the Orinoco from San Félix (one hour by *por puesto*, US$3, or take a tour).

Tucupita → *Phone code: 0287, Population: 67,000.*
A worthwhile side trip along asphalted roads can be made to Tucupita (*Climate: very humid*), on the Orinoco delta. Though capital of Delta Amacuro state and the main commercial centre of the delta, there's a one-horse feel about it. The **tourist office** is at Calle Dalla Costa beside Sonido Color 2000, fondomixtodeltaamacuro@hotmail.com. Tourists should go there first for tour information. **Note** Banks won't change traveller's cheques.

For a three to four day **trip to see the delta**, its fauna and the indigenous *Warao*, either arrange boats through the tourist office (see Ins and outs, above). Boats are not easy to come by and are expensive except for large groups. Bargain hard and never pay up front.

Excursions often only travel on the main river, not in the *caños* where wildlife is most often be seen. To avoid disappointment, be sure to determine where your guide intends to take you before you leave. If the river level rises after a downpour, arrangements may be cancelled. On all trips agree in advance exactly what is included, especially that there is enough food and water for you and your guide. Hammocks and mosquito repellents are essential.

Barrancas → *Population: 13,000.*

An interesting and friendly village, founded in 1530, Barrancas is one of the oldest villages in the Americas, but its precolonial past dates back to 1000 BC. Situated on the Orinoco, it can be reached by road from Tucupita (63 km), or from Maturín. It has two basic hotels (**$**). The village has a large community of Guyanese people who speak English. It is possible to take a boat to the *Warao* villages of **Curiapo** and **Amacuro** (near Guyana border), check at harbour.

It is possible to take a cargo boat to Mabaruma in Guyana from Curiapo. A trustworthy boatman is Bimbo, who lives at Wirma's guest house, where you can sleep if stuck in Curiapo (very likely). Contact Bimbo in advance through his sister in Tucupita; just ask for the "English woman" on Calle Amacuro – everyone knows her. In Curiapo, find Miss Teresa to get your exit stamp; she is rarely at home at the weekend. Take plenty of dollars cash, be prepared to wait for a boat and to cover yourself with a large plastic sheet once at sea (the mid part of the trip is on the open ocean). If thinking of taking this route, visit the Guyanese Embassy in Caracas first.

Ciudad Guayana and the Orinoco Delta listings

For Sleeping and Eating price codes and other relevant information, see Essentials, pages 9-11.

🛏 Sleeping

Ciudad Guayana: Puerto Ordaz *p131*
$$$$ Venetur Orinoco, Av Guayana, Parque Punta Visat, T713 1000, www.venetur.gob.ve. It overlooks La Llovizna in Parque Cachamay, far from centre, highest standard in city but price is high for what is offered.
$$$ Roraima Inn Express, Carrera La Paragua, T923 28362, 0800-767 2462, www.roraimainn.com. Good rooms but pricey, W-iFi, airport transfer, buffet breakfast, cable TV. Casino and entertainment, can get wild.

$$ Dos Ríos, México esq Ecuador, T924 0679. New rooms have a/c, hot water, TV, pool, restaurant, *loncheria*, hairdresser, helpful.
$$ Posada Turística Alonga, Urb La Corniza, Av Canadá, manz 10, casa 14, T923 3154, 0414-898 2794 (mob). Quiet residential area, cable TV, internet.
$$ Residencias Tore, C San Cristóbal y Cra Los Andes, T923 0679, tore@cantv.net. Good rooms with a/c, hot water, TV, meals available.
$ in the house of Rolf and Rosa Kampen, C Surinam 03-07, Villa Antillana, 3 km from central Pto Ordaz, T/F923 0516. Room for 6 people, free pick up (best to contact by fax), breakfast US$4, dinner can be arranged. Rolf speaks English, German and Dutch.

$ with Wolfgang Löffler of *Lobo Tours*, C Zambia 2, Africana Manzana 39, T961 6286. Room for 8 people, free transfer from airport. 'El Lobo' speaks English and German. Recommended.

Tucupita *p131*
$$ Saxxi, on main road into Tucupita, 10 mins from centre, T721 2112, hotelsaxxi@cantv.net. Comfortable, hot water, a/c, bar/restaurant, disco Fri-Sat, pool. Also has camps *Mis Palafitos* and *Orinoco Bujana Lodge*, **$$$**, T721 1733. All inclusive.
$ Gran Hotel Amacuro, Bolívar 23, T721 0404. A/c, big rooms, dubious, **$** with fan.
$ Pequeño, La Paz, T721 0523. Basic but clean, fan, good value, safe, stores luggage, orchid garden, popular, closes at 2200.
$ Residencias San Cristóbal, San Cristóbal 50, T721 4529. Fan, parking.
$ Sans Souci, Centurión 30, T721 0132. Safe, a/c, OK, **$** with fan. French spoken.

🍴 Eating

Ciudad Guayana *p131*
There are plenty of restaurants and cafés on Cras Tumeremo and Upata, off Av Las Américas. There is a very good *churrascaría* on Av Las Américas 15 mins' walk from *Hotel Guayana* towards the airport, in an old hacienda building on the left, next to a *cervecería*, recommended. Fast food and upmarket eateries in Ciudad Comercial Altavista and surrounding streets.
    Mall Orinokia, on Av Guayana, Altavista. Huge, super-modern shopping centre with restaurants, cafés and travel agencies. Multi-screen cinema.
El Arepazo Guayanés, C La Urbana, Puerto Ordaz, T922 4757, the oldest and best *arepariía* in Ciudad Guyana, open 24 hrs.
Pollos y Parillas El Guayanés, next door to Arepazo, open until midnight. (Opposite is a good laundry, **Lavandería Villa Brasil.**)
Mi Rinconcito across the street from Mall Orinokia (Altavista), T962 1554, is famous for

its *cachapas* and live music at the end of the week.

Tucupita *p131*
🍴 **Capri**, on Paseo Manamo. Very good.
🍴 **Mi Tasca**, C Dalla Costa. Popular, varied menu, large portions. Recommended.
🍴 **Refresquería La Cascada**, on Paseo Manamo. English spoken.

⛰ Activities and tours

Ciudad Guayana *p131*
Anaconda Tours, PB, loc 2, CC Anto, Av Las Américas, T923 7966, anaconda2@cantv.net. Trips to Castillos de Guayana, Guri dam, Orinoco Delta, Gran Sabana and Canaima.
Bagheera Tours, p 2, of 86, C C Gran Sabana, Paseo Caroní, near airport, T952 9481, bagheera@telcel.net.ve. Tours to Gran Sabana, Angel Falls, Caura River and Orinoco Delta.
Lobo Tours, C Zambia No 2, Villa Africana Manzana 39, T961 6286. Wolfgang Löffler will tailor his tours to fit your demands. Trips organized to the Gran Sabana and Orinoco Delta, but will put together other excursions. Very helpful, all-inclusive, excellent cooking. English and German spoken. Recommended.
Oridelta, T961 5526, T0416-806 1211, www.deltaorinoko.com.ve. Roger and Ninoska Ruffenach arrange 1, 2 and 3-day tours to their Campamento in the less-visited southern part of the Orinoco Delta (T400 2649, 0414-868 2121, simple facilities), near Piacoa, 25 km from Los Castillos. German and English spoken.
Piraña Tours, at *Hotel Guayana*, Av Guayana, Parque Punta Vista, Puerto Ordaz, T923 6447, www.pirana tours.com. Local trips on the Caroní, Cachamay Falls and Orinoco, Delta and Gran Sabana tours, 25 years' experience.
Recommended guide Richard Brandt, T/F922- 4370 (or in Santa Elena de Uairén at *Cabañas Friedenau*), has own car, speaks English and tailors trips to your requirements.

Tucupita *p131*

Some boat owners visit hotels in the evenings looking for clients and may negotiate a price. Ask Pieter Rothfuss at *Gekko Tours/Posada La Casita* in Ciudad Bolívar and Roger Ruffenbach of *Oridelta* in Ciudad Guayana about a trip through the southern part of the delta and into the Sierra Imataca highlands. The following (and *Mis Palafitos* – see *Hotel Saxxi*) are registered with the tourist board and have insurance (this does not necessarily guarantee a good tour).

Aventura Turística, C Centurión 62, T/F721 0835, and at bus station, a_t_d_1973@ hotmail.com. Nicolás and Vidalig Montabric have 2 camps in the northern part of the delta, all-inclusive tours, English and French spoken.

Delta Sur, C Mariño and C Pativilca, T/F721 2666, oldest-established company, 3 day tours offered, English spoken.

Tucupita Expeditions, opposite hospital, T0414- 789 8343, www.orinocodelta.com. 2- to 5-night tours to lodges in the delta.

⊙ Transport

Ciudad Guayana *p131*

Air Daily flights from Puerto Ordaz to **Caracas, Maracaibo, Porlamar** and short-haul destinations with **Aserca, Aeropostal, Rutaca** and others. Car hire, **Europcar** and **Avis**. Walk 600 m to gas station on main road for buses to San Félix or Puerto Ordaz.

Bus Terminals at San Félix and close to Puerto Ordaz airport; long distance buses at both. Public transport in Ciudad Guayana is very limited. New, free local buses are infrequent. Minibuses are fast and cheap; San Félix-Puerto Ordaz, US$1.40; buses run until 2100. Several buses daily to **Santa Elena de Uairén** (via El Callao), US$21, 10 hrs, with **Caribe** (T951 8385, recommended) and **Turgar** (or night bus, which misses the fine scenery, 9 hrs). **El Callao** (US$6), **Tumeremo** (US$7.50), **El Dorado** (US$10) and Km 88

with **Turgar**. **Ciudad Bolívar** US$1.75 (*por puesto* US$5.75), 1 hr. Bus to **Maturín** US$8.75, 2½ hrs. 8 daily to **Caracas**, US$21 (**Aeroexpresos Ejecutivos**), 10 hrs. 8 daily to **Puerto La Cruz**, US$18, 6 hrs, with **Caribe**. 2 daily to **Cumaná**, US$16.30, 8 hrs, with **Caribe**. 5 daily to **Valencia**, US$20, 12½ hrs, with **Expresos Occidente**. To **Tucupita**, US$7, 3 hrs, leaving from San Félix bus terminal with **Expresos Guayanesa**, booking office opens 1 hr before departure, be there early, passport check just before Tucupita. San Felix bus terminal is not a safe place, especially at night.

International buses 1 bus daily to **Brazil**, US$33, 14 hrs including 3 stops, departs 2130, arrives Boa Vista 1130, with **Caribe** recommended, a/c (take warm clothes), toilets and reclining seats.

Taxi San Félix-Puerto Ordaz US$4 minimum, Puerto Ordaz-airport US$8, airport-centre US$14, San Félix bus terminal-Puerto Ordaz bus terminal US$11, bus terminal-centre US$6, centre-San Félix bus terminal US$6.50. Some hotels and the airport charge double and only allow their own taxis to enter. Radio taxi **Carlos Manuel Piar**, T931 3948.

Tucupita *p131*

Bus *Por puesto* from **Maturín** US$11, 2-3 hrs; bus to Maturín, US$5.75, 3-4 hrs, **Expresos Guayanesa**, US$7 with **Expresos Los Llanos** recommended. 2 daily to **San Félix**, US$7, 3 hrs, with **Expresos La Guayanesa**. 2 daily to **Caracas**, US$17, 12-13 hrs, with **Camargüi**. **Puerto La Cruz**, US$12, 7-8 hrs.

Barrancas *p132*

Bus **Tucupita**-Barrancas, US$2, return at 0945 and 1700.

⊙ Directory

Ciudad Guayana *p131*

Banks See also Money, page 11. **Corp Banca** (American Express), Av Cuchivero y C Caruachi, Edif Seguros Orinoco, PB, Urb Alta

Vista, and C Urbana, Edif Don An, Puerto Ordaz. **Banco de Venezuela**, Av Las Américas y Av Monseñor Zabaleta. Banks will not exchange Brazilian currency. **Car hire** Many agencies at airport, **Margarita Rentals** cars recommended; **Hertz**, Puerto Ordaz, rents 4WD vehicles. A car is very useful here, eg for the Cerro Bolívar mine and Guri dam, or taking a road trip through the Gran Sabana to Brazil. **Consulates** **Brazil**, Cra Tocoma, Edif Eli-Alti, of 4, Alta Vista, T961 2995, www.consbrasguayana.org.ve, 0900-1200-1400-1800. Friendly, helpful, visa issued in 1 hr, no onward ticket requested (some have to pay, eg Australians), good information. **Internet** Planet Web Café, Carrera Tumeremo, **Cyberarepa**, CC Altavista. **Internet y Comunicaciones 2015**, C La Urbana, Puerto Ordaz. Open till late. **Medical services** **Clinic Chilemex**, Av Las Américas.

Tucupita *p131*
Banks **Banesco** C Petíon 35, cash on Visa. **Banco de Venezuela**, Paseo Manamo, Delta a La Paz, ATM and cash advances. **Internet Compucenter.com**, in same Centro Comercial on Plaza Bolívar. **Delta Microsystems**, C Pativilca.

Ciudad Guayana to Santa Elena de Uairén

Travelling South from Ciudad Guayana to the Brazilian border is becoming an increasingly popular excursion for Venezuelan tourists, as well as for overland travellers heading into (or out of) Brazil via Boa Vista. The road to the border at Santa Elena de Uairén passes across the beautiful Gran Sabana and is completely paved, with all bridges in place.

Ins and outs

Getting around A 4WD is only necessary off the main road, especially in the rainy season. You may need spare tanks of gasoline if spending a lot of time away from the main road (eg in Kavanayen and El Paují) and have a gas-guzzling vehicle. Carry extra water and plenty of food. Small eating places may close out of season. There are Guardia Nacional checks at the Río Cuyuní (Km 8), at Km 126, and at San Ignacio de Yuruaní (Km 259), and a military checkpoint at Luepa (Km 143); all driving permits, car registration papers, and ID must be shown. ▸▸ *See also Transport, page 144.*

Advice Camping is possible but a good waterproof tent is essential. A small fee is payable to the *indígenas* living around Kaui, Kama and similar villages (see also under Parque Nacional Canaima). Insect repellent and long-sleeved/trousered clothes are needed against *puri-puri* (small, black, vicious biting insects) and mosquitoes (especially in El Dorado, at Km 88 and at Icabarú); or use baby oil mixed with vitamin B12. Arrange five-day/four-night tours of the Gran Sabana in Caracas or in Ciudad Bolívar (cheaper and easier). See www.lagransabana.com.

To Tumeremo

South from Ciudad Guayana Highway 10 is a four-lane *autopista* as far as **Upata** (*Phone code: 0288; Population: 51,500*). Buy provisions opposite the petrol station. **Note** Water is rationed in Upata and hot water in hotels is rare south of Ciudad Guayana, except in the better hotels of Santa Elena. From Upata to Km 88, the road is partly resurfaced with occasional broad hard shoulders.

At 18 km beyond **Guasipati** is **El Callao** on the south bank of the Río Yuruari, off the highway, a small, clean, bright town (*Population: 12,000*) whose pre-Lenten carnival has a touch of calypso from British Caribbean immigrants who came to mine gold in the late 19th century. The gold mine, 8 km away in El Perú, has a museum of geology and carnival (T762 0336). Sr Rafael, who lives opposite will show you the mine (T762 0662, evenings only). The town has many jewellery shops and restaurants. The *Banco de Venezuela* on main plaza may change US$ cash, but not traveller's cheques. There is a chronic water shortage, check when it's available in your hotel. All prices rise for carnival in February.

On another 41 km is **Tumeremo** (*Population: 25,000*), which is recommended as the best place to buy provisions. There is *Banco de Orinoco* (Amex, after 1500), and gasoline (all grades) at a normal price (better than El Dorado). About 5 km from Tumeremo towards the Fuerte Tarabay is the beautiful artificial lake of San Pedro with free campsite.

El Dorado → *Phone code: 0288. Population: 4000.*

This hot, dirty and very noisy miners' supply centre in dense forest is 76 km from Tumeremo, 278 km from Ciudad Guayana, and 7 km off the road on the Río Cuyuní. On a river island is the prison made famous by Henri Charrière/Papillon's stay there in 1945. The local gold seams have been largely exhausted but mining still continues and the town's nightlife is entirely for the miners, violence is in the air after nightfall. El Dorado's other economic mainstay is its gas station (open 0800-1900, daily).

El Dorado to Santa Elena de Uairén

The turn-off to El Dorado is marked Km 0; distances are measured from here by green signs 2 km apart. About 3 km south of the turnoff to El Dorado, is the Río Cuyuní crossed by a bridge.

Las Claritas, a gold-miners' town at Km 85 has a couple of places to stay, a restaurant, a big market for food and gold, and safe parking at Las Hermanitas de las Pobres (Convent), which can be better reached by the track from Km 88. At **Km 88** (also called **San Isidro**), there is gasoline, a garage, one of the last reliable telephones before Santa Elena and Banco Guayana. Everything is expensive; better food shops at Km 85.

The wall of the Gran Sabana looms above Km 88 and the highway climbs steeply in sharp curves for 40 km before reaching the top. The road is in very good condition and presents no problem for conventional cars. 4WDs may be better in the wet season (May-October). At Km 100 the huge **Piedra de la Virgen** (sandy coloured with black streaks) is passed before the steepest climb (La Escalera) enters the beautiful **Parque Nacional Canaima** (see page 126).

The landscape is essentially savannah, with clusters of trees, moriche palms and bromeliads. Characteristic of this area are the large abrupt *tepuis* (flat-topped mountains or mesas), hundreds of waterfalls, and the silence of one of the oldest plateaus on earth. At Km 119 (sign can only be seen going north) a short trail leads to the 40 m **Danto** ('**Tapir**') **Falls**, a powerful fall wreathed in mosses and mist. If you are paying for your ride, try to persuade the driver to make a short stop; the falls are close to the road (about five minutes slippery walk down on the left-hand side), but not visible from it. (Buses cannot be flagged down here because of dangerous bends.) The **Monumento al Soldado Pionero** (Km 137) commemorates the army engineers who built the road up from the lowlands, finally opened in 1973; barbecues, toilets, shelters are now almost all in ruins. Some 4 km beyond is **Luepa**; all travellers must stop at the *ciudadela* (military checkpoint) a little way south. There is a popular camping place at Luepa, on the right going south which belongs to a tour company. An informative guide on duty will rent you a tent or you can hang a hammock in an open-sided shelter (very cold at night, no water or facilities, possible to buy a meal from a tour group, but expensive). There is a breakfast place, US$4. The Inparques station at Luepa has some guestrooms which are intended for visitors of Inparques, but they may let you stay for a small fee. There is a kitchen at the station and a cafetería for employees of Inparques and Edelca. You can camp at a site right on the Río Aponwao on the left hand side of the road going south.

Some 8 km beyond Luepa, a poor, graded gravel road leads 70 km west to **Kavanayén** (little traffic, best to have your own vehicle with high clearance, especially during the wet season, take snacks; the road can be cycled but is slow, lots of soft, sandy places). Accommodation is at the Capuchin mission, **$**, very friendly, also in private homes. One of the two grocery stores will prepare food, or the restaurant opposite serves cheap breakfasts and dinners, order in advance. Medical post in front of the mission, where handicrafts are sold.

The settlement is surrounded by *tepuis*. Off the road to Kavanayén are the falls of **Torón Merú** and **Chinak-Merú** (also called Aponwao), 105 m high and very impressive. Neither is a straightforward detour, so get full instructions before setting out. Chinak-Merú is reached via the very friendly Pemón village of **Iboribó** (there is a small bakery near the junction to Torón). A day's walk west of Kavanayén are the lovely falls on the **Río Karuay**. Ask locals for details.

For the remaining 180 km to Santa Elena de Uairén few people and only a few Pemón Indian villages are to be seen. San Juan and San Rafael de Kamoiran and **Rápidos de Kamoirán** are passed. The 5-m Kawí falls on the **Kaüi** River are at Km 195, while at Km 201.5 are the impressive 55 m high **Kama Merú** falls (US$1 to walk to bottom of falls). Also a small lake, handicrafts, a small shop, canoe trips. Cabins and *churuatas* can be rented, also camping. *Puri-puri* flies descend at dusk. Buses can be flagged down going south or north three times a day; check times in advance.

At Km 237 the Río Arapán cascades over the charming **Quebrada Pacheco** ; pools nearby where you can swim. Tour groups often stop here. A path up the opposite side of the main falls leads to an isolated natural pool 20 minutes walk away, in the middle of the savannah. Nearby are more falls with waterslides and pools. **Warning** Do not go beyond the red line at Pacheco: there is a hidden fall which has claimed lives. A new camp is being built between Kama Merú and Quebrada Pacheco. There are plans for lodging and excursions in the savannah. Contact Oscar Romero on T0414-886 2034. Next is **Balneario Saro Wapo** on the Río Soruapé (Km 244), a good place for swimming and picnics, natural whirlpool, restaurant, 10 minutes downriver is a natural waterslide. At Km 250 is the Pemón village of Kumarakapai, San Francisco de Yuruaní (see page 146), whose falls (Arapena-merú) can be seen from the road bridge, followed, 9 km of bends later, by the smaller **San Ignacio de Yuruaní** (strict military checkpoint; excellent regional food).

A trail at Km 275 leads to the **Quebrada de Jaspe** where a river cuts through striated cliffs and pieces of jasper glitter on the banks. Visit at midday when the sun shines best on the jasper, or at 1500 when the colour changes from red to orange, dazzlingly beautiful.

Santa Elena de Uairén → *Phone code: 0289. Population: 9000.*
This booming, pleasant frontier town was established by Capuchin Monks in 1931. The mid-20th century **cathedral** ① *daily 0530-1900, mass Mon-Sat 0630 and 1830, Sun 0630 and 2030*, built from local stone, is a famous landmark. Thanks to its relaxed atmosphere and many hotels, Santa Elena is an agreeable place in which to spend time. Gold is a better buy here than in Ciudad Bolívar.

Border with Brazil
The 16 km road to the border is paved. The entire road links Caracas with Manaus in four days with hard driving; see Northern Brazil, page , for a description of the road from the border and Brazilian immigration formalities. New customs and immigration facilities are at the border and the crossing is straightforward on both sides. Staff at the Ministry of Justice and the Guardia Nacional headquarters (T960 3765/995 1189) have been recommended as helpful with entry and exit problems. The **Brazilian consulate** is at Edifício Galeno, C Los Castaños, Urb Roraima del Casco Central, T995 1256, vcsantaelena@mre.gov.br; open 0800-1200, 1400-1800. You can get a visa here.

For entry to Venezuela, some nationalities who cross the border from Boa Vista, Brazil, need a visa. It is not required by western Europeans, whose passport must be valid for a year, but check with a consulate before leaving home. Venezuelan consulates are listed in directories in the Brazil chapter. A yellow fever vaccination certificate is required. Ask well in advance for other health requirements (eg malaria test certificate). Entering by car, keep photocopies of your licence, the Brazilian permission to leave and Venezuelan entry stamp. Allow two hours for formalities when crossing by private vehicle and don't cross during the lunch hour. Fresh fruit and vegetables may not be brought into Venezuela. There are frequent road checks when heading north from Santa Elena. Seniat (the customs authority) has its Aduana Principal Ecológica outside the town and there may be up to eight more thorough searches, mainly for drugs. Luggage will be sealed before loading into the bus hold in Santa Elena. These checks may mean you arrive in Ciudad Bolívar after dark. There is no public transport on the Venezuelan side, hitch or take a taxi from Brazil.

Santa Elena de Uairén

Sleeping		
1 Augusta	8 Las 5 Jotas	17 Ya-Koo Ecological Camp
2 Cabañas Friedenau	9 Los Castaños	
3 Cabañas Roraima	10 Lucrecia	Eating
4 Gran Sabana	11 Michelle	1 Alfredo's
5 Jaspe	12 Tavarúa	2 Café Goldrausch &
6 Kiamantí	13 Temiche Camp	Michelle
7 La Posada Aventura &	14 Tres Naciones	3 El Ranchón Criollo
Adventure Tours	15 Villa Apoipó	4 Panadería Gran Café
	16 Villa Fairmont	5 Venezuela Primero

El Paují

A road leaves the highway 8 km south of Santa Elena and after passing through a tunnel of jungle vegetation emerges onto rolling savannah dotted with *tepuis*. The road has been considerably improved and has been paved for about 20 km. The rest is graded, but rapidly deteriorating. It can take between 2-4 hours to reach El Pauji. Take advice before setting out, as rain can rapidly degrade the road. At Km 58 is a Guardia Nacional checkpoint at Paraitepuí, waterfall nearby.

El Paují, 17 km further on, is an agricultural settlement with a growing foreign population. It is a lovely area, with good walking. Excellent sights: **Chirica Tepuy**, huge, beautiful, jet black, set in rolling savannah; **Río Surucún**, where Venezuela's largest diamond was found; **Salto Catedral** (61 km off the road), beautiful small hollow, lovely falls, excellent swimming (camping, shop); **Salto La Gruta**, impressive falls, but very slippery; and **Pozo Esmeralda**, 1½ km outside El Paují towards Icabarú (400 m south of road), fine rapids, waterfall you can stand under and pools. At Los Saltos de Pauji are many powerful falls; going from El Paují towards Santa Elena, before crossing the first bridge, take track on left for about 500 m. A good walk is to the small hill, 2 km from El Paují beyond the airfield; views from the crest over **El Abismo**, the plunging escarpment marking the end of Gran Sabana highlands and the start of the Amazon rainforest. It takes an hour to reach the top, and the walk is highly recommended. Guides, though not necessary, are in the village. A recommended guide is German-speaking Marco. Small campsite (lovely early morning or sunset).

Apiculture is the main activity of El Paují and there's an International Honey Festival every summer. The honey made in this area is delicious; buy it at the shop in El Paují or Salto Catedral.

Ciudad Guayana to Santa Elena de Uairén listings

For Sleeping and Eating price codes and other relevant information, see Essentials, pages 9-11.

⊙ Sleeping

To Tumeremo *p136*
Upata
\$\$ Andrea, Plaza Miranda, T221 3618. Decent rooms, a/c, hot water, TV, fridge in some rooms. Credit cards accepted, Chinese restaurant, safe parking, good.
\$ Comercio, C Piar, T221 1156. Excellent.
\$ Yocoima, C Ayacucho, T221 1305. 25 rooms with a/c, TV, Italian restaurant, accepts credit cards.

Guasipati
\$\$ Hotel La Reina, Av Orinoco, T767 1357. A/c, hot water, cable TV, good.

\$ El Mery de Oro, Av Orinoco, T767 1287. Hot water, a/c, helpful if bland.
\$ Residencias El Agua, southern end of town. Basic, a/c, OK.

El Callao
\$\$ Arte Dorado, C Roscio 51, 5 mins from Plaza Bolívar, T762 0535. A/c, TV, parking.
\$\$ New Millenium, Plaza Bolívar, T762 0448. Nice rooms, a/c, TV, laundry, parking, cheaper without hot water. Recommended.
\$ Elvira, C Bolívar, 2 blocks from the plaza, T0416-788 7617 (mob). Shared bath, laundry facilities. Recommended.
\$ Isidora, on the road to El Perú but in town, T762 0290. A/c.
\$ Italia Centro, C Ricuarte off Plaza Bolívar, T762 0770. Basic, a/c.
\$ Ritz, C Ricuarte, T762 0730. Basic, cold beer.

Tumeremo *p136*

Most hotels here are used for doing business with diamonds and as short-stay accommodation.

$$-$ Miranda, Zea 33, T771 0202. Cable TV, a/c, parking, comfortable.

$ Central, Piar y Miranda, T710 2064. Fan, OK, bakery and snackbar.

$ La Francia, C Bolívar, T711 1477. Clean, a/c, cheaper with fan, TV, basic.

$ Pan-hoc, C Piar at Miranda, next to plaza Bolívar, T771 0264. Good value.

$ Sinfontes, C El Dorado, T771 0739. Good value, good beds, a/c, TV, bath, has seen better days (1 block down from *Leocar*, Dorado y Paez, next to the bus stop, which is poor value, very basic).

$ Tumeremo City, on Zea, T771 0281. A/c, TV, parking. Recommended.

El Dorado *p136*

All hotels have problems with running water and there is lots of short-stay accommodation.

$$ El Encanto Cuyuní, a camp 3 km down the road at Puente Río Cuyuní, T0288-808 3845. Bruno and Vanessa will pick you up from El Dorado, or buses drop you at the bridge. Hammock space, camping, cabins, guests can prepare food. Boat trips and tours.

$ Agua Selva, on right when entering town, T991 1093. Rustic camp, with shared bathrooms, fan, includes breakfast, dinner available at extra cost. Hammocks for rent, **$** including breakfast. Welcoming owner, tours. Recommended.

$ Universo, C Cuyuní, running parallel to the river, T991 1151. Clean, safe, a/c, some rooms have TV, safe parking. Recommended.

El Dorado to Santa Elena de Uairén *p137*

$$$ Campamento Turístico Anaconda, Las Claritas, T0286-923 7996, anaconda@cantv.net. Cabins with bath, fan,

well-furnished, bar, including breakfast and dinner, reserved for tour groups (**$$** in low season).

$$$ pp La Barquilla de Fresa, at Km 84.5. Book via Alba Betancourt in Caracas T0212-256 4162, T0416- 709 7205, barquilladefresa@ cantv.net. Run by Henry Cleve, English and German spoken. Bird-watching tours and inventory of bird species for the jungle here has reached more than 300 species. Full board lodging, reservations and deposit required.

$ Landolfi, Las Claritas, left turn in the centre of town towards the indigenous village of San Lucia de Inaway. A/c, **$** with fan, parking.

$ La Pilonera, opposite Vargas store, Km 88. With a/c and hot water, **$** with fan and cold water, safe parking, some rooms with bath, restaurant with good fruit drinks; good food next door.

Rápidos de Kamoirán

$ Campamento Rápidos de Kamoirán, Km 172, T0289-805 1505. Clean, with fan, well-kept, cold water, camping US$4, also restaurant, gasoline, and picnic spot by rapids.

Santa Elena de Uairén *p138, map p139*

$$$ Gran Sabana, outside town, 10 km from border, T995 1810. Most luxurious in town, good service. Recommended.

$$$-$$ Villa Fairmont, Urb Akurimá, T995 1022, at north edge of town. Large, comfortable rooms, a/c, hot water, TV, restaurant, small craft shop.

$$ Lucrecia, Av Perimetral, T995 1105, near old terminal. A/c or fan, TV, restaurant, pool, parking, helpful, good.

$$ Temiche Camp, 5 mins from town on airport road, T962 2693/0414-886 2323. Nice rooms, hot water, meals and use of kitchen extra.

$$ pp Ya-Koo Ecological Camp, 2 km on unpaved road to Sampai Indian community, up mountain behind Santa Elena, T995 1742, www.ya-koo.com. *Cabañas* in beautiful 10-ha site, full board, spacious rooms, hot water, natural pool. Cheaper in low season. Recommended if you have a car.

$ Augusta, C Bolívar, next to *Panadería Rico Pan*, T995 1654. Hot water, fan, cable TV, clean, central.

$ pp Cabañas Friedenau, Av Ppal de Cielo Azul, off Av Perimetral, T995 1353, friedenau@cantv.net. Self-contained chalets, price includes breakfast, nice grounds, vegetarian food, parking, transfer to Puerto Ordaz, bikes, horseriding, trips to Roraima (see below), English spoken. Recommended.

$ Cabañas Roraima, up road behind old bus terminal, near *Villa Fairmont*, T996 1164. A/c, hot water, fridge, also cabins for up to 8.

$ Jaspe, on C Mcal Sucre, T995 1379, 150 m from old bus terminal on opposite side. Hot water, fan, TV, free coffee.

$ Kiamantí, outside town near new bus terminal, T995 1952, kiamanti77@hotmail.com. Full board, fan, hot water, comfortable, parking, pool.

$ La Posada Aventura, above *Adventure Tours* on Av Perimetral, T995 1574. Hot water, fan. Good.

$ Las 5 Jotas, near *Cabañas Roraima*, T0414-886 1524. Comfortable, good value.

$ Los Castaños, C Mcal Sucre, near old bus terminal, T995 1450. A/c, TV, cheaper with fan.

$ Michelle, C Urdaneta, next to *Café Goldrausch*, T995 1415, hotelmichelle@cantv.net. Spotless, hot water, fan, helpful, laundry, good value. Credit cards accepted, cash advances on Visa if you're desperate.

$ Tavarúa, near *Ya-Koo*, T808 8386, 0416-289 2600, robtavarua1@yahoo.com. Lovely rooms, hot water, meals available, pick-up from town, Roberto Campano is a guide.

$ Tres Naciones, on C Zea, T995 1190. Basic, with a/c, hot water, restaurant, parking.

$ Villa Apoipó, on the road to the airport, turn left at the *Hotel Gran Sabana*, T492 2626, 0414-886 2049. Very nice rooms, hot water, fan. For groups but will take independent travellers if you ring ahead. Use of kitchen or full board. Bunk beds or hammocks available in large *churuata*.

El Paují *p140*

$$$ pp Campamento Amaribá, 3.5 km outside El Paují on road from Santa Elena, transport available from airstrip, T0414-932 2169, Caracas T0212-753 9314, amariba@cantv.net. Comfortable cabins with mosquito nets, separate bathrooms, good facilities, full board, kitchen, tours arranged, very hospitable.

$$ Campamento El Paují, 3.5 km outside El Paují on road from Santa Elena, transport usually available from airstrip, T995 1431, or contact through Maripak. Beautiful cabins with spectacular views over the Gran Sabana, food available, camping US$6 per tent. Recommended.

$$ Weimure, 2 km out, outside El Paují on road from Santa Elena, pauji0@yahoo.com. Beautiful cabin close to river, dynamic architect owner.

$ Canta Rana tourist camp, 25 km from town. Basic accommodation, breakfast and dinner included in the price, owners, Alfonso and Barbara Borrero, speak German, English and Spanish, waterfall and lovely surroundings.

$ pp Chimanta and **Manoa**, T995 1431. Cosy rooms, restaurant serving vegan food.

$ Maripak, near the airstrip and small store, T808 1033, maripaktepuy@hotmail.com, or reserve in Caracas T0212-234 3631. Run by Marielis Gil, cabins for 2/3 with bath, US$10 per meal, good food, tours, camping US$6 per tent, phone.

🍴 Eating

Tumeremo *p136*
Restaurante Las Cuevas, near plaza. Popular, average food and prices, service slow, check your bill. **Restaurante Turístico**, expensive but OK.

El Dorado *p136*
Archiven, Plaza Bolívar. Good, helpful owner. **El Caney**, on right just down from *Agua Selva*, good food. Recommended. Restaurant by church serves delicious *criolla* food.

Santa Elena de Uairén *p138, map p139*
Several restaurants on Mcal Sucre, one of these **El Ranchón Criollo** serves good *criolla* fare. **Alfredo's**, Av Perimetral, at the end of C Urdaneta. Tasty pizzas at good prices. **Venezuela Primero**, Av Perimetral. Chicken, meat, and seafood. **Pizzería Darwing**, C Icabarú, in front of Parque Ferial, T0414-875 5457. Great pizza.

Cafés
On the Plaza is a pay-by-weight buffet restaurant serving very good local food. **Café Goldrausch**, C Urdaneta, next to *Restaurant Michelle* . Makes good breakfasts, also dinners, and internet. Good place to form tour groups with other travellers. **Panadería Gran Café**, C Icabarú. Good breakfasts and coffee. **Gran Sabana Deli**, C Bolívar, CC Augusta, T995 1158. Cosy and good.

⛰ Activities and tours

Santa Elena de Uairén *p138, map p139*
Santa Elena is the most economical place to book tours of the Gran Sabana, Roraima, and other tepuis. There are many tour operators and freelance guides. Shop around, form larger groups, and haggle. Many tour operators will tailor tours to fit your needs, contact by email to discuss plans before arriving.

Adventure Tours, Av Perimetral at the end of C Urdaneta, T995 1861, adventure3tours@ hotmail.com. Tours of Gran Sabana or El Paují, group discounts, all-inclusive 6 days to Roraima (minimum 4 persons). Sleeping bags and camping mats available for hire.
Backpacker Tours, C Urdaneta, T995 1415, T0414-886 7227, www.backpacker-tours.com. 1-5 day, all-inclusive jeep tours through the Gran Sabana, visiting little-known falls in the Kavanayen area. Trekking to nearby Chirikayen Tepuy, 3-4 days and to Roraima (minimum 4 persons), plus more. German and English spoken. Recommended. Also have own **Posada Los Pinos**, Urb Akurima, 10 mins from airport, T995 1524.
Kamadac, C Urdaneta, T995 1408, T0414-886 6526, www.abenteuer-venezuela.de. Run by Andreas Hauer, tours of Gran Sabana, US$300 pp per day for jeep (4 persons). 6-day, all-inclusive tour to Roraima, US$405 pp (for 4), and also more adventurous tours to Auyán Tepuy from which Angel Falls cascades (5 days, US$785 pp for 4 people), difficult; many other options. Recommended.
New Frontiers Adventure, also on C Urdaneta next to *Tommy Town*, T0414-886 6040, www.newfrontiers adventures.com. Ecotours and tours for small groups. All the usual tours at standard prices, and 4-day, inclusive walking tours, taking in the different ecosystems of the Gran Sabana, and staying in Pemón villages. English, French, and German spoken. Recommended.
Roberto's Mystic Tours, Icabarú y Urdaneta, mystic-tours@cantv.net. Roberto is very helpful and knowledgeable about local culture (and UFOs), great tours. Recommended.
Recommended guides Rawllins and his brother, **Terry** (Guyanese) speak English, excellent cooks, T0414-886 2669, rawllins@ yahoo.com, akawaio@hotmail.com. **Franklin Sierra**, T995 1686, 0414-886 2448, speaks English, Italian and other languages, tailor-made tours, good service and value.

Tumeremo p136

Bus To **Santa Elena**, US$14, 8-10 hrs, with Líneas Orinoco, 2 blocks from plaza near *Leocar*); **El Dorado**, US$1.75, 1½ hrs. Bus to **Ciudad Bolívar**, US$8.50-9.50, 6 a day, 6½ hrs or *por puesto* (via San Félix and Puerto Ordaz). Bus to **San Félix** (Ciudad Guayana), US$2.75, *por puesto* US$8. To **Caracas**, US$24, direct service at 1600, 14 hrs.

El Dorado p136

Bus All buses stop on main plaza. From **Caracas**, Expresos del Oriente, at 1830 daily, US$24.50, 14½ hrs, return at 1400 (925 km). The Orinoco bus links with **Ciudad Bolívar** (6 hrs) and **Santa Elena**, as does Transmundial (better, leaving 1100, US$11 to **Santa Elena**, US$8.60 to San Félix, 4 hrs).

El Dorado to Santa Elena de Uairén p137

Km 88 (San Isidro)

Bus Km 88-Caracas, US$24.50; to **Ciudad Bolívar** wait at gas station for buses from Las Claritas (depart 0900, 1100, 1500, 1800). Frequent *por puestos* from **El Dorado** to Km 88, 1 hr, US$2.75. Most non-luxury buses stop at the petrol station to refuel. Alternatively get a ride with jeeps and trucks (little passes after 1030).

Santa Elena de Uairén p138, map p139

Air Airport, 8 km from the centre. Transmandú (www.transmandu.com), the only company with flights from **Ciudad Bolívar** in small planes.

Bus The bus terminal on road to Ciudad Bolívar is 2 km/30 mins walk from town, taxi US$5. Get to terminal 30 mins in advance for SENIAT baggage check for contraband. From **Caracas** there are direct buses (eg **Expresos Los Llanos**), US$37, or you can go to Ciudad Bolívar and then take a bus direct to Boa Vista, or Santa Elena, or to Ciudad Guayana and

change there. 10 buses daily from Santa Elena to **Ciudad Bolívar**, US$21.50-26.50, with Expresos Los Llanos (recommended), San Cristóbal, and Línea Orinoco, 10-12 hrs. 10 daily to **Ciudad Guayana** and **San Félix**, US$21, 10-11 hrs, with **Caribe** (recommended) and Turgar. 10 daily to **Puerto La Cruz**, US$24, 14 hrs, with **Caribe** (recommended), Turgar, and **Línea Orinoco**. Expresos Maturín goes to **Maturín** daily. Expresos Los Llanos go to **Maracay** and **Valencia** 3 times a day, US$33, 18- 20 hrs. 3 buses daily to **Boa Vista**, US$8.25, 4 hrs, Eucatur; at 0700 to **Manaus** 15 hrs, US$35 (make sure ticket includes the exit tax).

Jeep To **El Paují** (see below), **Canta Rana** (US$17.75), and **Icabarú** (US$20) leave about 0700 from Plaza Bolívar. Also at *Panadería Gran Café*, C Icabarú. PDV gas station on road out of town.

El Paují p140

Road To get further than El Paují – to Canta Rana and Icabarú – a 4WD vehicle is necessary. From Santa Elena, US$8-11 by jeep if full, more if not, daily at around 0600-0700 and 1500-1600 from Plaza Bolívar. Taxi US$11.

El Dorado p136

Banks There is a **Banco de Venezuela**, accepts Visa and Mastercard; exchange with the gold buyer on the main street, cash only, poor rates.

Santa Elena de Uairén p138, map p139

Banks See also Money, page 11. ATMs are unlikely to accept non- Venezuelan credit cards. Try shops in the centre for dollars cash, Brazilian reais or TCs, eg *Casa de Los Cóchamos*, gold shop south of main plaza that changes TCs at lower rate than bank. **Inversiones Fortaleza**, C Urdaneta on plaza, cash dollars, TCs or reais. **La Boutique Zapatería** also changes TCs and cash at good rates. Grocery store **El Gordito**, C Urdaneta, for reais (English and French spoken). Try at border with Brazilians entering Venezuela. Ask the bus driver on the Santa Elena-Boa Vista bus the best place for favourable bolívares/reais rates: in Santa Elena at Sucre y Perimetral; in Brazil at the first stop after the border. Check with travellers going in opposite direction what rates should be.

Internet **Global de Communicaciones**, C Icabarú y Urdaneta. Another place opposite **Panadería Rico Pan**, C Bolívar.
Telephones **Global de Communicaciones**, **CANTV** at the old bus terminal for international calls and faxes. It is cheaper to buy a card and call from a street phone for international calls.

Mount Roraima → *Altitude: 2810 m.*

An exciting trek is to the summit of Mt Roraima, at one time believed to be the 'Lost World' made famous by Arthur Conan Doyle's novel. 'Roroima' is a word in the Pemón Indian language meaning 'The great blue-green'. Due to the tough terrain and extreme weather conditions, this hike is only suitable for the fit. Supplies for a week or more should be bought in Santa Elena. If a tour company is supplying the food, check what it is first; vegetarians may go hungry.

San Francisco de Yuruaní
The starting point is this Pemón village, 9 km north of the San Ignacio military checkpoint (where you must register). There are three small shops selling basic goods but not enough for Roraima hike. Meals are available and tents can be hired, US$5 each per day, quality of tents and stoves is poor; better equipment is available in Santa Elena.

Paraitepui
The road to Paraitepui (which is signposted), the nearest village to the mountain, leaves the highway 1 km south of San Francisco. It is in good condition, with three bridges; the full 25 km can be walked in seven hours. You can sleep for free in the village if hiring a guide; camping is permitted. Few supplies are available; a small shop sells basics. The villagers speak Tauripán, the local dialect of the Pemón linguistic group, but now most of them also speak Spanish.

Climbing Roraima
The foot trail winds back and forth on a more direct line than the little-used jeep track; it is comparatively straightforward and adequately marked descending from the heights just past Paraitepui across rolling hills and numerous clear streams. The goal, Roraima, is the mountain on the right, the other massive outcrop on the left is Mata Hui (known as Kukenán after the river which rises within it). If leaving the village early in the day, you may reach the Río Cuquenán crossing by early afternoon (good camping here). Three hours' walk brings you to a lovely bird-filled meadow below the foothills of the massif, another perfect camping spot known as *campamento base* (10 hours to base camp from Paraitepui). The footpath now climbs steadily upwards through the cloud forest at the mountain's base and becomes an arduous scramble over tree trunks and damp rocks until the cliff is reached. From here it is possible to ascend to the plateau along the 'easy' rock ledge which is the only route to the top. Walkers in good health should take about four hours from the meadow to the top. The summit is an eerie world of stone and water, difficult to move around easily. There are not many good spots to camp; but there are various overhanging ledges which are colourfully known as 'hoteles' by the guides. Red painted arrows lead the way to the right after reaching the summit for the main group of these. A marked track leads to the survey pillar near the east cliff where Guyana, Brazil and Venezuela meet; allow a day as the track is very rough. Other sights include the Valley of the Crystals, La Laguna de Gladys and various sinkholes.

The whole trip can take anywhere between five days and two weeks. The dry season for trekking is November-May (with annual variations); June-August Roraima is usually enveloped in cloud. Do not remove crystals from the mountain; on-the-spot fines up to US$100 may be charged. Thorough searches are made on your return. Take your rubbish back down with you.

Mount Roraima listings

For Sleeping and Eating price codes and other relevant information, see Essentials, pages 9-11.

😴 Sleeping

San Francisco de Yuruaní *p146*
$ Arapena Posada, T01414-890 3314 (mob). Run by Arepena Tours (see below), small, basic.
$ El Caney de Yuruaní, T995 1307. Clean, basic rooms, fan, restaurant.
$ Posada, run by *Roraima Tours* (see below). Dormitories, usually full.
Sr Casilda Rodriguez has a *churuata* where you can sling a hammock.
Camping Permitted just about anywhere, free. Plenty of mosquitos at night.

Climbing Roraima *p146*

Camping Full equipment including stove is essential (an igloo-type tent with a plastic sheet for the floor is best for the summit, where it can be wet), wear thick socks and boots to protect legs from snakes, warm clothes for the summit (much mist, rain squalls and lightning at night) and effective insect repellent – biting *plaga (blackflies)* infest the grasslands. The water on the summit and around the foot of Roraima is very pure, but as more do the trek, the waters are becoming dirtied. Bring bottled water or a purifier for the savannah. Fires must not be lit on top of Roraima, only gas or liquid fuel stoves. Litter is appearing along the trail; please take care of the environment.

⛰ Activities and tours

Climbing Roraima *p146*
Guides and tours The National Guard requires all visitors to have a guide beyond Paraitepui; you will be fined. Go with a guide or tour operator from Santa Elena (US$400, 6 days/5 nights) or from San Francisco; those hired on the street or in Paraitepui have no accident insurance cover. Guides can help for the hike's final stages (easy to get lost) and for finding best camping spots. Guides in San Francisco de Yuruaní cost US$40 a day, more if they carry your supplies. Check the camping gear for leaks, etc, and be clear about who is providing the guide's food.
Arapena Tours, T0414-890 3314, arapenatours@ latinmail.com. Tours to Roraima and Kavurin, US$40 per day for guide.
Roraima Tours, T808 1037, T0414-886 3405, recommended, Ana Fernández is very helpful, all-inclusive tour (group rates can be arranged), or US$45 per day for guide only.
 Guides in Paraitepui cost US$25 a day, Spanish speaking guides. The **Ayuso** brothers are the best-known guides. Ask for El Capitán, he is in charge of guides. Parking at Inparques US$9.

🚌 Transport

San Francisco de Yuruaní *p146*
Bus From **Santa Elena** will let you off here and pick up passengers en route northwards (no buses 1200-1900). Jeep to **Paraitepui** US$100. Cheapest is Oscar Mejías Hernández, ask in village.

Contents

Footnotes

Index

Titles available in the Footprint *Focus* range

Latin America	UK RRP	US RRP
Bahia & Salvador	£7.99	$11.95
Buenos Aires & Pampas	£7.99	$11.95
Costa Rica	£8.99	$12.95
Cuzco, La Paz & Lake Titicaca	£8.99	$12.95
El Salvador	£5.99	$8.95
Guadalajara & Pacific Coast	£6.99	$9.95
Guatemala	£8.99	$12.95
Guyana, Guyane & Suriname	£5.99	$8.95
Havana	£6.99	$9.95
Honduras	£7.99	$11.95
Nicaragua	£7.99	$11.95
Paraguay	£5.99	$8.95
Quito & Galápagos Islands	£7.99	$11.95
Recife & Northeast Brazil	£7.99	$11.95
Rio de Janeiro	£8.99	$12.95
São Paulo	£5.99	$8.95
Uruguay	£6.99	$9.95
Venezuela	£8.99	$12.95
Yucatán Peninsula	£6.99	$9.95

Asia	UK RRP	US RRP
Angkor Wat	£5.99	$8.95
Bali & Lombok	£8.99	$12.95
Chennai & Tamil Nadu	£8.99	$12.95
Chiang Mai & Northern Thailand	£7.99	$11.95
Goa	£6.99	$9.95
Hanoi & Northern Vietnam	£8.99	$12.95
Ho Chi Minh City & Mekong Delta	£7.99	$11.95
Java	£7.99	$11.95
Kerala	£7.99	$11.95
Kolkata & West Bengal	£5.99	$8.95
Mumbai & Gujarat	£8.99	$12.95

Africa	UK RRP	US RRP
Beirut	£6.99	$9.95
Damascus	£5.99	$8.95
Durban & KwaZulu Natal	£8.99	$12.95
Fès & Northern Morocco	£8.99	$12.95
Jerusalem	£8.99	$12.95
Johannesburg & Kruger National Park	£7.99	$11.95
Kenya's beaches	£8.99	$12.95
Kilimanjaro & Northern Tanzania	£8.99	$12.95
Zanzibar & Pemba	£7.99	$11.95

Europe	UK RRP	US RRP
Bilbao & Basque Region	£6.99	$9.95
Granada & Sierra Nevada	£6.99	$9.95
Málaga	£5.99	$8.95
Orkney & Shetland Islands	£5.99	$8.95
Skye & Outer Hebrides	£6.99	$9.95

North America	UK RRP	US RRP
Vancouver & Rockies	£8.99	$12.95

Australasia	UK RRP	US RRP
Brisbane & Queensland	£8.99	$12.95
Perth	£7.99	$11.95

For the latest books, e-books and smart phone app releases, and a wealth of travel information, visit us at: www.footprinttravelguides.com.

footprinttravelguides.com

Join us on facebook for the latest travel news, product releases, offers and amazing competitions: www.facebook.com/footprintbooks.com.